THE ACTS OF PETER AND THE TWELVE APOSTLES (NHC 6.1)

SOCIETY
OF BIBLICAL
LITERATURE

DISSERTATION SERIES
Saul Olyan, Old Testament Editor
Mark Allan Powell, New Testament Editor

Number 174
THE ACTS OF PETER AND THE
TWELVE APOSTLES (NHC 6.1)
Allegory, Ascent, and Ministry in the
Wake of the Decian Persecution

by
Andrea Lorenzo Molinari

Andrea Lorenzo Molinari

THE ACTS OF PETER AND THE TWELVE APOSTLES (NHC 6.1)
Allegory, Ascent, and Ministry in the Wake of the Decian Persecution

Society of Biblical Literature
Atlanta, Georgia

THE ACTS OF PETER AND THE TWELVE APOSTLES (NHC 6.1)
Allegory, Ascent, and Ministry in the Wake of the Decian Persecution

by
Andrea Lorenzo Molinari
Ph.D., Marquette University, 1996
Julian V. Hills, Advisor

Library of Congress Cataloging-in-Publication Data

Molinari, Andrea Lorenzo, 1967–
    The Acts of Peter and the Twelve Apostles (NHC 6.1) : allegory, ascent,
and ministry in the wake of the Decian persecution / Andrea Lorenzo Molinar
    p. cm. — (Dissertation series / Society of Biblical Literature ; no. 174)
    Originally presented as the author's thesis (Ph.D.)—Marquette
University, 1996.
    Includes bibliographical references.
    ISBN 0-88414-017-2 (alk. paper)
    1. Acts of Peter and the Twelve Apostles—Criticism, interpretation, etc.
I. Title. II. Dissertation series (Society of Biblical Literature) ; no. 174.

BT1392.A372 M65 2000
229'.925—dc21   00-026684

08 07 06 05 04 03 02 01 00   5 4 3 2 1

Printed in the United States of America
on acid-free paper

Table of Contents

Preface

I was first introduced to *ActsPet12Apost.* in a class on the Nag Hammadi literature in the Spring of 1991. The seminar leader, Julian V. Hills, requested that each class participant study and present a paper on one of the texts. He personally asked me to read *ActsPet12Apost.* and consider writing on it. I read it that evening and found its allegory and imagery captivating. I was particularly interested in Lithargoel's description of the Journey to Nine Gates:

> And also (concerning) the road to the city which you asked me about, I will tell you about it. No man is able to go on that road, except one who has *forsaken everything* that he has and has fasted daily from stage to stage. For many are the robbers and wild beasts on that road. The one who carries bread with him on the road, the black dogs *kill* because of the bread. The one who carries a costly garment of the world with him, the robbers *kill* [because of the] garment. [The one who carries] water [with him, the wolves *kill* because of the water], since they were thirsty [for] it. [The one who] is anxious about [meat] and green vegetables, the lions *eat* because of the meat. [If] he evades the lions, the bulls devour him because of the green vegetables. (5.19–6.8)

Peter and Lithargoel were in the island city of Habitation and yet the description of the journey included creatures that might more properly be found along a wilderness path. At first I assumed, as I would later find out that Hans-Martin Schenke had argued, that this discrepancy signaled a change in sources. However, upon rereading the text I realized that the animals mentioned by Lithargoel as infesting the way to Nine Gates had the power of cognition. Obviously, these were no ordinary animals. The story was inviting me, as its reader, to enter the realm of symbolism and allegory. If the truth be told, it was precisely this peculiar description that my instincts told me was the key to the entire tractate. There was something terrible, something brutal and savage about its tone. It depicted the ultimate predators: thinking, voracious hunters who are drawn to their prey, drawn like bees to flowers, attracted by their possessions. According to Lithargoel, there was no possible defense, no mystical, magical weapon forged in the fires of the armorer god, Hephaestus, that could save their victims. No physical force on earth was capable of stopping them. They were the worst kind of monsters, stripping their victims of the essentials of life and then, finally, violently, of life itself. But instead of fighting the inevitable, Lithargoel counseled the travelers to divest themselves of life's basic necessities and, seemingly, of life itself, in an almost suicidal, pre-emptive strike — becoming nothing so as to cease to be a target. I had to know what the author meant by his or her symbols. As I studied the text I came to the conclusions I have presented in the following chapters.

Over the years of my education I have been blessed with a number of excellent teachers, in both the lessons of life and of the sacred page. While mentioning them all would be ponderous I am constrained by extreme gratitude to honor: Fr. Richard "Giles" Dimock, O.P., who presented in his life and actions the very incarnation of Jesus; Fr. Terrence J. Keegan, O.P., who challenged my myopic credulity and opened my eyes to the Synoptics with all their mystery; Fr. Raymond F. Collins, the closest thing to Irenaeus, a perfect blend of scholar and pastor, I have ever met; Richard A. Edwards, who demanded that I actually learn to use the historical-critical methods and taught me how they complement and strengthen each other's results and Julian V. Hills, who introduced me to Gnosticism, Nag Hammadi and my beloved *ActsPet12Apost.* Hills taught me more than any other about NT and early Christianity and how to analyze critically their remains. Lastly, I would be remiss if I did not thank Douglas M. Parrott. In studying this document as well as other Nag Hammadi texts I came to appreciate his insight and dedication to this field. As his was the first English translation of *ActsPet12Apost.* (done by an American no less) and because his work so greatly influenced and stimulated my thoughts on this text, he became a kind of hero to me although it had never been my pleasure to meet him. However, this changed in November 1995, when he and I met in Philadelphia at the SBL/ AAR convention. He listened patiently to my ideas and offered encouragement to a young graduate student he did not know. Later, when I called on his expertise he returned my phone call at his own expense (California to Wisconsin) and further aided my research. These days it is not often that one's heroes turn out to be so selfless and humble. It is an honor to follow in such a scholar's footsteps.

While these men formed me academically, others supported me personally. Again the list is very long but I cannot help but mention: Thomas A. Szigethy, Rev. Allen Taylor, Larry G. Iversen, Br. David Erwin, Kevin Lowery and Chris D. Alfaro without whose friendships I could not have achieved my goals. Their brotherhood sustained and encouraged me in the darkest of times and I am forever in their debt.

All these and many others taught, supported and loved me but that process began many years earlier with my parents: Achille F. and Gatra M. Molinari. My father, an immigrant from Italy, was my first teacher of scripture and my exegetical style is very much a reflection of his practicality and imagination. My mother, a teacher with multiple graduate degrees, was the first scholar I knew. I am reminded of her love of books and learning every time I visit a library.

Lastly, I thank my wife, Myrna, for over ten years of love, patience and iron-willed patronage. Her belief in me superseded my own belief in myself and was strong enough to carry me through the hardest of challenges, academic and personal. She is truly Isis to my Osiris, bringing life from death. It is to her that I dedicate this work.

Abbreviations

AB	Anchor Bible
ABD	D. N. Freedman (ed.), *Anchor Bible Dictionary*
ACW	Ancient Christian Writers
ANRW	*Aufstieg und Neidergang der römischen Welt*
CBQ	*Catholic Biblical Quarterly*
CBQMS	*Catholic Biblical Quarterly* — Monograph Series
CH	*Church History*
CSCO	Corpus scriptorum christianorum orientalium
GCS	Griechischen christlichen Schriftsteller
HDR	Harvard Dissertations in Religion
HTR	*Harvard Theological Review*
HTS	Harvard Theological Studies
JBL	*Journal of Biblical Literature*
JEH	*Journal of Ecclesiastical History*
JRS	*Journal of Roman Studies*
JSNT	*Journal for the Study of the New Testament*
JTS	*Journal of Theological Studies*
LCL	Loeb Classical Library
LSJ	Liddell-Scott-Jones, *Greek-English Lexicon*
NHS	Nag Hammadi Studies
NovT	*Novum Testamentum*
NTS	*New Testament Studies*
RAC	*Reallexikon für Antike und Christentum*
RHR	*Revue de l'histoire des religions*
RTP	*Revue de théologie et de philosophie*
SBLDS	Society of Biblical Literature Dissertation Series
SBLMS	Society of Biblical Literature Monograph Series
SBLSBS	Society of Biblical Literature Sources for Biblical Study
SBLSP	Society of Biblical Literature Seminar Papers
SC	Sources chrétiennes
SNTSMS	Society for New Testament Studies Monograph Series

The Text of Acts of Peter and the Twelve Apostles (VI.1 1–12.22)

(It is not my intention here to offer a new translation of the Coptic text, although in several instances I do suggest alternate words or phrases. In each of these instances my reasons are clearly explained in the pages that follow. In the main, the translation that follows is that of Douglas M. Parrott and Robert McL. Wilson and can be found in the NHLE. My purposes for including it here are twofold: 1) to provide a complete text as part of my analysis for ease of reference when examining my argument and 2) to delineate clearly and visually my division of the text in regard to sources and redactional insertions.)

1. [...] which [...]
   purpose [...:
   after...]
   us [...]
5. apostles [...].
   We sailed [...]
   of the body. [Others] were not
   anxious in [their
   hearts]. And in our hearts, we were
10. united. We agreed to fulfill
   the ministry to which
   the Lord appointed us. And we made
   a covenant with each other.
       We went down to the sea at
15. an opportune moment, which came
   to us from the Lord. We
   found a ship moored at the shore
   ready to embark,

and we spoke with the sailors of

20. the ship about our coming aboard with them.
They showed great
kindliness toward us as
was ordained by the Lord.
And after we had embarked,

25. we sailed a day
and a night. After that,
a wind came up behind the ship and
brought us to a small city
in the midst of the sea.

30.   And I, Peter, inquired about the name
of this city from residents
who were
standing on the dock.

II.   [A man] among [them] answered, [saying,
"The name] of this [city is
Habitation, that is], Foundation [...]
endurance." And

5. the leader [among them
holding] the palm branch at the edge of [the dock].
And after we had gone ashore [with the]
baggage, I [went]
into [the] city, to seek [advice]

10. about lodging. A man came out
wearing a cloth
bound around his waist,
and a gold belt girded [it].
Also a napkin was tied over [his]

15. chest, extending over
his shoulders and covering his head
and his hands. **I was staring at the**

man, because he was beautiful in his
form and stature. There were four
20. parts of his body that
I saw: the soles of his
feet and a part of his
chest and the palms of his
hands and his visage.
25. These things I was able to see.
A book cover like (that of) a
ruler was in his left hand.
A staff of styrax wood was in
his right hand. His
30. voice was resounding as he slowly spoke,
crying out in the city,
"Pearls! Pearls!" I,
indeed, thought he was a man [of]
that city. I said
35. to him, "My brother and my friend!"

III.   [He answered] me, [then, saying,
"Rightly] did you say, '[My brother
and] my friend.' What is it you [seek]
from me?" I said to him, "[I
5. ask] you [about] lodging for me
[and the] brothers also, because we
are strangers here." He said [to] me,
"For this reason have I myself just said,
'My brother and my friend,'
10. because I also am a fellow stranger
like you." And
having said these things, he cried out,
"Pearls! Pearls!"
The rich men of that

15. city heard his voice.

   They came out of their hidden storerooms.

   And some were

   looking out from the storerooms

   of their houses. Others

20. looked out from their

   upper windows. And they did not see (that they could gain)

   anything from him, because

   there was no pouch on his back nor

   bundle inside his cloth

25. and napkin. And because of their

   disdain they did not

   even acknowledge him.

   He, for his part, did not reveal himself to them.

   They returned to their

30. storerooms, saying,

   "This man is mocking us."

      And the poor [of that city] heard

IV.   [his voice,

   and they came to] the man [who sells

   this pearl. They said],

   "Please take the trouble to [show us

5. the] pearl [so that we may], then, [see]

   it with our (own) eyes. For we are [the poor].

   And we do not have this [...] price

   to pay for it. But [show us]

   that we might say to our friends that [we saw]

10. a pearl with our (own) eyes." He

   answered, saying to them, "If

   it is possible, come to my city,

   so that I may not only show it

   before your (very) eyes, but give it to

15. you for nothing." And indeed they,
    the poor of that city, heard
    and said, "Since we are beggars, we surely
    know that a man does not give a pearl
20. to a beggar, but (it is) bread
    and money that is usually received.
    Now then, the kindness which we want to receive
    from you (is) that you show
    us the pearl before our eyes.
25. And we will say to our friends
    proudly that we saw a
    pearl with our (own) eyes" — because
    it is not found among the poor, especially
    such beggars as these). He answered
30. (and) said to them, "If it is
    possible, you yourselves come
    to my city, so that I may not only
    show you it, but give it
    to you for nothing."
    The poor and the beggars rejoiced because of

V.   the man [who gives for] nothing.
     [The man asked Peter] about the sufferings.
     Peter answered [and
     told] those things that he had heard about the [sufferings]
5. of [the] way. **Because they are [interpreters of the]**
    sufferings in their ministry.
    He said to the man who sells this
    pearl, "I want
    to know **your name and** the sufferings of
10. the way to your city because we
    are strangers and servants of
    God. It is necessary for us to spread

the word of God in
every city harmoniously." He
15. answered and said, "If you
seek **my name, Lithargoel**
is my name, the interpretation of which is,
the light, gazelle-like stone.
"And also (concerning) the road to the city
20. which you asked me about, I will tell you
about it. No man is able to go
on that road, expect one
who has forsaken everything that
he has and has fasted
25. daily from stage to stage.
For many are the robbers and
wild beasts on that road.
The one who carries bread with him
on the road, the black dogs
30. kill because of
the bread. The one who carries a costly garment
of the world with him,
the robbers kill

VI.   [because of the] garment. [The one who carries] water
[with him, the wolves kill because
of the water], since they were thirsty [for] it.
[The one who] is anxious about [meat] and
5. green vegetables, the lions eat
because of the meat. [If] he evades
the lions, the bulls
devour him because of the green vegetables."
        When he had said [these] things to me, I sighed
10. within myself, saying, "[Great]
hardships are on the road! If only

Jesus would give us power to walk it!"
He looked at me since my face was sad, and I
sighed. He said to me, "Why
15. do you sigh, if you, indeed, know
this name 'Jesus' and believe him?
He is a great power for giving strength.
For I too believe in the Father
who sent him." I replied,
20. asking him, "What is the name
of the place to which you go,
your city?" He said to me,
"This is the name of my city,
'Nine Gates.' Let us praise God
25. as we are mindful that the tenth
is the head." After this I went away
from him in peace. As I was
about to go and call my friends, I
saw waves and large
30. high walls surrounding
the bounds of the city. I
marveled at the great things I saw.
I saw an old man
sitting and I asked him if the name of the
35. city was really

VII. [Habitation]. He [...],
"Habitation [...]."
He said to me, "[You
speak] truly, for we [inhabit] here
5. because [we] endure." **[I
responded], saying, "Justly
[...] have men named it
[...], because (by) everyone**

[who] endures his trials
10. cities are inhabited,
and a precious kingdom
comes from them, because
they endure in the midst of the
apostasies and the difficulties of the storms.
15. So that in this way, the city of everyone
who endures the suffering of his yoke
of faith will be inhabited,
and he will be included in
the kingdom of heaven." I hurried
20. and went and called my
friends so that we might go to the city
that he, Lithargoël, appointed for us.
In a bond
of faith we forsook
25. everything as
he had said (to do). We evaded
the robbers, because they did not
find their garments with us.
We evaded the
30. wolves, because they did not find the water
with us for which they thirsted.
We evaded the lions,
because they did not find the desire
for meat with us.

VIII. [We evaded the bulls...
...] [...
they did not find] green vegetables.
A great joy [came upon] us [and a]
5. peaceful carefreeness [like
that of] our Lord. We [rested

ourselves] in front of the gate, [and]
we talked with each other [about that]
which is not a distraction of this [world].
10. Rather we continued in contemplation
of the faith. As we discussed the
robbers on the road, whom we
evaded, behold
Lithargoel, having changed, came out to
15. us. **He had the appearance of a physician,
since an unguent box was under
his arm, and a young disciple was
following him carrying a pouch
full of medicine.**
20. We did not recognize him.
Peter responded and said to him,
"We want you to do
us a favor, because we are
strangers, and take us to the house of
30. Lithargoel before evening comes."
He said, "In uprightness
of heart I will show it to you.
But I am amazed at how
you knew this good man.
35. For he does not reveal himself to
every man, because he himself
is the son of a great king.
**Rest yourselves a little so
that I may go and heal this man
40. and come (back)." He hurried and came (back)**

IX.   **quickly.** He said to Peter,
"Peter!" And Peter was frightened,
for how did he know

that his name was Peter?
5. Peter responded to the Savior
   "How do you know me,
   for you called my name?"
   Lithargoel answered, "I
   want to ask you who gave the
10. name Peter to you?" He
   said to him, "It was Jesus Christ, the
   son of the living God. He
   gave this name to me." He answered
   and said, "It is I! Recognize me,
15. Peter." He loosened the garment,
   which clothed him — the one into which
   he had changed himself because of us —
   revealing to us in truth that
   it was he. We prostrated ourselves
20. on the ground and worshiped him. We
   comprised eleven disciples
   He stretched forth his hand
   and caused us to stand. We spoke with
   him humbly. Our heads were
25. bowed down in unworthiness
   as we said, "What you
   wish we will do. But
   give us the power to do
30. what you wish at all times."
He gave them the unguent box
and the pouch
that was in the hand of the young disciple.
He commanded them like this,

X.   saying, "Go into [the]
city from which you came,

which is called Habitation.
Continue in endurance as you

5. teach all who have believed
in my name, because I have endured
in sufferings of the faith. I
will give you your reward. To the
poor of that city give

10. what they need in order to live
until I give them what is better
which I told you that I will give
you for nothing." Peter answered
and said to him,

15. "Lord, you have taught us to
forsake the world and
everything in it. We have renounced them
for your sake. What we are concerned about (now)
is the food for a single day.

20. Where will we be able to find the needs that you ask
us to provide for the poor?"
   The Lord answered and said,
"O Peter, it was necessary
that you understand this parable

25. that I told you! Do you not understand
that my name, which you teach,
surpasses all riches,
and the wisdom of God
surpasses gold, and silver

30. and precious stone(s)?"
   He gave them the pouch
of medicine and said,
"Heal all the sick
of the city who believe

XI.   [in] my name." Peter was afraid
       [to] reply to him for a second time.
       He signaled to the one who was beside
       him, who was John: "You
5. talk this time."
       John answered and said,
       "Lord, before you we are afraid
       to say many words.
       But it is you who asks us
10. to practice this skill. We have not been
       taught to be physicians. How then
       will we know how to heal bodies
       as you have told us?"
       He answered them, "Rightly have you
15. spoken, John, for I know
       that the physicians of this world
       heal what belongs to this world.
       The physicians of souls, however,
       heal the heart. Heal
20. the bodies first, therefore, so
       that through the
       real powers of healing
       for their bodies, without medicine of
       the world, they may believe in you,
25. that you have power to heal
       the illnesses of the heart also. The
       rich men of the city, however, those
       who did not see fit
       even to acknowledge me, but who
30. reveled in their
       wealth and pride —
       with such as these, therefore

XII.   do not dine in [their] houses
      nor be friends with them,
      lest their partiality
      influence you. For many in the churches have

5. shown partiality to the rich, because
      they also are sinful,
      and they give occasion for
      others to sin. But judge
      them with uprightness, so

10. that your ministry may
      be glorified, and that
      my name also, may be glorified in the
      churches." The disciples
      answered and said, "Yes,

15. truly this is what is fitting
      to do." They prostrated themselves on the ground
      and worshiped him. He caused them
      to stand and departed from
      them in peace. Amen.
      The Acts of Peter
      and the Twelve
      Apostles

Introduction

For approximately 1500 years the sands of Upper Egypt concealed the fifty-two texts that would eventually come to be known as the Nag Hammadi library. While the exact circumstances which led to their burial (ca. mid-fourth century) may never be brought to light, James M. Robinson described the general situation in his 1988 introduction to the *Nag Hammadi Library in English*:

> Just as the Dead Sea Scrolls were put in jars for safekeeping and hidden at the time of the approach of the Roman Tenth Legion, the burial of the Nag Hammadi library in a jar may also have been precipitated by the approach of Roman authorities, who by then had become Christian. The fact that the Nag Hammadi library was hidden in a jar suggests the intention not to eliminate but to preserve the books. For not only were the Dead Sea Scrolls put in such jars for safekeeping, but biblical manuscripts have been found similarly preserved up and down the Nile, in some cases dating from the same period and buried in the Nag Hammadi region.[1]

---

[1] Robinson further elaborates on his belief that the burial was intended to preserve the texts: "The Bible refers to burial in a jar as a way to preserve a book and to burning as the way to eliminate one (Jer 32:14–15; 36:23). *The Life of St. Pachomius* reports that he got rid of a book by Origen, whom he considered a heretic, by throwing it in the water, with the comment that if the Lord's name had not been in it he would have burned it. The burning of the greatest library in antiquity at Alexandria by Christians late in the fourth century C.E. suggests that such a ready solution would hardly have been overlooked if the intent had been to get rid of the Nag Hammadi Library. If the codices had been part of a Pachomian library, they must have been removed not by heresy-hunters, but by devotees who cherished them enough to bury them in a jar for safekeeping, perhaps for posterity" (*The Nag Hammadi Library in English* [2d ed.; San Francisco: Harper, 1988] 20–21).

1

Given these thoughts of Robinson, a question naturally presents itself: If these texts were so important to those who buried them, why were they not recovered by their protectors following the period of persecution? Assuming that these individuals cared for these codices and considering the time and expense involved in producing such manuscripts, it is surely unlikely that these people intended to bury their texts as if in some kind of ancient time-capsule, waiting to be revealed to some future generation. The people who hid these texts were scholars, philosophers and dreamers, who sought to preserve their literary treasures. Such people would not have completely abandoned their books. It seems only rational to conclude that they were somehow prevented from returning. Either they died for their beliefs or they were forced to flee the region. In any event, they never returned to reclaim their library.

Such devotion and commitment to these sacred books demands that they be given a fair hearing. These texts deserve to be allowed to transmit their unique philosophies and world-views and be subsequently judged on their individual merits. While most interpreters of the Nag Hammadi texts would agree with such sentiments in theory, in past decades there has been a marked tendency to value Nag Hammadi only insofar as its works demonstrate the use and/ or knowledge of the New Testament. In some cases, scholarly studies on various Nag Hammadi texts have degenerated into catalogs of NT "echoes" and "allusions," in which the author argues for the dependence of a given Nag Hammadi tractate upon some NT passage.[2] I have often wondered if the unfortunate label "heretical texts"

---

[2] An early example of this tendency is Antoine Guillamont, Henri-Charles Puech, Gilles Quispel, Walter C. Till and Yassah 'Abd al Masīh, trans., *The Gospel According to Thomas* (Leiden: Brill, 1959). This was the first available English translation of this work and while the text received only the briefest of introductions (with promises of a further study to follow) the translators managed to include three and a half pages of what they call "Scriptural Parallels and Echoes" (ibid., 59–62). A more recent example of this approach is Jacqueline A. Williams, *Biblical Interpretation in the Gospel of Truth from Nag Hammadi* (SBLDS 79; Atlanta: Scholars Press, 1988). In her introduction, Williams states that "the present study demonstrates conclusively that Valentinus did in fact use many of the writings that would form the New Testament" but admits that "there

which is borne by the Nag Hammadi codices has not made various would-be interpreters nervous. It seems as if some scholars absolutely must find a NT dependency so as to justify their interest in such dubious books. Thankfully, there has been a growing appreciation of the integrity and unique witness to the Jesus tradition that these texts provide. Such awareness seems to be spearheaded by some of those scholars who are currently working on the *Gospel of Thomas* as was evidenced by papers and discussions that took place at the November 1995 SBL "Nag Hammadi and Gnosticism" section in Philadelphia. In these debates such scholars as Paul-Hubert Poirier, Ron Cameron, Philip H. Sellew, Stephen J. Patterson and Jean-Marie Sevrin called for and debated a status for Thomas on equal par with the four canonical gospels.[3]

This debate was of great interest to me as I accept a first century dating for *Gos. Thom.* and have no hesitation in accepting its traditions as equal to those found in the canonical gospels. Upon discussing this with other graduate students in attendance (some of whom were from Claremont), I realized that there were many younger students of Nag Hammadi who shared my view. Essentially, my judgement on the Jesus

---

are no verbatim quotations or quotation formulae" (ibid., 8). Once again the reader is led along the slippery slope of NT "allusions" and "echoes," many of which are arbitrary. This is by no means to assert that such analysis does not have its place in Nag Hammadi research. Certainly such studies are valuable (e.g., Robert L. Webb, Craig A. Evans and Richard A. Wiebe, *Nag Hammadi Texts and the Bible: A Synopsis and Index* [New Testament Tools and Studies 18; Leiden: Brill, 1993]) just as those which collect NT quotations in the Church Fathers.

[3] Patterson had already voiced this opinion: "Although Thomas's sayings generally show the same sorts of secondary developments one finds in the synoptic tradition, it is clear that they have undergone this process of development independently from the parallel synoptic tradition" ("The Gospel of Thomas: Introduction," in John S. Kloppenborg et al., eds., *Q-Thomas Reader* [Sonoma: Polebridge, 1990] 87). Marvin Meyer, also a participant in the SBL debate, expressed a similar position: "An excellent case can be made for the position that the Gospel of Thomas is not fundamentally dependent upon the New Testament gospels, but that it preserves sayings that at times appear to be more original than the New Testament parallels" (*The Gospel of Thomas: The Hidden Sayings of Jesus* [San Francisco: Harper, 1992] 13).

traditions that are found embedded at various levels in many, albeit not all, of the Nag Hammadi tractates is one of parallelism, not dependency.[4]

I would explain this view as one in which the Jesus Movement could be likened to a bicycle wheel. Jesus and his actual ministry would be the center of the wheel, while the subsequent traditions about him would be represented by the spokes. The synoptic gospels could be described as three spokes of that wheel that are adjacent to one another (at twelve, one and two o'clock), while John might be best viewed as a spoke somewhat separated yet not too distant (possibly at five o'clock). Other materials, such as the *Secret Gospel of Mark* and *Gos. Pet.* would be spokes located next to those of the Synoptic Gospels and John respectively (eleven and four o'clock). *Gos. Thom.* and the rest of the Jesus Traditions found in the Nag Hammadi library (such as the resurrection appearance I shall examine in *ActsPet12Apost.* 9.1–29) can go a long way toward helping NT scholars fill in other hitherto unavailable sections of the bicycle wheel and therefore advance our overall knowledge of the ways in which the Jesus traditions were used and transmitted.

Unfortunately, the desire to find NT connections has affected even the fledgling study of *ActsPet12Apost.* (NHC 6,1) 1.1–12.22. The process began as early as 1971, when Martin Krause and Pahor Labib published the first German translation of this text.[5] Krause and Labib identified

---

[4] For examples of studies which follow much the same approach see: Charles W. Hedrick, "Kingdom Sayings and Parables of Jesus in the Apocryphon of James: Tradition and Redaction," *NTS* 29 (1983) 1–24; Ron Cameron, *Sayings Traditions in the Apocryphon of James* (HTS 34; Philadelphia: Fortress, 1984); and much of the modern research on the *Gos. Thom.* which is cited in this study.

[5] The first English translation of *ActsPet12Apost.* appeared in James M. Robinson, ed., *The Nag Hammadi Library in English* (Leiden: Brill, 1977) 265–70. In the same year a Polish version also appeared (Wincenty Myszor, "Dzieje Piotra: Przeklad z koptyjskiego," *Studia theologica Varsaw* 15 [1977] 169–75). Three years later, an introduction and translation of the text was published in Italian (F. Salvoni, "Un nuovo Apocrifo: Gli atti di S. Pietro e dei 12 Apostoli," *Ricerche bibiche e religiose* 15 [1980] 35–42). To the best of my knowledge there is no French translation at this time. However, I have every confidence that the scholars of l'Université Laval will rectify this situation in due

possible echoes of forty-three NT passages in the twelve Coptic leaves of *ActsPet12Apost.*[6] Following in this general path, Jesse Sell, in a series of three articles, described "a striking Johannine echo,"[7] "an almost verbatim quotation of Simon Peter's 'confession,'"[8] and the term "'fellow stranger'...a Greek technical term which has 'migrated' — from the LXX through the NT and the patristic literature — into this Coptic 'Gnostic' text!"[9] While the usefulness and persuasiveness of these studies is varied, the pinnacle of eisogesis was attained by James E. Furman. After bombarding the reader with a chain of dubious NT connections, Furman, in a 1985 article which reads like a cross between a televangelist's sermon and a pamphlet expounding popular spirituality, stated: "My point is that here and elsewhere the author of 'Peter and the Twelve' says much through what he 'echoes,' teaching through allusion and reference." Furman more fully revealed his position in his conclusion:

> I see "Peter and the Twelve" as the product of a pious author summing up Gospel themes in a brief, colorful document. If this judgment is correct, "Peter and the Twelve," is something more than just another tract recovered from dusty antiquity. I suggest that "Peter and the Twelve" is a masterpiece of Coptic creativity, a spiritual treasure of light that gently leads forward to the greater

---

time.

[6] Krause and Labib, *Gnostische und hermetische Schriften aus Codex II und Codex VII* (Abhandlungen des deutschen archäologischen Instituts Kairo, koptische Reihe 2; Glückstadt: Augustin, 1971) 107–19. Twenty of these "echoes" are from Matthew.

[7] Sell, "A Note on a Striking Johannine Motif Found at CG VI:6,19," *NovT* 20 (1978) 233.

[8] Sell, "Simon Peter's 'Confession' and the Acts of Peter and the Twelve Apostles," *NovT* 21 (1979) 350.

[9] Sell, "Jesus the 'Fellow-Stranger': A Study of CG VI:2,35–3,11," *NovT* 23 (1981) 173–74.

light of canonical Scripture — no little achievement for a book found on a Gnostic shelf.[10]

While the work of Krause and Labib and Sell can hardly be grouped with such condescending statements as those made by Furman, Furman's remarks do betray what has been for certain scholars a general way of approaching these documents. Undoubtedly, the texts which would eventually become the NT did influence some of the Nag Hammadi tractates. However, I suggest that, especially in the case of *ActsPet12Apost.*, such searches for NT "allusions," "echoes" and "parallels" are premature. For example, in 1978, when Sell wrote the first of his articles suggesting a "Johannine echo," research on *ActsPet12Apost.* lacked detailed studies in every major form of criticism: source, form, redaction, narrative. To be sure, suggestions as to genre and sources had been made, but only in the most basic and introductory fashion. It was only with the work of Stephen J. Patterson that *ActsPet12Apost.* received its first detailed source-critical analysis.[11]

Recognizing the responsibility that comes with writing the first full length study of this text, I have determined to put aside attempts to find NT echoes, allusions and parallels and, employing historical-critical methods, focus on understanding the text as it is presented. In seeking to accomplish this task, I will also address the one literary element which could be described as *ActsPet12Apost.*'s defining characteristic — its use of allegorical imagery.

Since Krause's 1972 ground-breaking work, "Die Petrusakten in Codex VI von Nag Hammadi," there has followed a fairly small body of scholarly literature in which a variety of attempts have been made to grapple with some of the key issues confronting the modern interpreter.

---

[10] Furman, "Leading to Light: A Christian Reading of a Nag Hammadi Text," *Coptic Church Review* 6 (1985) 26.

[11] Patterson also provided a brief theory of redaction ("Sources, Redaction and Tendenz in The Acts of Peter and the Twelve Apostles [NH VI,1]," *VC* 45 [1991] 1–17).

In the last several decades there has been an effort to understand the structure of *ActsPet12Apost.* by examining the voice changes which occur at peculiar, sometimes unexpected and puzzling intervals. The first to discuss this problem was Krause, whose 1972 article was the impetus for such scholars as Douglas M. Parrott, Schenke and Patterson. These scholars presented differing solutions to the questions of form and source posed by these voice changes. One advantage of the approaches used by these writers was that the narrative voice changes and textual aporias were taken seriously as possible indicators of textual seams, and hence as evidence of a redactional hand at work. Unfortunately, the danger of this type of approach is that voice shifts and aporias can be given too much weight while an attempt to understand the text as it stands is neglected. Thus, the scholars's own judgments about what constitutes smooth narrative can lead to claims that a section is secondary, while in fact that section may make sense if one placed within an overall understanding of the text.

Certainly, other approaches have been taken. An example of this is the work of Sell. However, the work of Antoine Guillamont[12] and Carl A. Keller was possibly more beneficial at this early stage.[13] These two scholars have contributed more than anyone to the understanding of *ActsPet12Apost.* as an allegory. The value of their work lies in their recognition of the text as literature with all its ability to refer to something beyond that which is obvious. Therefore it is logical to attempt to use the strengths of all the studies previously published and produce an analysis that understands the structural peculiarities of the text in light of its allegorical message and meaning within its communal context. It will be my objective to demonstrate that there are two sources at work in the text: 1) an older, allegorical Christian-Gnostic text describing an otherworldly

---

[12] Guillamont, "De nouveaux Actes Apocryphes: Les Actes de Pierre et des Douze Apôtres," *RHR* 4 (1979) 141–52.

[13] Keller, "De la Foi à la Connaissance: Le Sens des 'Actes de Pierre et des Douze Apôtres' (NHC VI,1)," *RTP* 110 (1978) 131–37.

ascent; and 2) a resurrection appearance scene. These two sources were sewn together and altered by a redactor who both inserted material into these sources and attached a substantial section at the end. This editorial addition altered the emphasis of the first text.

The first text was driven by a Gnostic escapism, seeking to provide its readers with a method by which to leave this world and return through the hostile cosmic realms, infested as they are with evil archons. The editorial addition altered this trajectory by providing a new motivation for turning the disciples around and sending them back to the world. This return to the world was not merely for the purpose of transmitting the information about how to make the treacherous journey through the realm of the archons (as it had been in the first source) but for the purpose of earthly Church ministry (albeit aimed only at their own community and not to the world at large). This change is worth exploring in that this redactor was at ease enough with the idea of ascent to leave it in his or her new hybrid text. However, this ascent is not so literal as it must have been in the first text. Instead, its mysticism is now given practical expression and purpose: the mythology of the original is transformed into a literal, earthly commission.

Obviously these questions lead to a consideration of the community behind this text, a subject which, probably related to the relative newness and obscurity of this text, has been largely ignored. It is my contention that the text itself, especially those sections added by the redactor, provides ample clues to the actual historical situation which inspired or provoked its creation. These clues suggest a historical situation marked by recent persecutions, apostasies by the wealthy and both spiritual and physical disease — all of which, I shall argue, fit the years immediately following the Decian persecution (i.e., ca. 251–256 A.D.).

This dissertation will employ historical-critical methods and focus its energy upon answering basic questions, concerning issues such as sources, genre(s), the shape of the underlying tradition and compositional redaction. These investigations will be followed by a detailed analysis of a theoretical community that might have valued this text and a subsequent theory regarding its date and historical setting. More specifically, I will show that *ActsPet12Apost.* is primarily made up of a Christian-Gnostic allegory of the ascent of the soul which underwent a later adaptation. This adaptation shifts the center of gravity from an otherworldly escapism to a mysticism grounded by earth-based pastoral ministry.

Chapter 1
The Division of the Text by Sources

The *Acts of Peter and the Twelve Apostles*, discovered along with 46 other tracts at Nag Hammadi, Egypt, in 1945, is still very much in its infancy of scholarly analysis. While with some early Christian texts scholarly history is measured in centuries, the study of *ActsPet12Apost.* must be measured in decades. Until now the scholarly approach has been primarily that of introductions to the text (i.e., brief summaries of the narrative with short descriptions of the literary problems and peculiarities of the text); indeed, fully half of the available literature serves this purpose. Most of these introductions and several of the other studies have focused upon dividing and describing the text in light of its most obvious problem, the problem of peculiar voice shifts — apparent changes in the identity of the narrator. The narrative voice of the text begins in the first person plural, then shifts to the first person singular. After a peculiar shift to the third person, the text successively shifts back to the first person plural, then to the first person singular, finally ending in the third person.

In the following pages I shall begin to address these peculiar voice shifts by discussing the methodological characteristics of source criticism and the difficulties in the text that suggest the need for a source-critical analysis. Then I shall discuss the profitability of using source criticism as a point of departure for critical study of *ActsPet12Apost.* by briefly examining other source-critical studies of early Christian texts that have borne fruitful results. Next, I shall describe the various positions that have been proposed as solutions to this problem. Finally, after reviewing these theories, I shall present my own theory as to how the divisions in the text and corresponding source questions should be treated.

WHY SOURCE CRITICISM?

When a reader comes in contact with *ActsPet12Apost.* he or she is immediately confronted with sudden, rather distracting voice changes. These are hard to miss, even for the most unsophisticated reader. At times, these voice changes seem to coincide with other changes in the text, such as the change from "narrative" to "instruction" in 9.29–30. Such voice changes, coupled with changes in the roles of these sections, lead the scholar to suspect the introduction of a different source. Furthermore, there are changes in time frame that also seem to coincide with these voice changes. For example, there are statements of Peter in 1.10–11 ("we agreed to fulfill the ministry to which the Lord appointed us") and 5.12–14 ("It is necessary for us to spread the word of God in every city harmoniously") which imply that the disciples are just beginning their ministry. However, in 12.4, 13 churches are mentioned as already functioning, a definite contrast from the earlier sections. Thus one is forced to explore these and other problems in the text and question whether or not our text is actually the result of the combination of several sources.

In 1992, John Barton wrote a brief but enlightening article on source criticism. In this article Barton made an important observation on the differences between ancient and modern literary conventions and how these conventions relate to source criticism:

> Modern literary conventions forbid plagiarism, and require authors to identify and acknowledge any material they have borrowed from another writer. But in ancient times it was common to "write" a book by transcribing existing material, adapting and adding to it from other documents as required, and not indicating which parts

were original and which were borrowed.... Source criticism seeks
to separate out these originally independent documents...[1]

Barton delineates three major categories used by source critics which
provide evidence of the composite character of a given text:
inconsistencies, repetitions and doublets, and stylistic differences. Using
examples from the OT, Barton notes that inconsistencies can be
manifested by the difficulty in extracting a coherent sequence of narrative
events, such as the discrepancies found in our text when Peter describes
the appearance of Lithargoel, now in the guise of a physician, and
mentions that the group did not recognize him. ("As we discussed the
robbers on the road, whom we evaded, behold Lithargoel, having
changed, came out to us. He had the appearance of a physician, since an
unguent box was under his arm, and a young disciple was following him
carrying a pouch full of medicine. We did not recognize him," 8.11b–20.)
Later, the physician is "recognized" as Jesus and not as Lithargoel at all
(cf. 9.1–19a), leaving the reader to ask, "How did Peter know it was
Lithargoel disguised as a physician?" Barton also discusses thematic
inconsistencies, "when a text seems to give expression to two
incompatible points of view."[2] Thematic inconsistency is also found in
our text (e.g., the rich reject the merchant and are rejected by him as well
[3.25–28]; however, the rich are mentioned as being somehow in
relationship with the churches [11.27–12.8]). There are also smaller

---

[1]Barton, "Source Criticism," *ABD* 6.162. An excellent example of the
absorption of an originally separate source is found in Lucius Apuleius,
Metamorphoses 4.22–6.23. In this section the strange tale of Apuleius, a man
turned into an ass by the witch Pamphiles, is interrupted by the story of Cupid and
Psyche. Only the most passing of attempts is made to link this story with the
preceding material. Another example is Aristides' *Apology*. According to
Eusebius (*Hist. eccl.* 4.3.3), this apology was directed to Hadrian. However, a
Greek text of this work has been discovered in a speech of the medieval monastic
romance, *Barlaam and Josaphat*; see Helmut Koester, *Introduction to the New
Testament* (2 vols; Philadelphia: Fortress, 1982) 1.340–42.

[2] Barton, "Source Criticism," 163.

inconsistencies of detail, such as the use of the term "Lord" throughout the text (1.12, 16, 23; 8.6; 10.15, 22; 11.7) and the solitary use of the term "Savior," which, interestingly enough, occurs in a section of text that is different from any other section in our text in both voice (third person) and perspective (a narrator other than Peter).

As for repetitions and doublets, this type of textual phenomenon arises when "two versions of the same story have both been allowed to remain in the finished form of the book."[3] Barton cites the two creation accounts of Genesis 1–2 as an example, where "in 1:27, 'God created man in his own image,' but then in 2:7, 'the Lord God formed man of the dust of the ground,' just as if the man's creation had not been mentioned before." Once again, an example of this, albeit on a much smaller scale, can be found in our text. In 2.10b–29, two separate descriptions of the merchant are placed side by side. This goes beyond simple narrative expansion, since the merchant's head and hands are actually redescribed in the second version (2.17b–29).

Stylistic differences identified by Barton range from "a preference for particular words or phrases to peculiarities of grammar and syntax...recurring formulas, lists, and technical terms."[4] Certainly, such stylistic tendencies as using the first or third person could be placed under this category. Another example of this is the apparent preference for the use of the titles "brothers," "stranger(s)," and "friend(s)," in the first person narrative sections (2.35–3.10; 6.28; 7.21; 8.24) and their replacement in the later sections with the term "disciple" (9.20 and 12.13, but not in 8.17 and 9.32, which use, ⲀⲖⲞⲨ "a child, servant").

Clearly, Barton's three main indicators are all present in our document. Therefore it is reasonable to conclude that the evidence provided by *ActsPet12Apost.* warrants an examination with a view to the detection of its underlying sources. It is important to recognize the continued validity of the insights which can be gained by a source-critical

---

[3] Ibid., 163.

[4] Ibid., 163.

inquiry. This is especially necessary in light of such new types of criticism such as: reader-response and narrative criticism, which have risen in popularity over the last twenty years. These methods tend to overlook questions regarding sources and focus upon the text as it currently exists.[5] However, the source-critical method has a long and significant history of scholarly contribution to the study of scripture.

Over the last century source criticism has been a great aid to biblical studies in helping to expand biblical scholars's understanding of both the OT[6] and NT.[7] However, more recent studies have employed source-critical methods to other early Christian texts and also have provided important insights. Within the Nag Hammadi corpus itself, source

---

[5] See Terence J. Keegan, *Interpreting the Bible: A Popular Introduction to Biblical Hermeneutics* (New York: Paulist, 1985). This introduction is an example of how proponents of narrative-critical methodologies can sometimes downplay the value of source-criticism and other historical-critical methods.

[6] For example there is the classic work of S. R. Driver, who actually diagrams the intertwining of the J, E and P sources and states, "That P and JE form two clearly definable, independent sources, is a conclusion abundantly justified by the facts" (*An Introduction to the Literature of the Old Testament* [9th ed. rev.; Edinburgh: T. & T. Clark, 1929] 19). Also in the Pentateuch there is the work of Julius Wellhausen on the four-source hypothesis (J, E, D and Q/P); e.g., see *Geschichte Israels* (Berlin: Reimer, 1878). It should be observed that in recent years the propriety of accepting these Pentateuchal sources as such has been called into question by scholars such as, Thomas L. Thompson, *The Origin Tradition of Ancient Israel* (JSOTSS 55; Sheffield: JSOT Press, 1987). Source Criticism also has contributed greatly to the study of the prophets, e.g., see Bernhard von Duhm, *Die Theologie der Propheten als Gundlage für die innere Entwicklungsgeschichte der israelitischen Religion* (Bonn: Marcus, 1875) and *Israels Propheten* (Tübingen: Mohr, 1922).

[7] For example, there is the work of Adolf von Harnack, *Die Apostelgeschichte* (Beiträge zur Einleitung in das Neue Testament 3; Leipzig: Hinrichs, 1908). In the Synoptics there are those such as Heinrich-Julius Holtzmann, *Die synoptischen Evangelien: Ihr Ursprung und ihr geschichtlicher Charakter* (Leipzig: Engelmann, 1863) and B. H. Streeter, *The Four Gospels: A Study of Origins* (London: Macmillan, 1924).

criticism has proved to be a helpful method of coming to understand these newly discovered texts so as to prepare for more textual analysis.

Probably the most dramatic example of source criticism at work in the Nag Hammadi corpus is provided by the two documents *Eugnostos* and *Sophia of Jesus Christ*.[8] *Eug.* appears in two recensions (NHC 3.3 and NHC 5.1), while *SJC* has also two versions (NHC 3.4 and Papyrus Berolinensis 8502.3, both in Coptic) and is attested in a Greek fragment (Oxyrhynchus papyrus 1081). The two copies of *Eug.* are different,[9] while both versions of *SJC* agree essentially.[10] Parrott explains that *Eug.* (NHC 5) represents the most ancient version (ca. 1st century B. C.), while *Eug.* (NHC 3), a revised version, is closer to the text which was used by the author of *SJC*, and should be dated during the late 1st century A. D.[11]

---

[8] See Michel Tardieu, *Écrits gnostiques: Codex de Berlin* (Sources gnostiques et manichéennes 1; Paris: Cerf, 1984) 54–60.

[9] Douglas M. Parrott explains that *Eug.* NHC 3 differs from NHC 5, "Eug-III was apparently edited in the light of SJC by sharpening the prediction at the end. Since that sharpening is only apparent because of the parallel in Eug-V, the latter's reading is probably is to be thought of as earlier here. In addition to the prediction, there are two other places, which we noted, where Eug-V seems earlier than Eug-III, namely, the titles in the incipit and subscript" (*Nag Hammadi Codices III,3–4 and V,1 with Papyrus Berolinensis 8502,3 and Oxyrhynchus Papyrus 1081* [NHS 27; Leiden: Brill, 1991] 16).

[10] Except for what Catherine Barry describes as "differences, imputable certainly to the process of translation from the original Greek, [which] are of two orders: relative to the work of the translators or inherent in the order of the words. Moreover, the witness of BG contains repetitions, attributable not so much to the translation, but to glosses inserted by a thoughtful revisionist so as to lay stress on certain passages" (*La Sagesse de Jésus Christ* [Bibliothèque Copte de Nag Hammadi Section Textes 20; Quebec: Les Presses de l'Université Laval, 1993] 18).

[11] This is the earliest dating for *SJC*, as is described by Barry (ibid., 35–36). On the issue of dating, Barry (ibid., 36) sides with Michel Tardieu and Jean-Daniel Dubois in attributing SJC to the middle of the third century A. D. (*Introduction à la littérature gnostique* [Initiations au christianisme ancien; Paris: Cerf, 1986] 131–32).

These multiple versions have been instrumental in helping scholars evaluate the history of transmission of these texts and their traditions.

As a second example, John D. Turner, in his work on *Thomas the Contender*, begins his commentary by stating that "taken as a whole" *Thom. Cont.* "cannot be considered a unity."[12] Turner argues that the text is a composite of two texts: Section A (138.4–142.26), a revelation dialogue, and Section B, made up of an introductory apocalypse (142.26–143.7), a collection of woes (143.7–145.1) and beatitudes (145.1–8), and a concluding admonition and promise of salvation (145.8–17). After describing a five-step process of composition, Turner lists the three main justifications for his hypothesis: 1) the language of the incipit is unique when compared with the rest of the work; 2) the dialogue includes only three-fifths of the text; and 3) motifs important to Section B are absent from Section A and visa versa.[13] Thus, Turner concludes:

> In the commentary we have offered reasons for considering Thomas the Contender to be the sum of two originally separate works. One work, section A, was a dialogue between Thomas and the Savior, perhaps entitled "The Book of Thomas the Contender writing to the Perfect." The other work, section B, was a collection of the Savior's sayings gathered into a homiletical discourse, perhaps entitled "The Hidden Words which the Savior spoke, which I wrote down, even I, Mathaias." A redactor has prefixed section A to section B, and prefaced the whole with an incipit title composed on analogy with the original title to section B, and designating Mathaias as the scribe of the whole. The subscript title, designating Thomas as the scribe of the whole, was borrowed from the original title to section A, and suffixed to the newly-formed whole.[14]

---

[12] Turner, *The Book of Thomas the Contender* (SBLDS 23; Missoula, MT: Scholars Press, 1975) 106.

[13] Ibid., 108–9.

[14] Ibid., 215.

A third example of fruitful source-critical work within the Nag Hammadi corpus is that of Charles W. Hedrick on the *Apocalypse of Adam*.[15] Hedrick recognizes significant changes in setting (from a primordial garden to a "historical" situation) and actors (from a scene which includes Adam, Eve and Seth to one which isolates Adam and the three men) and argues that *Apoc. Adam* is a composite text made up of two sources and material added by a redactor.[16] While recognizing a certain subjectivity in his judgments, Hedrick defends his use of source criticism:

> This approach takes the many anomalies of the text seriously and attempts to make sense of them. In some cases it clears up ambiguities in the tractate. For example, it explains the contradictory use of the title "god of the aeons." Most students of Adam have, no doubt, already recognized and pondered this particular problem: How can the tractate apply this same title to both the demiurge (74.26–27) and the eternal God (85.4–5) with no sense of discontinuity? The solution is made possible by source analysis. Apparently the rather unsophisticated redactor simply failed to adjust his Vorlage (source A 74.26–27) to his own theology (85.4–5) at this point.[17]

---

[15] Hedrick, "The Apocalypse of Adam: A Literary and Source Analysis," *SBLSP* 2 (1972) 581–90, later expanded as *The Apocalypse of Adam* (SBLDS 46; Atlanta: Scholars Press, 1980).

[16] Hedrick, "Analysis," 587–88. Hedrick divided the text into Source A (64.6–65.23; 66.12–67.12; 67.22–76.7; 83.7–84.3; 64.1–6; 85.19–22); Source B (65.24–66.12; 67.12–21; 76.8–83.7) and material added by the redactor (84.4–85.18; 85.22b–31 and approximately ten other polemical passages).

[17] Ibid., 589.

While there are a number of other ground-breaking studies that employ source criticism to interpret Nag Hammadi tractates,[18] source criticism has also been used on other early Christian texts as is evidenced by the work of R. H. Charles on *The Ascension of Isaiah*.[19] Still a more recent example of work on this text is an article by Robert G. Hall. In this study Hall admits, following other scholars such as Charles, that the author probably wrote the first part by interpolating a pre-existing Jewish source.[20] However, he claims that the Vision of Isaiah need not have been the result of redactional incorporation of a previous Jewish source. He argues that the community behind the *Ascension of Isaiah* could have also produced the Vision of Isaiah.

These examples of source-critical studies in early Christian literature are by no means unique in their usage of source criticism. They demonstrate that much has been and can be gained from such studies. Regardless, source criticism is only one possible tool for unlocking the secrets of our text. Therefore it is important to establish at this juncture that I see source-critical analysis as only the first step in a process of study that also requires form and redactional studies so as to understand more fully the nature of *ActsPet12Apost*. Having said this we can now proceed to an examination of the proposals that have been made which attempt to address the source critical problems evidenced by the text.

---

[18] See, e.g., Scott Kent Brown, "Jewish and Gnostic Elements in the Second Apocalypse of James," *NovT* 17 (1975) 225–37; John Horman, "The Source of the Version of the Parable of the Sower in the Gospel of Thomas," *NovT* 21 (1979) 326–401; Gesine Robinson, "The Trimorphic Protennoia and the Prologue of the Fourth Gospel," in J. E. Goehring and C. W. Hedrick, eds., *Gnosticism and the Early Christian World: In Honor of James M. Robinson* (Sonoma, CA: Polebridge, 1990) 37–50.

[19] See Charles, *The Ascension of Isaiah Translated from the Ethiopic Version* (London: Black, 1900) xxxvi–xlv.

[20] Hall, "Isaiah's Ascent to See the Beloved: An Ancient Jewish Source for the Ascension of Isaiah?" *JBL* 113 (1994) 463–84. Hall lists scholars who have employed the source-critical method on page 463.

MARTIN KRAUSE

In 1972, Martin Krause argued that the title itself reflects the composite nature of the text. He argued that the text actually contains two separate "acts": first, an act of Peter, and second, an act of the apostolic group.[21] Krause divides the text into three originally independent parts: a contextual framework (1.3–1.29), a first narrative (1.29–7.23) and a second narrative (8.13–12.19).[22] Observing that there are inconsistencies in the text, Krause notes the changes in the voice of narration: the first person plural ("we") is used in the framework, the first person singular ("I") is used in the first narrative, and the voice of narration changes from the first person plural to the third person singular in the second narrative section.[23] Krause hypothesizes this process of composition of the text:

> The third part has apparently been redacted to the second part through references which point back to it. This, however, has created contradictions between the two narratives. Through this, the pearl in part three has been Christianized through its reinterpretation as the name Jesus. A contextual framework, the first part, was then placed in front of the two narratives.[24]

HANS-MARTIN SCHENKE

In 1973, Hans-Martin Schenke published a short study in which he proposed, then rejected, an explanation of the text's peculiar voice shifts as a choir-sermon with Peter as soloist. Instead, he found the text to be half sermon, half narrative, the original framework being that of a

---

[21] Krause, "Die Petrusakten in Codex VI von Nag Hammadi," in idem, ed., *Essays on the Nag Hammadi Texts in Honor of Alexander Bohlig* (NHS 3; Leiden: Brill, 1972) 38.

[22] Ibid., 49–51.

[23] Ibid., 49.

[24] Ibid., 51.

sermon.[25]   Later, in 1989, Schenke wrote an introduction to *ActsPet12Apost.* in volume 2 of the revised edition of *Neutestamentliche Apokryphen*. In his more recent work Schenke contends, apparently building from the work of Krause, that *ActsPet12Apost.* came into existence through the combination of three different texts. The first text was a "legendary narrative" of a fantastic voyage involving Peter and the other apostles. In this material the apostles are brought "out of time and space" to an imaginary island which signifies the world. This island is symbolically named according to its situation.[26] Schenke views the statement, "So that in this way, the city of everyone who endures the burden of his yoke of faith will be inhabited, and he will be included in the kingdom of heaven" (7.15–19), as the original ending of this story.

Schenke's second text was not added to the first (as if it were merely "tacked" on to the end) — it was inserted into it. This second text was the description of a vision (presumably by Peter) of a pearl-merchant named Lithargoel who appears in a strange city offering a mysterious pearl to rich and poor alike. Schenke argues that this was a transparent allegory of Jesus' preaching of salvation and its reception in the world. For Schenke this second text originally had no relationship with the first.[27]

---

[25] Schenke sees this sermon as having been altered at the end into a narrative. This sermon was originally only Peter's, although the other apostles were dealt with in the text ("Die Taten des Petrus und der zwölf Apostel," *TLZ* 98 [1973] 15).

[26] Schenke sees the key aspects of this story as being: a) the imparting of the name "since the island city still endures although it ought properly to be swallowed up by the sea"; b) the statements concerning the power and significance of endurance; and c) a sermon-like application of the name ("The Acts of Peter and the Twelve Apostles," in Wilhelm Schneemelcher, ed., *New Testament Apocrypha* [2 vols; Louisville: Westminster/ Knox, 1992] 2.417).

[27] The thinking behind Schenke's position is that there is a "breakdown in the internal logic of the imagery." Since there are no black dogs, wolves, lions or bulls on the sea the original location of Lithargoel's city "must be conceived as lying in the midst of a desert." For Schenke, Peter's intervention in his own vision makes the whole description less clear; "the only logical sequence — and so it may originally have been related — is that the poor themselves ask the pearl-

Schenke's third text demonstrates its specific characteristics by a collection of motifs typical of canonical Easter stories. Imagining this text as an Easter or Pentecost story, Schenke believes its original setting to be before the gates of Jerusalem, where Peter and the disciples meet the risen Jesus. Schenke states that a hint of the third text's original character is betrayed in that "the central figure wears one disguise too many."[28]

As for a possible motivation for three so supposedly different texts to be united, he suggests that

> what is common to all three, and could arouse the temptation to form such a hybrid, was *probably* that in all of them a city stood mysteriously at the centre, and *possibly* also that all three, although in different ways, may have been Peter texts. The second and third must also have been bound together through the name Lithargoel, which the central figure in each case bears. Each text was marked by characteristic clusters of motifs, specific to the genre or peculiar to that text, and here it is not difficult to recognize where they really belong, even when they have been displaced in the weaving-together of the texts.[29]

DOUGLAS M. PARROTT

In 1979, Douglas M. Parrott offered an analysis of the source question that differed slightly from that of Krause. Although, as he states, it is not his intention to offer a detailed source analysis, Parrott does make some

---

merchant his name and that of his city, and also about the way to that city." He is also disturbed by what he terms "the inconceivable clothing of Lithargoel." He determines that the reference to "a napkin" (σουδάριον; 2.14) is actually a reference to "grave clothes" used to help the reader or listener recognize the merchant as the crucified Jesus. According to Schenke, this reference migrated into this section from the third text ("The Acts of Peter and the Twelve Apostles," 418).

[28] The physician, identified as Lithargoel in 8.14, presents himself not as Lithargoel but as Jesus (ibid., 418).

[29] Ibid., 417.

suggestions that further the source-critical discussion. He begins by noting that Krause's analysis is weakened by its reliance upon divisions that are suggested by a secondary and inaccurate title.[30] Instead, he suggests a structural division of the text into four major units: 1) an introductory section, which sets the stage for the tractate (beginning to 2.10); 2) a section in which Peter meets a pearl merchant and sees the response of the rich and poor to him (2.10–5.18); 3) the journey of Peter and his friends to Lithargoel's city (5.19–8.11), following instructions by Lithargoel; and 4) the appearance of Lithargoel as physician, his revelation of himself as Jesus Christ, and the commissioning of the eleven disciples (8.11–12.19).[31]

In regard to the sources underlying *ActsPet12Apost.* Parrott, like Krause, does not see the text as a seamless garment. Parrott argues that the text is comprised of four originally independent accounts: 1) the story of a pearl merchant who is rejected by the rich but accepted by the poor; 2) a story about a city called Habitation; 3) a story about a journey which, contrary to the expected command to seek provisions requires the abandonment of food and possessions for successful completion; and lastly 4) an account of Christ's commission of his disciples so that they may undertake a mission of preaching and healing among poor and sick Christians. Parrott believes that the first three of these four "probably

---

[30] Parrott holds that the title must be secondary because of the contradiction between the explicit statement of the text ("we comprised eleven disciples") and the title's reference to twelve. He concludes, "The title, then, was probably provided by someone who had not read the tractate carefully or who followed the common practice of the second and third centuries of using the number twelve to refer to the apostles as a group" ("The Acts of Peter and the Twelve Apostles [VI,1:1.1–12.22]," in idem, ed., *Nag Hammadi Codices V,2–5 and VI with Papyrus Berolinensis 8502,1 and 4* [NHS 11; Leiden: Brill, 1979] 189).

[31] Unfortunately, Parrott does not provide specific reasons why the text should be divided into these four sections. Rather, one is left with the impression that these sections represent Parrott's assessment of the major movements in the text.

began as parables or allegories, somewhat resembling those found in the *Shepherd of Hermas*."[32]

Basing his judgement upon three key factors, Parrott asserted in 1979 that the sections where Lithargoel-Christ is identified as a physician are secondary.[33] His first reason for considering this material to be secondary is that "it compromises the identification of Lithargoel with Jesus, which is most important for the narrative."[34] For Parrott this perplexing identification problem disappears if the physician passages are removed. Parrott's second reason is the apparent peculiarity of Lithargoel, an already disguised figure, appearing in yet another disguise, that of a physician. His third reason is that the physician material produces three significant contradictions with other parts of the texts.[35] Parrott concludes

---

[32] Parrott, "The Acts of Peter and the Twelve Apostles (VI.1)," in James M. Robinson, ed., *The Nag Hammadi Library in English* (2d ed.; San Francisco: Harper, 1988) 287–88. Parrott argues that an editor related these accounts to one another. This editor used the common presence of 1) Peter and the other disciples, 2) the name Lithargoel, which links the pearl merchant (Parrott's second section) with the one who gives directions about the way to the city (third section) and 3) Christ (section four) who commissions the disciples to connect his or her sources.

[33] This includes 8.15–9.1; 9.30–32; and 10.31–32; see Parrott, *Nag Hammadi Codices V,2–5 and VI*, 201.

[34] Parrott argues that within the narrative the physician is never recognized as Lithargoel by Peter and the disciples — only as Jesus. He notes Peter's identification (as narrator) of the physician with Lithargoel (8.13–15). However, he dismisses this identification: "we do not know how, since the text says explicitly, 'We did not recognize him' (the physician as Lithargoel) (8.20). Only in 10.12–13 do the words of the Lord himself make clear the connection, and these are not said in such a way as to make the reader think that something new is being revealed to the disciples" (ibid., 201).

[35] These three contradictions are as follows: "a) In 8.20 the assumption is that all the disciples were involved in the earlier discussion with Lithargoel and therefore might have been able to recognize him. In fact, however, only Peter was present earlier. b) In 8.28–32 Lithargoel-Christ, as the physician, wonders how Peter came to know Lithargoel, since he does not reveal himself to everyone. But Lithargoel had appeared to both rich and poor and he himself told Peter his name (5.16). c) In 9.30–32 and 10.31–32 Christ gives the eleven various medicines for use in healing, but when they ask him how to heal bodies he tells them to do it

that the intent of this added physician material was to identify Christ with Asclepius, a practice common to the second through fourth centuries.[36]

STEPHEN J. PATTERSON

Until the work of Stephen J. Patterson published in 1991 the ideas of Krause and Parrott went virtually unchallenged (barring the 1989 study of Schenke). Patterson's work may well mark a new era in scholarly consideration of this text. In his analysis of the various literary and source theories, Patterson reviews and critiques the work of Krause, Parrott and Schenke in the most comprehensive treatment of the source question to date.[37]

Patterson begins his treatment of literary and source theories by referring to a study by Vernon K. Robbins which helps explain some of the "we passages" in *ActsPet12Apost.* by analyzing similar "we passages" in the canonical Acts of the Apostles.[38] By reviewing a variety of ancient

---

'without medicine of the world' (11.23–24)" (ibid., 201).

[36] For examples, H. J. Rose, *Religion in Greece and Rome* (New York: Harper, 1959) 112; and Adolf von Harnack, *The Mission and Expansion of Christianity in the First Three Centuries* (New York: Harper, 1961) 101–24. See also Everett Ferguson, *Backgrounds of Early Christianity* (2d ed.; Grand Rapids, MI: Eerdmans, 1993) 207–12. Ferguson includes helpful bibliographical references including both ancient sources and modern commentators. However, the most thorough source on Asclepius is Emma J. and Ludwig Edelstein, *Asclepius: A Collection and Interpretation of the Testimonies* (2 vols; Baltimore: Johns Hopkins Press, 1945). The Edelsteins supply a discussion of the clash between Christ and Asclepius (ibid., 2.132–38), stating, "The decisive reason for the disquiet aroused in Christian writers by Asclepius lay in the fact that in the early Gospel Jesus appeared as a physician, as a healer of diseases. It was such an interpretation of the new god's mission that made him resemble Asclepius, the god of medicine, more than any other pagan divinity. It was the similarity between the deeds of Christ and Asclepius that was bound to heighten the controversy between the Christian faith and the Asclepius religion" (ibid., 133).

[37] Patterson, "Sources, Redaction and Tendenz," 5–9.

[38] Robbins, "By Land and By Sea: The We-Passages and Ancient Sea Voyages," in Charles H. Talbert, ed., *Perspectives on Luke-Acts* (Perspectives in Religious Studies 5; Edinburgh: T. & T. Clark, 1978) 215–42. While this study

sea voyage accounts which have been discussed by commentators for decades (including Homer's *Odyssey*, Virgil's *Aeneid*, and Aeschylus's *Seven Against Thebes*), Robbins reaffirms that it was a common literary convention for ancient narrators to shift from either a first person singular or third person singular to a first person plural when narrating a sea voyage.[39] Robbins also offered another possible explanation of this convention in terms of social relationships:

> Since first person narration emerged naturally in relation to sea voyage literature, there could be no complete reversal of the trend. The dynamic of voyaging on the sea brings with it the experience of working with others to achieve a safe voyage and of sharing with others the fear and desperation when storm threatens to end the voyage in shipwreck. The social setting that emerges through a voyage on the sea gave rise to the sea voyage genre recounted

---

by Robbins presents an original solution to the "we passages" in Acts, the discussion of the source or sources behind these texts is an old one; for a summary of past discussion see Jacques Dupont, *The Sources of the Acts* (New York: Herder and Herder, 1964) 75–112; also Stanley E. Porter, "The 'We' Passages," in Bruce W. Winter, ed., *The Book of Acts in its First Century Setting*, vol. 2: *Graeco-Roman Setting* (Grand Rapids: Eerdmans, 1994) 545–74. Both texts include extensive bibliographies.

[39] For example, in Virgil's *Aeneid* 3.1–9 Aeneas describes the fall of Troy and the subsequent voyage that ends in a shipwreck off the coast of Dido's Carthage. Once the preparation for the journey is described, the use of the first person plural becomes typical (I have underlined the first person plural suffix):

> With Asian power and Priam's tribe uprooted,
> though blameless, by heaven's decree; with Ilium's pride
> fallen, and Neptune's Troy all smoke and ash,
> God's oracles drove us (*agimur*) on to exile, on
> to distant, lonely lands. We built a fleet (*classem... molimur*)
> down to Antander and Ida's Phrygian peaks,
> uncertain which way Fate led or where to stop.
> We marshalled our men (*contrahimus... viros*).
> When summer first came on,
> Anchises bade us trust our sails to fate.

with the personal plural dynamic: "We thought we were lost, we
did what we could, and we made it through."[40]

Robbins does examine *ActsPet12Apost.* and suggests that this ancient
literary convention may explain the use of the first person plural in the sea
voyage sections of *ActsPet12Apost.* Patterson agrees with this suggestion.
He notes that the shift from the first person plural to the first person
singular voice of Peter at 1.29–30 occurs at the moment in the text that the
sea journey comes to an end. Likewise, at 7.23–8.20 the shift from first
person singular to first person plural occurs at the point in the story when
Peter and the disciples journey to Lithargoel's city, although this is not
specifically presented as a sea journey.[41]

Patterson notes that, while Robbins's study is helpful in the above-
mentioned cases, it does not serve to explain all the narrative shifts in
ActsPet12Apost.: "in contrast to the we-passages in Acts, the narrative
shifts in the *ActsPet12Apost.* often involve not simply a shift in voice
(third person to first, or singular to plural), but an actual shift in the

---

[40] Robbins, "By Land and By Sea," 223. It should also be noted that
Porter has argued against Robbins's conclusions. He cites: 1) mix of literatures
(Egyptian, Greek and Latin); 2) range of centuries (1800 B.C. to third century
A.D.); and 3) variety of genres (epic, poetry, prose narrative, oratory, etc.) as key
weaknesses in Robbins's theory, Porter, "By Land and By Sea," 554. However,
I am not entirely convinced by Porter's arguments. I do not view any of his three
objections as damaging to Robbins's thesis. While I hesitate to describe, with
Robbins, the use of the first person plural in such set terms as "literary
convention," I would agree with Robbins and C. K. Barrett in suggesting a
sociological motivation for this recurring trend. See Barrett, "Paul Shipwrecked,"
in B. P. Thompson, ed., *Scripture: Meaning and Method: Essays Presented to
Anthony Tyrrell Hanson for his Seventieth Birthday* (Hull: Hull University Press,
1987) 53–54.

[41] Patterson, "Sources, Redaction and Tendenz," 6. It is important to
point out that Patterson does not include 7.23–8.20 as I have written but rather
9.17–26. I have made this change because Patterson describes 9.17–26 as "the
point where Peter and the disciples undertake the journey to Lithargoel's city."
These line quotations are incorrect. Therefore, I have assumed a publishing error
and replaced 9.17–26 with 7.23–8.20, which properly fits Patterson's point.

narrative perspective of the text." Thus, Patterson distinguishes between shifts in voice and shifts in identity of the narrator (Peter vs. a narrator) and concludes that while Robbins's study is helpful in explaining the existence of the we passages in the canonical Acts and even the two shifts in *ActsPet12Apost.*, something more is required to explain the other shifts present in this text.

Patterson proceeds briefly to examine the theories of Krause, Parrott and Schenke. He groups Krause's theory with Parrott's, describing them (and in doing so oversimplifying their theories) as seeing *ActsPet12Apost.* as composed of two originally separate acts, a Petrine act and an apostolic act. He critiques these theories as not being nuanced enough to deal with the complexities of shifts in voice and identity present in the text.

Patterson seems more amenable to the theory of Schenke, which he describes as "a more fruitful attempt to deal with this problem."[42] He views Schenke's idea of multiple levels of composition, with one level inserted into another and separate material attached at the end of the text, as possibly offering the basis for a solution to the problem. Before offering his own solution, Patterson makes four methodological observations which he believes must be seen as lessons learned from the previous attempts to solve this problem. The first is related to the work of Robbins. Patterson notes that Robbins's study has shown us that not every shift in narrative voice in this text need signal a different source or redactional layering. Some shifts can be attributed to ancient literary convention. Patterson's second observation is that, although some shifts can be attributed to literary convention, there are other aporias in the text that must be otherwise explained. Therefore, any compositional theory must take these aporias into account. Patterson's third observation builds upon the preceding: "the aporias alone will not always provide one with the neat divisions in the text one would hope for in trying to clarify where

---

[42] Ibid., 8.

one voice stops and another begins."[43] For Patterson, the aporias signal a shift in the textual sources but do not necessarily mark where the shift has taken place. Thus Patterson urges the interpreter to pay attention not only to aporias and places where new voices emerge but also to the episodic structure of the text as a whole and the places where these elements coincide. Patterson's fourth observation is that any theory which attempts to explain the compositional history of this text must have the necessary complexity to deal with the various voice shifts which can be found in the text. He argues that there are at least three different voices to be found in the text: 1) the "I, Peter" voice; 2) the first person plural voice of the disciples; and 3) the anonymous third person voice. Patterson concludes that at least three sources are required.

With these considerations in mind Patterson then proposes a "Three-Source Hypothesis." The first of these three sources Patterson calls his "I, Peter Source," consisting of 1.1–3.11 and 5.5–8.9. Originally, this source consisted of the encounter of Peter with the angel Lithargoel in a symbolic city, Habitation. A discussion occurs about a heavenly city called Nine Gates and ascetical instructions are given as to how to safely arrive at this city. The cities and the ascetical instructions were the principal content of this story. Patterson compares this source with such heavenly journey texts as *The Installation of the Archangel Michael* and *The Book of the Installation of the Archangel Gabriel*.

Patterson calls his second source the "Third Person Source" because it is characterized by this voice. Primarily, Patterson sees two episodes as stemming from this proposed source: 1) the story of the pearl merchant (3.11–5.5), which Patterson sees as having been "inserted" into the "I, Peter" text; and 2) the more obvious commissioning scene (9.30–12.29).[44]

---

[43] Ibid., 9. Patterson argues that only once in *ActsPet12Apost.* can a narrative aporia be said to mark a textual seam: the shift between first and third person which occurs at 9.29–30.

[44] While Patterson sees the commissioning scene as obviously from another source, he recognizes that the story of the pearl merchant is far less easy to identify as such. By way of explaining this point, Patterson notes that the shift

Patterson views these sections as deriving from the same source because
of their common third person voice and their common concern for the
poor. Patterson envisioned the original version of the story as featuring
Jesus himself as the pearl merchant. Thus, the instructions to shun the
rich in 11.26–12.8, would have been a calculated repayment for their
rejection of the pearl merchant in 3.14–31.

The third source is called the "We Source." Patterson insists that
what he calls "the resurrection appearance" in 8.10–9.29 was part of this
material.[45] Although Patterson is unsure whether 1.1–29 should be
included in this source, he suggests that if the "resurrection appearance"
scene of the "We Source" originally came out of an Easter text, then it
may have included a commissioning and sending-out scene of which
1.1–29 may be a remnant.

In drawing together the loose ends of his theory Patterson points out
a number of changes and additions which, he conjectures, were made to
these three sources by the hand of a redactor: 1) a lengthy description of
Lithargoel's appearance (2.14–29);[46] 2) the cry "Pearls, Pearls" in 2.32;

---

to third person at 3.11 is presented as Peter's third person remembrance of the
event. However, Patterson reminds his reader that at 5.1 a "source using a non-
Petrine third person voice" has been inserted. Patterson argues that this
"insertion" has already occurred back at 3.11. The three points he puts forward
in favor of this thesis are: 1) this story of the pearl merchant does not need to
include Peter, since he only appears at the end as a "tutor" for the poor; 2)
3.11–5.5 is tangential to the main Petrine narrative, since one could pass from
3.11 to 5.5 and not miss the intervening section; and 3) the presence of "a
redactional seam" in 5.4–5. This seam is indicated by Peter telling the poor about
the hardships of the way to Lithargoel's city and then turning around and asking
Lithargoel about these same hardships (ibid., 11–12).

[45] Patterson recognizes the tenuous location of the "We Source" seam
at 8.10. Part of the problem is that the "I, Peter" source exhibits its plural voice
at this point (until 8.21, where Peter is specifically mentioned) and it is hard to tell
where a new source is being inserted.

[46] Patterson claims that this "added" material serves to identify
Lithargoel with Jesus. However, to anticipate later discussion, I fail to see the
connection. Lithargoel's hands and feet are plainly seen and described but no
mention is made of any tell-tale nailprints. It appears that Patterson, like Schenke,

3) the third person voice in 5.5–7, which Patterson attributes to a redactor's attempt to smooth out the problem of voice; and 4) the difficulty created between 8.13 and 9.19, where the physician is identified first as Lithargoel in disguise and then as Jesus. Patterson describes these lines as the section where the redactor attempted to splice together the "I, Peter" source and the "resurrection appearance" of the "We Source."

A DIFFERENT PROPOSAL

To address the text's division/source question it is important to reconsider the question of voice shifts and their usefulness in dividing the text and recognizing underlying sources. In light of Patterson's detailed study of the various types, I suggest that there are five different varieties of voice shifts in *ActsPet12Apost.* I would stress that these are not necessarily indications of sources, but rather types of voice shifts present in the text. It is my contention (in agreement with Patterson) that these voice shifts are only one factor to be considered when examining the question of sources in *ActsPet12Apost.* As I hope to demonstrate, aporias, shifts in vocabulary and thematic discrepancies are of equal significance. I shall argue ultimately that there are three main blocks of material in *ActsPet12Apost.*, and that the first two of these have undergone redaction by the author. These three are: 1) *The Story of the Pearl Merchant* (1.1 to 9.1, except for redactional additions); 2) *A Resurrection Appearance* (9.1 to 9.29; also except for redactional additions); and 3) *The Author/Redactor's Theology* (9.30–12.19). To begin this analysis I shall delineate the five types of voice shifts present in *ActsPet12Apost.* and then proceed to an examination of the specific parameters of these texts.

The five voice shift types are: 1) *I, Peter* — first person narration from Peter's perspective; found in 1.30–3.11 and 6.9–7.22; 2) Robbins's *"We of journeys"* — first person plural narration often found in travel literature of the Greco-Roman period; found in 1.1–29 and 7.23–8.20; 3)

---

fixes his attention upon Lithargoel's sweat-cloth (σουδάριον), which he claims to be grave-clothes.

We - apostolic voice — first person plural narration which could be considered the voice of one in the apostolic group due to its proximity to lines which refer to Peter in the third person; found only in 9.15–29; 4) *The Narrator* — third person narration which refers to Peter as a character and not as the storyteller; found in 5.1–14; 8.21–9.15 and 9.30–12.19; and 5) *Problematic Sections* — passages in the third person yet difficult to classify under "The Narrator" because they could be understood as being connected with the "I, Peter" texts (i.e., third person narration by a first person narrator); found in 3.11–5.1 and 5.14–6.8. In summary the following voice shift types are found:

1) *I, Peter* — **a**. 1.30–3.11; **b**. 6.9–7.22

2) *We of Journeys* — **a**. 1.1–29; **b**. 7.23–8.20

3) *We - Apostolic Voice* — **a**. 9.15–29

4) *The Narrator* — **a**. 5.1–14; **b**. 8.21–9.15; **c**. 9.30–12.19

5) *Problematic Sections* — **a**. 3.11–5.1; **b**. 5.14–6.8

Having now become aware of the variety of voice shifts in *ActsPet12Apost.* and their exact locations in the text, it is possible to take the next step, namely, to determine the relationships, if any, between these voice shifts and any underlying sources.

A UNITY FROM 1.1 TO 8.20?

There may be more unity in *ActsPet12Apost.* than one might first suppose when encountering the variety of voice shifts in the text. For example, in shift types 1) and 2) there is a consistent first person voice of narration (singular and plural). To these sections might be added 3.11–5.1, which was classed above as part of shift type 5). This text follows directly upon an "I, Peter" section (1.30–3.11) and could easily be seen as Peter narrating events as they unfolded around him. Therefore it would not be incorrect (in terms of literary technique) for these lines to be written in the third person yet to occur within the larger context of a first person narrative.[47] The second "Problematic Sections" text (5.14–6.8) might for the same reason also be added to the texts associated with the first person. However, it's relationship with 5.1–14, a text classed under "The Narrator" shift type (third person), must be explained.

First Person Narration: Greek, Roman and Early Christian Texts. To understand 5.1–14, a text which breaks up an otherwise continuous first person narrative flow spanning 1.1 to 8.20, a brief examination of other occurrences of first person narration in Greek, Roman and especially early Christian literature is helpful. According to Robert Scholes and Robert Kellogg, scholars of literary technique, first person narration and all eye-witness narrative forms reached their first significant development in Roman times. Scholes and Kellogg do not claim that first person narration did not exist before, rather that "narrative forms designed to exploit first person presentation in one way or another had not been developed before; so that a Xenophon, writing of his own experiences in Asia Minor in the *Anabasis*, automatically wrote of himself in the third person, just as Caesar later did in *De Bello Gallico*.... Such men chose this mode of narration not out of pride or humility, but because they associated the third person with formal narratives of the epic and historical kind, with which they associated their own works."[48] According to Scholes and Kellogg the first person is less formal and more intimate:

> In early literature the first person is generally associated with such
> loose and personal forms as the epistle and the memoir, the forms
> of the amateur rather than the professional author. We find

---

[47] So Patterson: "At 3.11 there is a shift from the first to third person, but the third person narrative is placed ostensibly on the lips of Peter, who tells the story of Lithargoel now as an observer of events, not as a participant in them. Narratively this poses no problem" (ibid., 9).

[48] This statement is incomplete in its reference to Caesar's literary works. Caesar writes also of himself in the third person in *Civil Wars*. Scholes and Kellogg, *The Nature of Narrative* (New York: Oxford University Press, 1966) 72. The third chapter of this book, "The Classical Heritage of Modern Narrative," is especially helpful in its overview of Greco-Roman literary development.

occasionally a sense of self-awareness in the authors of works which are essentially neither first person in form nor autobiographical in spirit, as when Hesiod opens the Theogony with a reminiscence of the time when a delegation of Muses visited Hesiod (referring to himself in the third person) and persuaded him to enlighten the world with the true histories of the deathless gods; but we find almost no first person narrative in early Greek literature, with the important exception of the story of his travels told by Odysseus to the Phaeacians, which is embedded in the larger narrative structure of Homer.

This portion of the Odyssey is of great interest. It is the most magical, fabulous, and romantic thing in Homer. It is a traveler's tale, a road or journey narrative, and it is told in the first person. The traveler's tale is a persistent oral form in all cultures. It is, in a sense, the amateur's answer to the professional rhapsodist, skald, or jongleur. Its form is the simple linear form of voyage by land or sea, and in it fiction, which in its highest sense involves ordering and shaping for an esthetic end, is reduced to its most humble form — the lie. Traveler's tales in all countries are notoriously untrustworthy, and untrustworthy in proportion to the distance of the travels from familiar territory, just as ancient maps become less reliable toward their edges. The prose writers of the Roman Empire developed the first person journey narrative as an art form and also established the pattern of the inward journey, the autobiography, in its two usual forms — the apology and the confession.[49]

To illustrate their point, Scholes and Kellogg refer to several examples. Among these are Petronius Arbiter, *Satyricon* (ca. 64), Lucius Apulieus, *Metamorphoses* (ca. 150), and Lucian of Samosata, *A True Story* (ca. 180). Each of these is written almost exclusively in the first person, as a personal account of the main character's adventures while traveling.

In the NT, the "we source" texts in Acts 16:10–17; 20:5–15; 21:1–18 and 27:1–28:16, mentioned above, are the most famous examples of first

---

[49] Ibid., 72–73.

person narration. Furthermore, the book of Revelation, like other apocalypses,[50] also includes extensive first person narration. David E. Aune has described the function of the first person in apocalypses: "the autobiographical style of apocalypses requires emphasis since this feature is an important aspect of the legitimization of the revelatory experience, and the first-person style in oral performance enables the audience to experience the vividness and vitality of the original revelatory experience."[51] The first person is also present in the various epistles of the NT, whether authentic or pseudepigraphal,[52] a typical aspect of a personal letter. There are also brief occurrences of the first person in Luke 1:1–4 and John 21:24–25.

While these examples are helpful, the closest parallel I have found to the oddly placed voice shifts in *ActsPet12Apost.* 5.1–14 also occurs in the Nag Hammadi literature.[53] In the *Apocryphon of James* the reader is, much as in the text surrounding *ActsPet12Apost.* 5.1–14, confronted with a confusing voice shift from first to third person, then back to first again. *Ap. Jas.* begins with a pseudepigraphal letter in which "James" claims to be sending a book containing material revealed to Peter and himself (1.8–12):

---

[50] For example, the Coptic *Apocalypse of Paul* and *Apocalypse of Peter* (both from Nag Hammadi) and the Greek *Apocalypse of Paul*. In other non-canonical early Christian texts, related to apocalyptic literature, there are such examples of first person narration as *Shepherd of Hermas* and *Ascension of Isaiah* 7.1–11.35.

[51] Aune, "The Apocalypse of John and the Problem of Genre," *Semeia* 36 (1986) 87.

[52] See Raymond F. Collins, *Letters That Paul Did Not Write* (Good News Studies 28; Wilmington, DE: Michael Glazier, 1988) 69–86; also William G. Doty, *Letters in Primitive Christianity* (Guides to Biblical Scholarship, New Testament Series; Philadelphia: Fortress, 1973), for a detailed description of ancient letter writing technique as well as the practice of pseudepigraphy.

[53] By "oddly placed" I refer to the peculiar and unexpected switch to third person narration in the middle of an otherwise first person text.

Since you asked that I send you a secret book which was revealed to me and Peter by the Lord, I could not turn you away or gainsay you; but [I have written] it in the Hebrew alphabet and sent it to you, and you alone. But since you are a minister of the salvation of the saints, endeavor earnestly and take care not to rehearse this text to many — *this that the Savior did not wish to tell to all of us, his twelve disciples.* But blessed will they be who will be saved through the faith of this discourse.

I also sent you, ten months ago, another secret book which the Savior had revealed to me. Under the circumstances, however, regard that one as revealed to me, James; but this one [untranslatable fragments] *the twelve disciples [were] all sitting together and recalling what the Savior had said to each one of them,* whether in secret or openly, and [putting it] in books — [But I] was writing that which was in [my book] — lo, the Savior appeared, [after] departing from [us while we] gazed after him. And five hundred and fifty days since he had risen from the dead, *we said to him,* "Have you departed and removed yourself from us?"

But Jesus said, "No, but I shall go to the place from whence I came. If you wish to come with me, come!" *They all answered* and said, "If you bid us, we come."

He said, "Verily I say unto you, no one will ever enter the kingdom of heaven at my bidding, but (only) because you yourselves are full. Leave James and Peter to me that I may fill them." *And having called these two, he drew them aside* and bade the rest occupy themselves with that which they were about. (1.8–2.39)

In this letter James refers to the twelve disciples as "us" (first person plural; 1.24–25), thereby establishing his "identity" as one of Jesus' inner circle. However, this identity begins to break down in 2.12, when the twelve are referred to as "them" (third person plural). This peculiar shift is followed by a return to the first person as the plural is once again used to refer to the group of disciples. This return is short-lived, because in 2.26 the disciples are referred to, once again, in the third person plural. In 2.36–37, the identity of the narrator is compromised, revealing itself not to be James. James is shown to be separate from the narrator as he and Peter are referred to as "these two" and "them." From this point on, the voice of narration remains constant in referring to James as "I" and Peter and James as "we" and "us" while referring to the rest of the twelve as "they."

A second example of voice shifting from the Nag Hammadi literature is from the *1 Apocalypse of James*, which contains both first person narration and an abrupt shift from the first to the third person. *1 Ap. Jas.*, cast in the form of a dialogue within a narrative framework, has narration which begins with the first person singular "me" in reference to James (24.11; see also 25.12; 27.18).[54] However, the text then switches over

---

[54] As far as I am aware, the most complete explanation of this voice shift to date is provided by Scott Kent Brown. Brown offers two possible explanations which are related to the question of sources: "We could urge that these constitute traces remaining from a much earlier period when the memory of James was so strong that the story was told as if by himself. With the passage of time, this set of incidents came to be narrated as if observed by a third party. These stories, then, were not completely readapted and the three instances represent traces left over from the earliest stages of the tradition's life. It is more likely, however, that it was done the other way around. The overwhelming evidence from the apocalypse itself points to the fact that the account had always been told about James, not as if by him. At a period sometime after the *Urtext* of our document appeared, an attempt was possibly made to edit the story to appear as if related by James himself. But with any tradition which has become crystallized enough to be written down, the resistance to this type of alteration was strong enough that it was not carried through completely" ("James: A Religio-Historical Study of the Relation Between Jewish, Gnostic, and Catholic Christianity in the Early Period Through an Investigation of the Traditions About James the Lord's Brother" [Ph.D. dissertation; Brown University, 1972] 74–75). Likewise, William R. Schoedel detects editorial activity, claiming that "although most of the report is in the third person, there are three places where the author speaks of himself in the first person. This may indicate the artificiality of the narrative framework" ("The First Apocalypse of James, V,3:24.10–44.10," in D. M. Parrott, ed., *Nag Hammadi Codices V,2–5 and VI with Papyrus Berolinensis 8502,1 and 4* [NHS 11; Leiden: Brill, 1979] 5). Regrettably, the most recent full-length study on this text offers little insight on this occurrence in the text. Armand Veilleux, while dismissing the proposals of Brown, avoids the question by suggesting that because of the internal cohesion of the text there is no need to propose an explanation (*La Première Apocalypse de Jacques [NH V,3]. La Seconde Apocalypse de Jacques*

almost completely to the third person, using "James said" (**ⲡⲉⲝⲉ ⲓⲁⲕⲱⲃⲟⲥ**) to introduce James's questions to the Lord, leaving the reader to ask the reason for this sudden shift in narrative technique.

A third example of first person narration and abrupt voice shifts from within the Nag Hammadi corpus is *Hypostasis of the Archons*. *Hyp. Arch.* begins as a "learned treatise in which a teacher addresses a topic ostensibly suggested by the dedicatee of the work." This introduction is written in the first person singular (86.22, 26). The work then proceeds to switch to the third person, only to resume the first person in what Bentley Layton has called "an angelic revelation dialogue" from 93.13 until the end of the text.[55]

The *Epistula Apostolorum* provides us with yet another interesting parallel shift in voice which can be compared to that found in *ActsPet12Apost.* 5.1–14. Julian V. Hills analyzes a peculiar occurrence in this document. The *Epistula*, as a whole reported from the point of view of the disciples, contains a list of miracles in chapter 5:

> Then there was a marriage in Cana of Galilee. And he was invited with his mother and his brothers. And he made water into wine and awakened the dead and made the lame to walk; for him whose hand was withered, he stretched it out again, and the woman who suffered twelve years from a haemorrhage touched the edge of his garment and was immediately whole; and while *we reflected* and wondered concerning the miracle he performed, he said to us, "Who touched me?" And *we said* to him, "O Lord, the crowd of people touched you." And he answered and said to us, "I noticed that a power went out from me." Immediately that woman came before him, answered and said to him, "Lord, I touched you." And he answered and said to her, "Go, your faith has made you

---

[NH 5,4] [Bibliothèque Copte de Nag Hammadi Section Études 17; Quebec: Les Presses de l'Université Laval, 1986] 65.

[55] Layton, *The Gnostic Scriptures* (Garden City, NY: Doubleday, 1987) 65.

whole."... Then he walked on the sea, and the winds blew, and he rebuked them, and the waves of the sea became calm. And when *we, his disciples, had no denarii, we said to him*, "Master, what should we do about the tax-collector?" And he answered and said to *us*, "One of you cast the hook, the net, into the deep and draw out a fish, and he will find a denarius in it. Give that to the tax-collector for me and you." *Then we had no bread* except five loaves and two fish, he commanded the people to lie down, and their number amounted to 5000 besides children and women, whom *we served* with pieces of bread; and they were filled, and there was (some) left over, and *we carried* away twelve baskets full of pieces, asking and saying, "What meaning is there in these five loaves?"

This list begins: "Then there was a marriage in Cana of Galilee. And he was invited with his mother and his brothers. And he made water into wine...." Hills notes the connection of this Cana wedding to its canonical counterpart in John 2:1–12 and observes the change in terminology from "disciples" in John to "brothers" in the *Epistula*. Hills explains:

> In relating the presence of "his brothers," however, either the author is drawing on material independent of John, or he is making a conscious change; or, finally, a later hand has been at work. It has long been noted that Jesus' brothers, perhaps understood by John to be the disciples, appear in John 2:12, and it was even affirmed by Bultmann that John's source at 2:2, and therefore possibly the Epistula's source, read "and his brothers."[56]

---

[56] Hills, *Tradition and Composition in the Epistula Apostolorum* (HDR 24; Minneapolis: Fortress, 1990) 48. For the reference to Bultmann see Rudolf Bultmann, *The Gospel of John: A Commentary* (Philadelphia: Westminster, 1971) 114 and n. 6.

Hills notes the peculiarity that in three separate places the *Epistula* expressly calls the disciples "brothers."[57] If in the *Epistula* "disciples" and "brothers" are related, even interchangeable, terms then the question arises, Why doesn't this section of the text use "we" or "us" (in place of "brothers") as are found in eight other places within this same list of miracles? Thus, there is a subtle (and short-lived) switch in from the first to third person narration.[58]

From these examples of first person narration there are several conclusions that can be drawn. First, first person tends to be associated with travel/ adventure literature (e.g., Lucian, *A True Story*; Lucius Apulieus, *Metamorphoses*). Second, it is also associated with revelatory literature (e.g., Revelation; *Ascension of Isaiah*; *Apocryphon of James*). Third, it tends to represent a less formal (as compared to Homer, *Iliad*), more amateurish literary effort, being influenced by the form of the traveler's tale. Fourth, in some of these works there are peculiar and sometimes sudden shifts in the voice of narration (from first to third). It would seem that *ActsPet12Apost.* has connections with each of these four aspects.

First Person as a Literary Device. Now that I have briefly discussed the uses of first person narration in both Greek, Roman and early Christian literature, it is possible to more closely examine the voice change that occurs in 5.1–14. Until this point in the text the voice of narration has been consistently first person, both plural and singular. However, at 5.1–14, especially at 5.2–7, the voice switches to third person for no obvious reason.

---

[57] These three are 1) 10.2 (part of a retelling of Jesus' appearance to three women outside the tomb, "go to your brothers and say, 'Come, our Master has risen from the dead'"); 2) 19.5 ("Truly I say unto you, you will be my brothers and companions"); and 3) 32.4 ("Truly I say unto you, you are my brothers, companions in the kingdom of heaven").

[58] Hills suggests that this section may represent a later addition to the text. However, in recent discussion with me he acknowledges that this occurrence is difficult to explain and may represent an authorial mistake or "slip."

There are three possible explanations for the change in voice at 5.1–14: 1) a change in sources (as in the *Apocalypse of Adam*, according to C. W. Hedrick's study); 2) a deliberate literary choice on the part of the author,[59] and 3) a mistake or "slip" on the part of the author (i.e., sloppy pseudonymity). I reject the first of these explanations because I see nothing other than this change in voice that would suggest a change in source. The material included in 5.1–14 is in agreement with previously given information: when the merchant offers the pearl to the poor, he clearly indicates that he does not actually have the pearl on his person. Rather, he expressly invites the poor to come to his city "so that I may not only show it before your (very) eyes, but give it to you for nothing" (4.10–15, 30–34). We assume that Peter, as a member of the assembled crowd, was also extended this invitation. Therefore, the question Peter asks of the merchant in 5.7–14 as to the way to the merchant's city is a logical progression or response to the merchant's appeal to the people present in Habitation. One must go to the merchant's city to receive the

---

[59] This understanding of voice changes in literature is explored by the comments of French literary theorist Gérard Genette (*Narrative Discourse: An Essay in Method* [Ithaca, NY: Cornell University Press, 1980] 246). (Note, however, that Genette admits the possibility of a deliberate literary choice on the part of the author but only for modern literature.) Genette writes concerning unexpected shifts in voice that a, "glaring violation is the shift in grammatical person to designate the same character: for instance, in *Autre étude de femme*, Bianchon moves all of a sudden from 'I' to 'he,' as if he were unexpectedly abandoning the role of narrator; for instance, in *Jean Santeuil*, the hero moves inversely from 'he' to 'I.' In the field of the classical novel, and still in Proust, such effects obviously result from a sort of narrative pathology, explicable by last-minute reshufflings and states of textual incompleteness. But we know that the contemporary novel has passed that limit, as it has so many others, and does not hesitate to establish between narrator and character(s) a variable or floating relationship, a pronominal vertigo in tune with a freer logic and a more complex conception of 'personality.' The most advanced forms of this emancipation are perhaps not the most perceptible ones, because the classical attributes of 'character' — proper name, physical and moral 'nature' — have disappeared and along with them the signs that direct grammatical (pronominal) traffic."

pearl. Thus, if anything is ever to be made of this invitation, it is necessary to know the way to this city.[60]

As for the second possible explanation, a deliberate literary choice on the part of the author, I am at a loss as to how this switch in voice could serve the progression of the story. Any possible explanation of 5.1–14 in light of this suggestion is further complicated by the reappearance of the first person in 6.9–8.20. The immediate reappearance of the first person in 6.9–27 assumes a dialogue between the merchant and Peter that has been narrated in the first person. In short, there is no special indication of a return to the first person. It is as if the voice change of 5.1–14 never happened. Obviously, lack of understanding of a literary motive for the voice change in 5.1–14 does not eliminate its possibility. However, any theory which attempts to adopt this explanation must explain the immediate return to the first person in 6.9, a task which will not be easy.

I propose that the third explanation, a mistake or "slip" (i.e., sloppy pseudonymity) on the part of the author, makes the most sense of this perplexing voice shift in 5.1–14. To understand this suggestion it is important to consider the literary role of first person narration. Despite the above examples, the typical voice in which the majority of ancient narratives are written is third person. Virgil's *Aeneid*, Thucydides' *Peloponnesian War*, Genesis, the canonical gospels and the majority of the Nag Hammadi documents may be used as examples. However, the writer of this text made a conscious decision to write in the first person — a voice typically reserved for personal testimony. This literary decision creates the narrative illusion of a personal account of actual events occurring in the life of the narrator (in this case, Peter). In short, this

---

[60] In 5.7–14, it is interesting to note that Peter does not mention the pearl. His interest in the merchant's city is not basely associated with a desire for gain. (Frankly, this would be rather embarrassing for the community, their role-model scurrying off like some crazed bargain shopper in search of the ultimate sale.) Rather, his thought is to pursue the commission given him in 1.10–11. However, he still needs to know the way to the city. Thus two different motivations are given for attaining "Nine Gates": a spiritual one (evangelism) and a simpler, more common motivation (lifting the poor out of their beggarly state).

technique has the effect of historicizing the story by personalizing it. Clearly this is a deliberate literary device. This is not to imply that the third person cannot also be used as a literary device (cf. Julius Caesar's references to himself in the third person in *Civil Wars* and Hesiod's similar technique in *Theogony*).

Recognition of the first person as a literary device may be an important step to understanding the intrusion of the third person in 5.1–14. If the author was not Peter, then he or she had not experienced these events first hand. Thus, writing in the first person may have been more demanding[61] in that it required (and still does require) the writer to "get inside" the character and "see" the events through the character's eyes. I would oppose this to third person narration which allows the author to visualize the characters's actions and statements as occurring before his or her imagination as actors on a stage.

The work of literary theorist Ellen Peel sheds some interesting light on the consideration of sudden shifts in voice. Peel describes such sharp shifts between first person narration by the protagonist and third person narration about the protagonist as "alternating narration." While she recognizes the presence of this literary technique in works with male protagonists, Peel suggests that alternating narration in modern literature is part of a feminist aesthetic (a way of writing characteristic of feminist texts):

> I considered the tendency toward alternating narration in contemporary novels about women to be merely interesting until I began to wonder what the technique signified in these writings. The answer seems to lie in the female protagonists's uneasy view of themselves as both subject and object, both self and other. First person point of view presents the protagonist as subject (at least of narration); third person narration presents her as object (at least of

---

[61] Consider some of the difficult textual transitions caused by using first person narration, such as description of actions unfolding before the eyes of the main character and description or narration given by a character other than the main character.

narration); and sharp alternation between the two vividly presents her unease.[62]

Peel connects this narrative unease between the protagonist's view of herself as both subject and object with the actual situation of women in a patriarchal society:

> The answer lies in the feminist analysis of women's role as subject and object. A woman may consider herself a subject but face strong pressure from a society that urges her to see herself as object, as other. Simone de Beauvoir says that woman "is defined and differentiated with reference to man and not he with reference to her; she is the incidental, the inessential as opposed to the essential. He is the Subject, he is the Absolute — she is the Other." Probably the issue of self and other, like the related issue of subject and object, has concerned every human being. But, for the reasons articulated by Beauvoir, the issue has particular urgency for women in a sexist society.... I contend that alternating narration is a particularly effective technique for expressing a feminist awareness of women's condition.[63]

Peel's work is a literary theorist's study intended to develop the second possible explanation for sudden voice shifts or "alternating narration," a deliberate literary choice on the part of the author. However, her discussion of subject and object has something to contribute to my suggestion that 5.1–14 represents a mistake or "slip" (i.e., sloppy pseudonymity) on the part of the author. Peel's principle suggests that alternating narration can be deliberately used by an author to reflect a character's unease with himself or herself (i.e., tension between the

---

[62] Peel, "Subject, Object, and the Alternation of First and Third Person Narration in Novels by Alther, Atwood, and Drabble: Toward a Theory of Feminist Aesthetics," *Critique* 98 (1989) 108.

[63] Ibid., 118–19. De Beauvoir's insightful comments are from her work, *The Second Sex* (New York: Vintage-Random House, 1974) xix.

character's view of self as subject and external pressure to view their self as object). Is it not possible to argue that an author might experience this same unease in relation to one of his or her own characters? In our case the author is using Peter as the subject ("I, Peter"), yet the author is not Peter. Therefore, from the author's perspective, Peter is really not subject (self), but object (other). It is precisely this tension between the subject of the author and the subject of the character that makes writing a story in first person narration difficult and always susceptible to a "slip" into the author's natural view of the character — as object (i.e., third person).[64]

Thus, the third person in 5.1–14 may represent the writer "slipping" into a more natural third person, natural, I assert, for a person who is not describing personally witnessed events.[65] This "slip" was either unnoticed

---

[64] In discussing this concept with my wife, a social worker, I was unexpectedly given a modern example of just such a circumstance. My wife is required to write reports detailing the specific steps she has taken in aiding her various clients. These reports, as formal documents, are supposed to be written in the third person, in which the social worker is supposed to refer to himself or herself as "this social worker." However, my wife related that upon rereading her reports and the reports of many other social workers she noticed that virtually every report fluctuated between the third and first person. When asked to explain this phenomenon my wife stated that the third person did not seem natural and, try as she might, over the course of a long report she and other social workers could not help but revert back to the first person, which seemed more natural. I recognize that this does not conclusively prove the validity of my argument. However, it does show that such unintentional "slips" in voice do happen in real life circumstances.

[65] Patterson argues that "somewhere between 3.7 and 5.3 there has been a shift from the first person voice of Peter to the third person voice of an anonymous narrator." However, Patterson is unsure as to where this transition has actually taken place. He attributes this discrepancy to a redactor: "It is as though a redactor was able to accomplish a smooth transition from one source to another, but once he/she was well into the second source the identity of the voice in the original narrative was soon forgotten as the scribe dutifully copied exactly what was on the page before him/her. By 5.3 the redactor has simply forgotten that it is Peter who is telling the story" ("Sources, Redaction and Tendenz," 9–10). Patterson attributes the words "Peter" in 5.3 and the Coptic prefix "he" in 5.7 to error.

or simply disregarded by the author due to the complications inherent in using first person narration.

Difficulties Posed by 5.1–6. A second area of concern when dealing with voice shifts in 5.1–14 is the difficulties posed by 5.1–6. The problems of 5.1–6 are twofold: 1) the change in voice, an explanatory theory for which has been proposed above, and 2) a peculiar narrative order, which presents Peter answering the poor's questions about "the hardships of the way" only to turn around in 5.7–10 and ask the merchant about these same hardships.[66]

This second problem could lead an interpreter to posit a literary seam indicating a change in sources. However, the difficulty may not be so much a narrative issue as a discrepancy in the translation of the Coptic text. Much of the first few letters in the sentence that begins in 5.1, translated in NHS 11 as "The men asked Peter about the hardships,"[67] is gone. Therefore, the prefix plus word for "the men" is only a theoretical reconstruction of how the text might have read. In fact, the textual fragments merely reveal the two letters Rho and Omega, the first two letters in the Coptic ⲢⲰⲘⲈ "man." Certainly, the translator's assumption that the original text included ⲢⲰⲘⲈ is well within the realm of possibility. In fact, I agree that the text did in fact read ⲢⲰⲘⲈ. However, I disagree with the translator's assumption that at the end of 5.1 the original text included a plural Coptic prefix. I suggest that the original text used the Coptic singular prefix and originally read "The man asked Peter..." (ⲁ[ϥϣ]ⲓⲛⲉ ⲛ̄ϭⲓ ⲡⲓ]ⲢⲰ[ⲘⲈ... ⲉ[ⲡⲈⲦⲢⲞⲤ).

This slight change is quite significant in determining who is asking Peter about the hardships. The grammatical tendencies manifested in

---

[66] Patterson labels this narrative problem a "jolting aporia." This leads Patterson to suggest that there has been a shift in sources, yet he finds it difficult to locate this seam with much specificity (ibid., 3, 9–10).

[67] The translation in *The Nag Hammadi Library in English* mirrors this wording. Schenke's translation is slightly different: "The people asked Peter about the hardships" ("The Acts of Peter and the Twelve Apostles," 421).

ActsPet12Apost. to this point in the text suggest that it is not the poor who are asking this question, but rather "the man who sells this pearl" (i.e., the pearl merchant). I have come to this conclusion based upon the following three considerations.

First, the translators assume that the text is referring to the poor and the beggars, and thus postulate a plural prefix for ⲡⲱⲙⲉ. However, the Coptic text never refers to these groups as "the men." Rather, they are systematically referred to as the "poor of the city" (3.32; 4.16) or simply "the poor" (4.6, 28, 35). The beggars are referred to as such (4.29, 35).[68] In fact, the logic of referring to any group within the city of Habitation as "the men" (i.e., in generic terms) lacks precision in that it defeats the strict dichotomy the author has set up between the rich, who reject the pearl merchant, and the poor, who rejoice because of his promise.[69]

The second reason the text originally referred to "the man who sells this pearl" is that to this point it has been typical for the author to refer to the pearl merchant by using the word ⲡⲱⲙⲉ. Granted, ⲡⲱⲙⲉ may have different prefixes as is called for by its respective situations in the text, but the pattern is undeniable (see 2.10; 2.17; 2.33; 3.31; 4.2 and even 5.7).

The third reason has to do with narrative flow — the coherence of the story or plot. In the text leading up to 5.1–14, Peter meets and converses with the pearl merchant (2.17–3.11). This conversation is interrupted by the intrusions of Habitation's two factions, the rich and the poor. While the rich disdain the merchant and do not acknowledge him (3.25–27), the

---

[68] In the Coptic there are two terms translated in the English as "beggar." In 4.18, 20 ⲱⲁⲧⲙⲛ̄ⲧⲛⲁⲉ is used by the poor to describe themselves and their condition, while in 4.29, 35 the term ⲡⲉϥⲧⲱⲃⲁ̄ϩ is used to describe a distinct group among the poor. It is possible that both of these words translated the original Greek word προσαίτης — "a beggar" (Crum, *Dictionary*, s.v. 217b, 402b).

[69] My theory of a singular subject ("the man") is allowed by the remaining fragment of the verb "to ask." The alpha of its prefix could easily be third person singular, allowing the prefix+verb to read "he asked."

poor converse with him (4.3–34). Meanwhile, Peter apparently remains close so as to narrate the action and conversation. At 4.35–5.1, the conversation between the poor and the merchant is resolved in a positive manner ("the poor and the beggars rejoiced"). Thus the poor as a group recede from view and, logically, the merchant resumes his conversation with Peter.

The author, then, originally intended to present the reader with a solidly first person narrative from 1.1 to 8.20. It is here that the pattern of first person narration begins to break down permanently (excepting the "We - Apostolic voice" passage in 9.15–29) and it is here that our most intriguing shifts occur.

A PROBLEMATIC SECTION (8.21–35) — THE CASE OF THE MISSING TEXT

In addition to the obvious voice shift at this juncture there is a more subtle indicator of a possible transition in the underlying sources. A key to understanding this transition lies in a careful reading of the Coptic in 8.21. When these lines are more closely examined a rather peculiar use of the verb **ⲞⲨⲰⲰ︢ⲂⲈ** ("to respond") is discovered. This verb is not uncommon to *ActsPet12Apost.*, appearing 13 times over its twelve pages.[70] What is peculiar to this instance is that in every other occurrence it refers to a "response" by a character to a statement, request or question posed by another character.[71] It is only at 8.20–21 that it is used to initiate

---

[70] 3.1; 4.10–11, 29–30; 5.3, 15; 7.6; 8.20–21; 9.4–5, 8, 13; 10.13, 22; 11.14. Patterson also noted this peculiarity, describing this use in 8.21 as an "aporia" ("Sources, Redaction and Tendenz," 4).

[71] Coptic **ⲞⲨⲰⲰ︢ⲂⲈ** regularly translates Greek ἀποκρίνεσθαι (Crum, *Dictionary*, s.v. [502b]). In the four gospels, forms of ἀποκρίνεσθαι appear 211 times. Of these, it is used to initiate a character's response on 200 occasions; at least three of the 11 other occurrences can be taken in this sense. When these gospels are examined in the Coptic, **ⲞⲨⲰⲰ︢ⲂⲈ** appears as the translation of ἀποκρίνεσθαι in 195 of these 211 instances. Therefore it is correct to state that **ⲞⲨⲰⲰ︢ⲂⲈ** typically translates ἀποκρίνεσθαι and is used to initiate a reply in all but 5% of the 195 occurrences examined. Here and elsewhere the text of the

dialogue. Based on previous usage, it would appear that there is some text missing, though it is virtually impossible to guess how much preceded 8.21. Furthermore, it is difficult to determine this missing section's relationship to the surrounding texts. The possibility of text, originally preceding these lines, but now missing, coupled with an obvious voice shift leads me to want to separate it, as having been altered by the hand of the redactor, from the Petrine narration spanning 1.1 to 8.20. Yet the issue is far from decided by this point. There are several significant thematic aspects which link it with the previous text: 1) the use of the term "stranger" (8.24 to 3.7, 10); 2) the reference to Lithargoel (8.25 to 5.16); and 3) the reference to medical topics (8.34 to 8.15–19). Until an overall theory of the text's redaction is presented a more complete understanding cannot be achieved. Suffice it to say here that I consider this text to be related to the rest of the pearl merchant story in 1.1–8.20.

AN INSERTED RESURRECTION APPEARANCE (9.1–29)
At 9.1, there appears to be yet another indication of a textual break. Following the rather plastic "He hurried and came (back) quickly" in 8.35–9.1, there is a rather abruptly introduced section to which I shall refer, following Schenke and Patterson's lead,[72] as a resurrection appearance. In this section, I include 9.1 to 9.29, which contains my third voice shift type, "We - Apostolic Voice." My reasons for regarding this as stemming from an originally separate source are fourfold.

The first reason is related to the voice shift present within this section, "We - Apostolic Voice." As Patterson has noted, "the narrative shifts in *ActsPet12Apost.* often involve not simply a shift in voice (third

---

Coptic NT is from George Horner, ed. and trans., *The Coptic Version of the New Testament in the Southern Dialect: Otherwise Called Sahidic and Thebaic* (7 vols; Oxford: Clarendon, 1911–1924).

[72] Patterson describes this resurrection appearance as being in 8.10–9.29 and links it with his proposed third source — the "We Source" (ibid., 12). Schenke's view is similar. He calls the text "an Easter and Pentecost story" ("The Acts of Peter and the Twelve Apostles," 418).

person to first, or singular to plural), but an actual shift in the narrative perspective of the text." Patterson notes that in this text the voice is one of the apostolic group — not Peter.[73] Thus, this narrative perspective (that of one of the apostolic group) is unique to this section of *ActsPet12Apost.*, a fact which sets it apart from the rest of the document.

The second reason has to do with the problematic relationships between Lithargoel, the physician and Jesus. In 8.11–20, Lithargoel is introduced for the first time as a physician. The narrator (presumably Peter — still in the "We of Journeys") notes that the group did not recognize him. The reader expects a recognition scene where the physician is revealed as Lithargoel and, presumably, Lithargoel's relationship with physicians is explained. Instead, Lithargoel is referred to as "the Savior" in 9.5, a term that is otherwise foreign to *ActsPet12Apost.* Thus, Lithargoel is never "recognized" as the physician and subsequently drops out of the narrative.[74]

Third, there is a natural break in the text as it now stands. Lithargoel, now a physician, leaves and promises to return. My judgment is to regard the cursory mention of Lithargoel's departure and return as secondary. It just doesn't seem to make a great deal of narrative sense. Why take the trouble to narrate a departure of a key character and then not do anything with the other characters in the meantime?

The fourth reason is admittedly a minor point. In 9.20 the "we" is referred to as eleven "disciples." This term, a Greek loanword, μαθητής appears only twice in *ActsPet12Apost.* (9.20; 12.13) and it is only in 9.20 that a numerical designation is associated with the term "disciples."

---

[73] Patterson, "Sources, Redaction and Tendenz," 6–7. Patterson groups this first person plural voice in 9.15–29 with his third source, the "We Source."

[74] The significance of this point should not be overlooked. This is nothing less than the absorption of the character of the pearl merchant, Lithargoel and the physician into Jesus. Lithargoel was to be revealed as a heavenly physician but now it is Jesus who is depicted as the physician. As Schenke states, "the central figure now wears one disguise too many" ("The Acts of Peter and the Twelve Apostles," 418).

Elsewhere those with Peter are called brothers (3.6), strangers (3.7; 8.25), friends (6.28; 7.21) and possibly even apostles (1.5) and yet none of these terms has any kind of numerical designation as in 9.20.

THE AUTHOR/ REDACTOR'S OWN MATERIAL

The final section to be examined is 9.30–12.19. As noted above, this is one of those sections which I have classed under "The Narrator" voice shift type. These lines are the defining section of *ActsPet12Apost.* and representative of the author/ redactor's own hand. The section begins with a reference to the unguent box (ⲚⲀⲢⲀⲞⲤ; ⲚⲀⲢⲦⲞⲤ in 8.16) and pouch (ⲄⲖⲞⲤⲤⲞⲔⲰⲘⲞⲚ) that were mentioned in 8.16–19. However, it is clear from what follows that this is merely the author's attempt to link his/her work with the previous material. This is apparent in that when reference is made in 9.30–31 to the unguent box and pouch it is not expanded upon. Instead, it is not until 10.31–32, when the text presents Jesus as once again giving the pouch to Peter and the others, that the subject of healing is seriously broached. It is only in the following text that it becomes clear that the author's own views on healing are more complicated than just the simple performance of medical techniques and remedies. While the author is obliged by his or her use of the previous material to mention the unguent box and pouch, it is clear in 11.14–26 (especially lines 19–23) that the author envisions bodily healing as being able to be brought about "without medicine of the world."[75] Certainly, there are other ways that this section is tied to the previous material and ways in which it differs, but this leads us to a consideration of a redactional theory for *ActsPet12Apost.*

In summary, I suggest that in *ActsPet12Apost.* two originally separate bodies of source material have been brought together, edited and then built upon by an author/redactor. I do not consider that these two

---

[75] Presumably this envisioned healing would be like many of the miracles of Jesus as reported by the canonical gospels where no aids are used (e.g., Mark 1:29–31; 40–42 but not John 9:1–7).

previously separate source units have remained untouched by the author/ redactor's hand. On the contrary, the author/ redactor has added material and thereby altered these sources. However, these are questions that are best addressed later in this study. For now it is sufficient to paint with broad strokes, and hence to describe the primary units as follows:

1) *The Story of the Pearl Merchant* (1.1 to 9.1, except for redactional additions): A first-person narrative, parable-like or allegorical in nature, involving a mysterious pearl merchant and two symbolic cities. A mystical journey must be undertaken to one of these cities so as to attain "the pearl," which is most likely salvation of the soul (i.e., heaven, oneness with God). There was probably a return from the heavenly city so as to pass on the knowledge of how to make the journey and any other knowledge that might have been revealed at "Nine Gates."

2) *A Resurrection Appearance* (9.1 to 9.29): This is told from the perspective of one of the followers of Jesus, but not Peter. It is written in the first person yet employs third person within its overall structure. It is possibly docetic or gnostic in tone, and its reference to the "eleven disciples" associates it with a post-crucifixion period and with the traditions associated with that period that appears in the canonical gospels.

3) *The Author/Redactor's Theology* (9.30–12.19): A third person narration, didactic or hortatory in tone, that attempts to echo themes from the pearl merchant source. It shifts the emphasis of the first source from a heavenly hereafter to an earthly or pastoral focus.

Chapter 2
Classification by Genre

In this chapter my objective is to reconsider the question of the genre of *ActsPet12Apost.* I shall begin by describing, then evaluating the two major theories that have been proposed for this text. The first proposal was advanced by Martin Krause in 1972. Krause suggests that *ActsPet12Apost.* is a gnostic apocryphal act. He draws exclusively upon the research of Rosa Söder, who worked toward defining the formal characteristics of the genre, apocryphal act. The second proposal was presented by Pheme Perkins in 1980. She argues that *ActsPet12Apost.* is a gnostic revelation dialogue. This conclusion was reached by first considering the formal characteristics of revelation dialogues and then by application of these characteristics to a number of Nag Hammadi texts, including *ActsPet12Apost.* I agree with Perkins's assessment but only as a partial answer to the question of genre. Like Perkins, I view 9.1–12.19 (Resurrection Appearance and the Author/ Redactor's Theology) as a revelation dialogue. However, I will argue that this part of our text is a revelation dialogue with a unique church order-like focus.

Although I recognize validity in the latter of these theories, alone it fails to explain sufficiently the strong allegorical character of *ActsPet12Apost.* (specifically that found in 1.1 to 9.1), an element of the text that any consideration of genre must address. Therefore, in an attempt to treat this problem, I propose that the first section of *ActsPet12Apost.*, which corresponds to the first source division I have suggested above (The Story of the Pearl Merchant, 1.1–9.1), is a composite of two major types of forms. First, there are the symbolic elements of the story (e.g., the cities of Habitation and Nine Gates, the Pearl and the divisions of rich and poor within Habitation). These are story components which serve as one-to-one representations of perceived real-world realities or constructions of mythic reality. This literary technique is described by the fourth century (A.D.) grammarian Diomedes as *homoeosis*. Second, there is the dominant story aspect which deals with the ascent of the soul. (This includes both of the apostles's journeys: to Habitation and Nine Gates.) Based on the correspondences between the content of *ActsPet12Apost.* and the definitions provided in various ancient works on literary technique, the most accurate formal definition I have been able to locate in antiquity is that of Macrobius's (ca. fourth or fifth century A.D.) *narratio fabulosa*. Thus, I suggest that *ActsPet12Apost.* is essentially the combination of two major forms: a *narratio fabulosa* (built upon a foundational *homoeosis*) and a unique revelation dialogue. This connection, or rather, combination of forms was a result of the redactor's work.

MARTIN KRAUSE: A GNOSTIC APOCRYPHAL ACT

In his 1972 article, "Die Petrusakten in Codex VI von Nag Hammadi," Krause never questions his first assumption that the genre of *ActsPet12Apost.* is what its title claims. He assumes *ActsPet12Apost.* is an apocryphal act or, more accurately, two acts: 1) an act of Peter, and 2) an act of the twelve apostles inclusive of Peter.[1] In addition, he concerns himself with the relationships between *ActsPet12Apost.*, the *Act of Peter* found in BG 8502.4 and the commonly known Vercelli *Acts of Peter*. Following the work of Carl Schmidt, he views the *Act of Peter* as part of the long-lost beginning of the *Acts of Peter*.[2] Furthermore, Krause finds

---

[1] Krause makes this clear at the end of the first section of his study: "In accordance with the content of the tract, I explain the title as follows: the plural ΝΙⲠⲣⲀⲌⲓⲤ (12.20), 'the acts,' already distinguishes between several acts, at least two. The one act is that of Peter, the other is that of the twelve apostles inclusive of Peter" ("Die Petrusakten," 38).

[2] Schmidt first published the *Act of Peter* in 1903. At that time he presented his initial argument for an original unity between the apocryphal *Acts of Peter* and the Act of Peter (*Die alten Petrusakten im zusammenhang der apocryphen Apostellitteratur nebst einem neuentdeckten Fragment* [TU 24; Leipzig: Hinrichs, 1903]1–25). Then, as a response to the actions and arguments of Gerhard Ficker, Schmidt refined and restated his argument ("Studien zu den

points of contact between the *Act of Peter* and *ActsPet12Apost.*[3] and
concludes that *ActsPet12Apost.* preceded the *Act of Peter* chronologically
as part of the lost beginning section of the *Acts of Peter*. In the
introduction to his article, Krause provides a clue to his motivation for
having detected links between these texts. He notes that his observations
are to be part of a (then) forthcoming commentary on the *Acts of Peter*.[4]

---

alten Petrusakten," *ZKG* 43 [1924] 321–48). The history of that debate is as
follows: There are three works by Ficker that come into play here. The first two
were published in 1904, the third in 1924. In the first analysis (a brief
introduction in the first edition of *Neutestamentliche Apokryphen*), Ficker
hesitatingly accepted Schmidt's proposal of an original unity between the Coptic
Act of Peter and the *Acts of Peter*, albeit with some reservations. In this collection
the text of the *Act of Peter* was published in German as part of the *Acts of Peter*
("Petrusakten," in Edgar Hennecke, ed., *Neutestamentliche Apokryphen in
Verbindung mit Fachgelehrten in deutscher Übersetzung und mit Einleitungen*
[Tübingen: Mohr, 1904] 383–423). However, in the same year (1904), Ficker also
published a rather extensive analysis of the *Acts of Peter* as part of a handbook
intended to accompany the texts provided in the previous volume. In this study
Ficker included a brief critical analysis of Schmidt's 1903 article in which he
concluded, contrary to Schmidt, that the *Act of Peter* was probably not the long-
lost first part of the *Acts of Peter* ("Petrusakten," in E. Hennecke, ed., *Handbuch
zu den Neutestamentlichen Apokryphen in Verbindung mit Fachgelehrten*
[Tübingen: Mohr, 1904] 395–491; see especially 400–4). Finally, in 1924, Ficker
pushed Schmidt too far. In the second edition of *Neutestamentliche Apokryphen*,
Ficker, acting upon his previously stated conviction, refused to publish the *Act of
Peter* as part of the *Acts of Peter* ("Actus Vercellenses," in E. Hennecke, ed.,
*Neutestamentliche Apokryphen in Verbindung mit Fachgelehrten in deutscher
Uebersetzung und mit Einleitungen* [2d ed.; Tübingen: Mohr, 1924] 226–49).

[3] Krause notes the following: 1) the emphasis on Peter's ability to heal
the sick (cf. *Act Pet.* 128.1–7; 130.1–9 and *ActsPet12Apost.* 10.33–34; 11.19–26);
2) the basis for healing is the same: it is to awaken faith (cf. *Act Pet.* 129.17–9 and
ActsPet12Apost. 11.19–26); 3) the use of the formulation "to believe on the name"
(cf. *Act Pet.* 129,1 and *ActsPet12Apost.* 10.5–6); and 4) the emphasis on the soul
(cf. *Act Pet.* 129.17; 132.3; 138.10 and *ActsPet12Apost.* 11.14–19) (ibid., 56–57).
While these parallels exist, they cannot prove any more than that both documents
emerged from a milieu common to early Christianity. Krause is mistakenly
assuming that just because two documents share the same hero they must share the
same author or community.

[4] Ibid., 36.

Therefore, it comes as no surprise that, given his assumption of a textual relationship between the *Acts of Peter* and *ActsPet12Apost.*, Krause would seek to demonstrate that both texts share the same formal characteristics, i.e., those of an apocryphal act.

To demonstrate that *ActsPet12Apost.* is an apocryphal act Krause relies completely upon the work of Rosa Söder. Her 1932 study is an attempt to define the genre, apocryphal acts, by comparing various motifs that these texts have in common with the Greek novel. While she does not argue for a direct relationship between the Greek novel and the apocryphal acts, she does delineate five main elements (held in common with the Greek novel) which, in her opinion, are to be regarded as typical of the genre, apocryphal acts.[5] They are as follows: 1) the travel motif; 2) the aretalogical element (i.e., the interest in the miraculous powers of the apostle); 3) the teratological element (i.e., the fantastic aspects of the world in which the apostle acts such as talking animals and cannibals); 4) the tendentious element (contained in the teaching, preaching and speeches); and 5) the erotic element (which can be manifested in ascetic and/or encratite aspects of the text or in romantic aspects).[6] In an attempt

---

[5] Söder, *Die apokryphen Apostelgeschichten und die romanhafte Literatur der Antike* (Würzburger Studien zur Alterumswissenschaft; Stuttgart: Kohlhammer, 1932) 21–148.

[6] It is well known that the value of Söder's five elements for understanding the apocryphal acts has been severely criticized by scholars such as Wilhelm Schneemelcher and Jean-Daniel Kaestli. See Schneemelcher, "Introduction: Second and Third Century Acts of Apostles," in idem, ed., *New Testament Apocrypha* (2 vols; Louisville: Westminster/ Knox, 1992) 2.78–83; and Kaestli, "Les principales orientations de la recherche sur les actes apocryphes des apôtres," in François Bovon, ed., *Les Actes Apocryphes des Apôtres* (Geneva: Labor et Fides, 1981) 57–67. See also the more recent discussion of Christine M. Thomas, "The Acts of Peter, the Ancient Novel, and Early Christian History" (Ph.D. dissertation; Harvard University, 1995) 1–25; especially 8–14. Of these three the work of Kaestli is indispensable for several reasons the most important of which are 1) his review of the history of the scholarly discussion on the question of the genre of the apocryphal acts and 2) his point by point critique of Söder's five elements. Even though I am well aware of the debate that has resulted from Söder's thesis, I accept her categories as the parameters of Krause's

to demonstrate that *ActsPet12Apost.* has the formal characteristics of an apocryphal act, Krause proceeds to compare systematically Söder's five elements with his three segments of *ActsPet12Apost.*: the framework section (1.3–1.29); the first narrative (1.29–7.23) and the second narrative (8.13–12.19). He begins by noting the presence of the travel motif with many of its topoi in the framework section (1.3–1.29). Krause lists the following travel topoi as being present in *ActsPet12Apost.*:

1) *The motivation for the journey is the command of God.* Krause quotes 1.9–12 as evidence: "And in our hearts, we were united. We agreed to fulfill the ministry to which the Lord had appointed us."[7]

2) *The journey leads to the sea* (cf. 1.14–16).[8]

3) *The waiting and ready ship* (cf. 1.16–23).[9]

4) *The presence of a traveling companion or companions* (cf. 1.4–5; 9.21–22).[10]

5) *The storm at sea* (cf. 1.26–29).[11]

Primarily basing his argument on the presence of these travel topoi, Krause concludes that the framework section should be regarded as an apocryphal acts narrative.[12] In the case of this first point, it is important

---

argument and intend to demonstrate his mistaken association of *ActsPet12Apost.* with the genre, apocryphal acts, based on the very categories Krause treats as authoritative — those of Söder.

[7] "The apostle does not generally set out on his own to his mission-area. Either it is decided by lot, and they must absolutely obey what God's will dictates or Christ himself divides the land" (Söder, *Die apokryphen Apostelgeschichten*, 44).

[8] "The journey of the hero of the novel generally comes to the sea" (ibid., 42). She cites numerous examples including both Greco-Roman novels and apocryphal acts, such as Peter's journey from Jerusalem by sea (*Acts of Peter* 5).

[9] Ibid., 42.

[10] Ibid., 46–47.

[11] Ibid., 48.

[12] Krause, "Die Petrusakten," 55.

to observe that the travel motif need not be considered a unique and/ or constitutive element of the genre, apocryphal acts. The concept of missionary travel need not be explained as having its roots in novelistic literature (or any other Greco-Roman literary genre) or be considered as a distinctive element of the apocryphal acts. In the case of the apocryphal acts, the idea of missionary activity and apostolic travels, has its roots in the gospel wanderings of Jesus himself (which the gospels describe as encouraged in his disciples, e.g., Mark 6:6–13; Luke 10:1). This same activity is characteristic of the canonical Acts and probably to be regarded as less an indicator of genre and more a reflection of the indelible mark that the actual, historical travels of apostles like Peter, Paul and John left on the Church's psyche.[13] Thus we should not be surprised that the disciples of Jesus are associated with travel. It is clearly not conclusive evidence that *ActsPet12Apost.* should be considered as belonging to the genre, apocryphal acts.

In addition, there is a flaw in Krause's conception of the text when one considers this issue of travel, its relationship to Söder's second key motif, the aretalogical element, and its association with *ActsPet12Apost.* At the beginning of his comparison of the framework section with the apocryphal acts genre, Krause states that the wandering hero travels through the world teaching and working miracles. While the apostles certainly receive a commission in 1.11–12, it does not seem to be a commission to work miracles. In fact, when Peter himself articulates his mission to the pearl salesman (Lithargoel), he states, "It is necessary for us to spread the word of God in every city harmoniously" (5.12–14). The initial mission is not that of "wunderwirkend" but of evangelism. While there is a second commission to a dual type of healing in 10.31–11.26, the emphasis is upon the commissioning itself, not upon miraculous works. Furthermore, by a careful reading of 10.31–11.26, it can be observed that the stress is upon the healing of souls rather than physical healing. The

---

[13]Cf. the remarks of Kaestli on this matter ("Les principales orientations," 64).

healing of bodies, while taken for granted as part of the disciples' ministry, serves only as an avenue for faith so as to bring about the ultimate goal of the mission, healing of souls (cf. 11.18–26). More specifically, it should be noted that a key difference in the presentation of the miraculous in the *ActsPet12Apost.* versus the apocryphal acts is that while miracles are obviously accepted as part and parcel of the Christian call to ministry in the former they are far from the ostentatious focus that they have become in the latter. In the former they are practical events that take place in the world outside the text, in the latter they are woven into the myth and legendary story world itself.

This consideration of the emphasis (or lack thereof) upon the miraculous in our text leads me to question just how strong Söder's aretalogical element is in *ActsPet12Apost.* Krause identifies the presence of the aretalogical element in his second narrative. He points to the transformation of Lithargoel into Jesus (9.15–19) and Lithargoel's supposed omniscience (9.2–4).[14] However, these examples are weak. This is especially the case when they are compared to incidents such as those found in the *Acts of Peter* (e.g., the smoked fish that swam again at the command of Peter [c. 13] or the young man bitten by the serpent and subsequently healed by Thomas [*Acts of Thomas* 30–33]). Upon working through the aretalogical topoi listed by Söder, I find that virtually none are found in *ActsPet12Apost.* The presentation of the apostles is less like the figures of superhuman proportion found in the apocryphal acts and more like the well-meaning yet often inadequate disciples found in the canonical gospels. For example, Peter is ignorant of the city of

---

[14] In Söder's description of the aretalogical element she describes the topos of the apostle's omniscience (e.g., *Acts of John* 46) (*Die apokryphen Apostelgeschichten*, 65). While Krause tries to argue for the presence of the topos "omniscience of the apostle," I fail to see its application. The "omniscience" (if any is actually present) is that of Jesus, not of Peter — and, frankly, I fail to see how Jesus' knowledge of one of his own disciples's name amounts to omniscience. The closest possible example of omniscience, on Lithargoel's part, not Peter's, is found in 2.32–3.11. This, of course, is assuming that Lithargoel's recognition of Peter's status as a stranger is somehow indicative of divine power!

Habitation's name (1.30–32) and needs to seek advice about lodgings
(2.8–10). He does not know Lithargoel or how to get to his city (5.8–12).
He feels inadequate to overcome the hardships on the road and is sad
(6.9–14). He marvels at the things he sees (6.31–32). He is frightened by
what he does not understand (9.2–4); yet he and the apostolic group
worship Jesus as soon as he reveals himself and express willing servitude
(9.19–29). He fails to understand the parable (10.23–31; cf. Mark
4:10–13). This less then glamorous portrayal of the apostle is a far cry
from the heroes presented for our consideration in the apocryphal acts.

As if sensing the weakness of the aretalogical element, Krause tries
to stress the presence of the tendentious element in both his first and
second narratives.   He identifies this element in the explication
concerning endurance in trials and temptations (7.6–19); in the basis for
healing (to awaken faith; 11.24–26) and in the high ascetic demands (to
renounce everything and fast daily; 5.23–25).[15] However, this element is
also weakened by the lack of apostolic preaching and teaching in
ActsPet12Apost. The only teaching presented comes in the form of a
commission by Jesus (not from Peter or any member of the apostolic
group) to teach, heal and judge the churches.[16] Certainly, this text is
unlike the majority of apocryphal acts in that preaching and teaching
placed in the mouth of an apostolic figure is absent.

The peculiar thing about both the aretalogical element (healing
specifically, 11.14–26) and the tendentious element (teaching, 10.5–7) in
ActsPet12Apost. is that they exist or happen *outside* the text. It is taken

---

[15] Krause, "Die Petrusakten," 55.

[16] Furthermore, it should be noted that Söder's tendentious element (as
well as her criteria in general) is not universally accepted as fundamental. For
example, Jean-Daniel Kaestli questions the value of Söder's tendentious element:
"However, is the use of this criteria to define novelistic literature truly pertinent?
At all events it is not of the same nature as the other four elements reserved by R.
Söder: these can be dismissed in effect by the thematic contents, while the
doctrinal and moral tendency designates the general intention of texts,
independent of their content. Moreover, the same criteria can be applied to other
genres of writing" (Kaestli, "Les principales orientations," 63).

for granted that they happen but there is no pressing need to portray them in the text. It is as if the teaching and healings do not need to be concretized in a story. For the writer's community, they are not dramatic or inspirational ideals but actual community occurrences. However, this leads us into areas that must be dealt with in an analysis of the community behind *ActsPet12Apost.*

Krause does not try to detect Söder's teratological or erotic elements in our text. This is probably because they are virtually non-existent. The only section that could be classified feasiblely under Söder's teratological element is Lithargoel's odd description of the strangely intelligent and perceptive animals on the road to his city (5.26–6.8).[17] This subtle and solitary instance pales before the talking animals, cannibals and other strange aspects of the story worlds presented in other apocryphal acts.[18] On the other hand, the erotic element can be fairly safely excluded. There are no clashes between an apostle and a jealous suitor or husband over the heart and soul of some young female convert as with Paul and Thecla or Andrew and Maximilla. While there is reference to fasting and asceticism in *ActsPet12Apost.* (5.21–25; 10.15–19), there is absolutely no reference to sexual asceticism. Besides, if the mere presence of ascetical teaching were enough to classify a text as having an erotic element, then much of early Christian literature would have to considered as possibly belonging to the apocryphal acts genre.

Armed only with a strong travel element, a marginal claim to Söder's aretalogical and tendentious elements and no ties to the teratological and erotic elements, Krause concludes that *ActsPet12Apost.* cannot be viewed as a normal acts of the apostles. It is a gnostic apocryphal act.[19]

---

[17] However, there is a better explanation for this peculiarity, which I shall present in my next section.

[18] Söder, *Die apokryphen Apostelgeschichten*, 103–12.

[19] Krause's conclusion is as abrupt as it is unsupported. Krause recognizes that *ActsPet12Apost.* could not be viewed as a normal example of the genre, acts of the apostles. He attributes this to the fact that it is Lithargoel and not the apostles who stands as the center of the action. This peculiarity, the fact

62   The Acts of Peter and the Twelve Apostles

However, it is apparent that if one uses Söder's criteria, which Krause himself relied upon, this conclusion is untenable.

Certainly, there are points of similarity between *ActsPet12Apost.* and the apocryphal acts (e.g., the motif of missionary travel which I have suggested is indicative of the historical reality of the apostolic mission and not an exclusive element of genre — and the central role played by the apostle). In addition, this association with the apocryphal acts is not limited to modern scholarship as is evidenced by the choice of titles (ⲚⲒⲠⲢⲀϢⲒⲤ Ⲛ̄ⲦⲈ ⲠⲈⲦⲢⲞⲤ ⲘⲚ̄ ⲠⲒⲘⲚ̄ⲦⲤⲚⲞⲞⲨⲤ Ⲛ̄ⲀⲠⲞⲤⲦⲞⲖⲞⲤ). However, when one moves beyond the surface similarities between *ActsPet12Apost.* and the apocryphal acts there are some disturbing differences that demand an accounting.

First, as has already been stated, Söder's aretological and tendentious elements are not significant aspects of *ActsPet12Apost.* The miracles, teaching, preaching and prayers so typical of apocryphal acts serve no dramatic role. They are referred to but are never actually given narrative expression. Second, and as a natural consequence of the lack of narrative preaching, there is no erotic element (i.e., Peter and the apostles never actually preach in the story and no one is converted — hence, no female converts are attracted to their message at the expense of their husbands, fiancés and lovers). Third, and as a result of the absence of these typical motifs, Peter and the apostles make no impact on Habitation. This point of difference cannot be overemphasized. Unlike the apostolic figures in the apocryphal acts who quickly polarize public opinion in their respective sites of ministry (e.g., female converts who adore them, Christians who follow their teachings, crowds who witness their miracles, authorities who jealously plot their downfall), Peter and the apostles pass through Habitation as strangers (Ⲁ[ⲚⲞ]Ⲛ [ϨⲈⲚϢ]Ⲙ̄ⲘⲞ Ⲙ̄ⲠⲒⲘⲀ; 3.6–7). Except for his dialogue with the merchant, Peter has no direct

---

that gnostic-like concepts are present and the text's discovery in the midst of a gnostic-hermetic library leads Krause to designate *ActsPet12Apost.* as a gnostic example of the genre, acts of the apostles ("Die Petrusakten," 55–56).

contact with *anyone* in Habitation, least of all the people of Habitation (recall my comments regarding the identity of the interlocutor in 5.1–2; ⲠⲓⲢⲰⲘⲈ as referring to the merchant). He is reduced to the role of an observer as events unfold around him — not unlike Dickens's immortal character, Scrooge, who, escorted by the three spirits, can hear and see events of the past, present and future but is powerless to interact with them.   Gone is the focus on the apostle's wondrous ministry and preaching. In its place there is an emphasis on proper understanding of one's own ministry, hence Jesus' detailed instructions regarding the nature and targets of ministry (10.1–11.26) and the censure aimed at current (in terms of the redactor) church leaders (12.4–13). From this we are led to believe that, unlike the apocryphal acts, what is crucial to *ActsPet12Apost.* is the transformation that comes about within Peter himself (and in terms of the redactor) the (prospective?) minister — not the transformation he causes by his ministry.

.   This shift in emphasis suggests a difference in intended audience, from a general Christian audience to a group of (prospective?) ministers. By way of explaining this assertion let us consider that the apocryphal acts present a largely idealized, even superhuman apostle. While their portrayal of the apostolic figure can best be described as fictional, these same documents tend to give a reasonablely accurate narrative description of a hypothetical Christian community both in terms of the types of people involved (e.g., elders, virgins, widows, new converts, martyrs, wealthy supporters, etc.) and their usual struggles with faith and doctrine. The hearers of these literary creations, Christians themselves, would have had no trouble seeing the many correlations between the community as pictured and their own experience — which would have served the dual function of entertainment and moral exhortation. Being able to relate to the broken humanity of the communities described (as well as their occasional heroism, e.g., the persecution for their beliefs as with Thecla) served the function of encouraging the listener to apply the preaching and moral exhortation of the idealized apostle. This universality is missing in *ActsPet12Apost.* Its message and informational relevance is aimed at a select group — the ministers of the community themselves. The humanness of Peter, described above, coupled with the apostles's general status of "student" served to encourage the ministers of the redactor's day to relate to the apostles and accept their experience as somehow normative.

Beyond these points of missing motifs and possible audiences, I suggest that it is the allegorical or symbolic character of *ActsPet12Apost.* that most differentiates it from the apocryphal acts. Unlike the apocryphal acts which, although exhibiting many fantastic elements, still present many realistic characters, narrative settings and circumstances, *ActsPet12Apost.* is characterized by a two dimensional quality. For example, Habitation, characterized as a place of endurance (2ΥΠΟΜΙΝΕ; 7.5, 9) and trials (ΠΙΡΑC[Μ]ΟC; 7.9–10), and Nine Gates, characterized by joy (ΡΑϢΕ; 8.4), peace (ΕΙΡ[ΗΝΗ]; 8.5) and rest (MTON; 8.6), lack the realistic feel of the Rome of *Acts of Peter* in which a variety of good and bad events can and do occur. Likewise, the rich and poor are nameless people, objects of exclusion or ministry, who are defined by one overriding characteristic, their social/ financial status. All in all, with the exception of the merchant/ Lithargoel/ Jesus character and Peter and the apostles, the focus of *ActsPet12Apost.* is on types of places and people — not specific characters and their growth and/ or development (cf. Marcellus in *Acts of Peter*). Because of the two dimensional way in which places and people are portrayed, both are reduced to the level of exemplar, and encourage the reader to seek an underlying meaning in their monochrome settings and characters. Certainly, more can and will be said on this issue in both the rest of this chapter and the next, but for now suffice it to say that there are good reasons to seek another understanding of genre than Krause's suggestion of apocryphal acts, gnostic or otherwise.

PHEME PERKINS: A REVELATION DIALOGUE

In 1980, Pheme Perkins analyzed the genre of revelation dialogue and examined a number of Nag Hammadi texts which Perkins concluded were

examples of this genre.[20]   Among these texts was *ActsPet12Apost.*, the
genre of which Perkins describes as "closest to that of apocryphal acts."[21]
Perkins views the text as based on two (possibly orally circulating)
allegories: 1) Jesus as pearl-merchant and 2) Jesus as physician of souls.[22]

Surprisingly, Perkins, like Krause before, recognizes this allegorical
element in *ActsPet12Apost.*;[23] but does not attempt to explain its
relationship to the genre, acts of the apostles.[24] Instead, Perkins accepts
Krause's genre evaluation with the provision that a "revelation dialogue
occurs in the second half of the work."[25]

Perkins includes in her study a chart listing the formal features
common to gnostic revelation dialogues.[26] A review of these features in
relation to *ActsPet12Apost.* is helpful in understanding the roles played by
the three blocks in the text. These features are as follows: 1) *a narrative
setting*; 2) *the involvement of the risen savior*; 3) *the revealer's
appearance* (which includes two components: the revealer's physical
appearance and the revealer's address); 4) *mention of opponents*
(sometimes with reference to persecution) *and preaching of gnosis*
(sometimes including a command to keep the revelation hidden); 5) a

---

[20] Perkins, *The Gnostic Dialogue: The Early Church and the Crisis of
Gnosticism* (Theological Inquiries; New York: Paulist, 1980).

[21] Ibid., 125.

[22] Ibid., 125.

[23] Krause notes that, "our text contains many images which are to be
understood as parables by the hearers and readers. They therefore have a deeper
meaning." He proceeds to list many of these images ("Die Petrusakten," 53).

[24] It is this failure to account for the presence of a strong allegorical tone
that weakens Perkins's genre evaluation of *ActsPet12Apost.* The presence of
allegory, a medium not normally typical of the straightforward presentation of the
genre, acts of the apostles (except for the *Acts of Thomas*, e.g., the Hymn of the
Pearl), should be taken in account.

[25] Perkins, *Gnostic Dialogue*, 127.

[26] These major features occur in at least sixty percent of all known
examples of this genre (ibid., 31).

post-resurrection commission; 6) *questions* (listed and/ or in erotapokriseis form);[27] and 7) *content* (including such topics as the Sophia myth, ascetic preaching, ascent of the soul, Christ as the Gnostic savior and Christian-Gnostic doctrine).[28] In the pages that follow I shall examine each of these features and consider their role within our text. If these features can, in fact, be shown to appear in *ActsPet12Apost.*, then Perkins was right in declaring it a revelation dialogue. This examination is necessary because Perkins's study was very general in its references to our particular text. As I have demonstrated in connection with Krause, if one is to make a claim as to a genre of a text, then that text should be carefully examined so as to learn whether or not it complies with the known (or argued) features of the genre. I shall demonstrate that while Perkins was correct in describing the latter section of our text as a revelation dialogue, the writing as a whole cannot be grouped with gnostic dialogues.

NARRATIVE SETTING

Perkins subdivides her first feature (Narrative Setting) into five related parts:

---

[27] Perkins describes the erotapokriseis type of question: "This type of writing is frequently used to give questions and answers to problems of Homeric exegesis or of jurisprudence. Thus, it is primarily instructional but lacks the introductory 'setting' characteristic of Platonic and other philosophical dialogues. Most Gnostic revelation dialogues invoke New Testament stories to provide a setting for the dialogue. Thus, they are not simply erotapokriseis, though some of their question/ answer content may derive from such a source" (ibid., 20).

[28] This is considerably more specific than the work of Krause, which Perkins drew upon in coming to these formal features. Krause divided the formal structure of the revelation dialogue into four main parts: 1) a narrative framework (which Krause found to be part of all the texts he compared except *The Dialogue of the Savior*); 2) a dialogue with predominant questions and direct answers to these questions; 3) action; and 4) a narrative framework at the end of the tractates with a departure to preach ("Der Dialog des Soter in Codex III von Nag Hammadi," in idem, ed., *Gnosis and Gnosticism* [NHS 8; Leiden: Brill, 1977] 19, 22). In keeping with his 1972 position on *ActsPet12Apost.* as an acts of the apostles, Krause did not use *ActsPet12Apost.* as one of his comparison texts.

1) *Location*: (typically either a mountain or the temple in Jerusalem);

2) *An indication of the time that has passed since Jesus' resurrection*;[29]

3 *The recipient(s) of the revelation*: In the overwhelming majority of texts Perkins examines this was a disciple, several disciples, the Twelve or the Twelve complemented by a group of women disciples;

4) *The activity of the disciples at the time immediately preceding the appearance*;[30]

5) *A description of the mental state of the recipient(s)*.

When *ActsPet12Apost.* is compared to these formal features the connections are not strong. Perkins herself observes that *ActsPet12Apost.* "is not tied to a traditional revelation site. It has used motifs from romance literature to tell the story of the dangers, hardship, and sea journeys faced by the apostles. The revelation itself occurs in a mysterious city in the middle of the ocean."[31] This need not be a problem. As I argued earlier, there are three sources at work in *ActsPet12Apost.* The section where the actual revelation of Jesus takes place is in my second source, *A Resurrection Appearance* (9.1–9.29). I view this as having been originally separate from the first source, *The Story of the Pearl Merchant* (1.1–9.1), of which the city of Nine Gates was a part. Regarding the site of the revelation I concur with Schenke's assessment: "We can well imagine that this text, as an Easter and Pentecost story, had its setting before one of the gates of the real Jerusalem, where the eleven disciples under Peter's leadership were to meet the risen Jesus."[32]

---

[29] Perkins made it clear that this feature is only occasionally present. It is found in *Apocryphon of James* 2.19–20 (550 days), *1 Apocalypse of James* 30.17–18 (several days) and *Pistis Sophia* 1.1 (eleven years) (*Gnostic Dialogue*, 47–48).

[30] This includes undergoing persecution, preaching writing and discussing Jesus' words (ibid., 42).

[31] The revelation takes place outside the city of Nine Gates (ibid., 48).

[32] Schenke, "The Acts of Peter and the Twelve Apostles," 418.

The second and third parts of Perkins's *narrative setting* are partially fulfilled by the same aspect of the text. The phrase, "We comprised eleven disciples" (9.20) indicates a time not long after Jesus' death (due to the presumed absence of Judas). It also makes clear who are the recipients of the revelation. Meanwhile, the fourth and fifth parts are not present in my second source. One must go back to the first source (8.4–11) to find references to the recipients's actions (talking and contemplating the faith) and their state of mind (joy/ peacefully carefree). The redactor who joined these two sources may have assumed these components from the first source and merely edited out any reference to the recipients's actions included in the second source.

THE INVOLVEMENT OF THE RISEN SAVIOR

In regard to Perkins's second feature, no explicit mention is made of Jesus' resurrection. In fact, when Jesus reveals himself to the disciples, the description is rather peculiar: "He loosened the garment, which clothed him — the one into which he had changed himself because of us — revealing to us in truth that it was he" (ⲁϥⲃⲟⲩϣϥ ⲛϯ ϩⲃⲥⲱ ⲉⲧⲥⲧⲟⲉ ϩⲓⲱⲱϥ ⲧⲁⲓ ⲉⲧⲁϥϣⲃⲧϥ ⲛⲧⲟⲟⲧⲛ ⲛϩⲏⲧⲥ ⲉⲧⲁϥⲟⲩⲱⲛϩ ⲉⲣⲟⲛ ϩⲛ ⲟⲩⲙⲛⲧⲙⲉ ϫⲉ ⲛⲧⲟϥ ⲡⲉ; 9.15–19). One expects the phrase, "He loosened his garment" (ⲁϥⲃⲟⲩϣϥ ⲛϯ ϩⲃⲥⲱ) to lead into a scene where, as in the canonical tradition, Jesus shows his wounds so as to identify himself (cf. Luke 24:39; John 20:27). As it now stands, the emphasis has completely shifted from Jesus' physical body (and the assumed tell-tale scars of the crucified one) to the interpretation of Jesus' garment. The text now equates the garment with a physical body which like clothes can be put on and taken off. Jesus is now a spiritual being capable of putting on and taking off flesh as one would a suit of clothes. The reader can only presume a risen Jesus because of the post-resurrection setting implied by the mention of the eleven disciples (9.20).

THE REVEALER'S APPEARANCE

Perkins includes two major components under this heading: the revealer's physical appearance and the revealer's address. According to Perkins, the revealer's appearance could comprise three elements: cosmic signs (rarely used OT-like metaphorical language, e.g., Is 24:18–23; 63:19–64:1; cf. *Pistis Sophia* 1.5 and *Apocryphon of John* 1.31–2.1), polymorphous shape, and luminosity.[33] According to Perkins none of these elements are present in *ActsPet12Apost.* However, as I noted in the previous section (Involvement of the Risen Savior), Jesus may well be presented in a polymorphous manner in that he "wears" the body of a physician and then "loosens" (ⲃⲱⲱⲗ) or removes his bodily disguise so as to reveal his true identity. Furthermore, Jesus is also linked with Lithargoel (in a forced manner; cf. 8.12–9.10). The reader is led to assume that Jesus was "wearing" the flesh of Lithargoel as yet another disguise.

In regard to the second component, the revealer's address, Perkins concludes that this consisted of three parts: a rebuke, an I AM statement and a statement of purpose. Of these three parts Perkins finds only the I AM statement in our text.[34] Once again, I must disagree with Perkins, because our text does contain a rebuke. My disagreement with Perkins is based on part of her own description of how the rebuke functions in some dialogues. She writes:

> In other dialogues, the rebuke has a dogmatic function more like the second rebuke in *NatArc.* [93.22–32]. The seer should have known the truth which will now be the subject of the revelation (cf. *ApocryJn* CG II 2.9–12; *PetPhil* CG VIII 134.15–18; *Zostr* CG VIII 3.31–4.12). Thus the rebuke is no longer concerned with the proper attitude in prayer. Rather it shifts the blame for the

---

[33] Perkins, *Gnostic Dialogue*, 49–52. Perkins gives examples of both polymorphous shape and luminosity.

[34] Ibid., 55.

necessity of this extra revelation to the recipients. God did not
intend for them to be in such a state of ignorance.[35]

This very type of rebuke is present in *ActsPet12Apost.* In 10.22–30, Jesus
rebukes Peter (albeit gently) for failing to understand the value of his
name ("The Lord answered and said: 'O Peter, it was necessary that you
understand the parable that I told you! Do you not understand
[**KCOOYN ∂N**] that my name, which you teach, surpasses all riches,
and the wisdom of God surpasses gold and silver and precious
stones?'").[36]

MENTION OF OPPONENTS AND PREACHING OF GNOSIS
Certainly opponents are mentioned in *ActsPet12Apost.* One need only
refer to 11.26–12.13, where both the rich and the "many" (presumably the
majority of the leadership) in the churches who have shown partiality
toward the rich are labeled sinful. Furthermore, the disciples are
encouraged to teach. As for the two more minor aspects, persecution and
the command to keep the revelation hidden, Perkins views the former as
problematic and the latter as not present in our text. Regardless of
Perkins's   conclusion   about   the   mention   of   persecution   in

---

[35] Ibid., 54. This is the rebuke to which Perkins refers in *Hyp. Arc.*
92.22–32: "But Norea turned to them [the rulers] and said to them, 'It is you who
are the rulers of the darkness; you are accursed. And you did not know my
mother; instead it was your female counterpart that you knew. For I am not your
descendent; rather it is from the world above that I am come.' The arrogant ruler
turned, with all his might, [and] his countenance came to be like (a) black [...]; he
said to her presumptuously, "You must render service to us , [as did] also your
mother Eve...."

[36] Perkins links this text with "the misunderstanding type of question so
common in Johannine discourse to initiate the reader into the symbolic truth about
Jesus that is presented by the narrative" (ibid., 127–28).

ActsPet12Apost., I am convinced that it is not at all foreign to the experience of the author/ redactor's community.[37]

A POST-RESURRECTION COMMISSION

Even a cursory reading reveals that there is a substantial commissioning element in *ActsPet12Apost.* The disciples are commissioned to teach (10.4–5); to care for the daily needs of the poor (10.8–10); to perform bodily healings (11.19–20); to heal souls (11.25–26); and to judge in uprightness (12.8–9).

QUESTIONS AND CONTENT

I shall treat Perkins's last two formal characteristics together because they are closely related. This is because the content of a revelation dialogue proceeds through its questions. Perkins describes the questions in our text as of the *erotapokriseis* (instructional) type. This type of question and answer form has an ancient and varied usage.[38] Among its many uses, none is more significant for our purposes than its employment in

---

[37] I will later argue (regarding the community behind *ActsPet12Apost.*) that this text received its final redaction shortly after a period of severe persecution. For now, suffice it to point to 7.6–19 as an indication of the intensity of the community's experience.

[38] As described by Heinrich Dörrie and Hermann Dörries, "Erotapokriseis," in *RAC* 6 (1966) 342–70.   According to Dörrie the *erotapokriseis* type of question has its essential starting point in Homeric exegesis, asking the question: "What did Homer mean by this saying?" Eventually, it would also be used in philosophical writings, ancient grammars and medical works ("Erotapokriseis," 342–46).

revelatory literature. It is found extensively in the *Corpus Hermeticum*[39] and, as Perkins notes, in the gnostic revelation dialogues.

The concept of asking the god or gods a question with the expectation of an answer is an ancient one. Its roots can be traced back to the oracle tradition, exemplified by Apollo's oracle at Delphi. However, the response gleaned from this type of questioning were far from clear in their meaning.[40] The use of the *erotapokriseis* schema afforded the ancient scholar the opportunity not only to ask the central theological questions but also to answer them by putting the desired response into the god's mouth.[41]

In the case of the gnostic dialogues this desired response included such topics as: *Urgeschichte* (e.g., the Sophia myth, the highest god); soteriology (e.g., the soul's ascent); doctrinal points (e.g., Christ as gnostic revealer, the proper understanding of the crucifixion) and eschatology. Perkins includes two very helpful charts which concretely diagram both the formal and topical content of the gnostic revelation dialogues.[42] However, her charts imply that *ActsPet12Apost.* lacks many major elements. Of the twenty-five categories listed by Perkins, our text

---

[39] An example of this type of questioning is provided by *Hermetica* 4, "A Discourse of Hermes to Tat": "For what reason, then, did god not share mind with all of them, my father?" "He wanted it put between souls, my child, as a prize for them to contest." "And where did he put it?" "He filled a great mixing bowl with it and sent it below, appointing a herald whom he commanded to make the following proclamation to human hearts: 'Immerse yourself in the mixing bowl if your heart has the strength, if it believes you will rise up again to the one who sent the mixing bowl below, if it recognizes the purpose of your coming to be" (4.3–4). See also *Hermetica* 10 and 11. The translation here is taken from Brian P. Copenhaver, trans., *Hermetica* (Cambridge: Cambridge University Press, 1992) 15. For an English translation of this literature that includes both Greek and Latin see Walter Scott, ed. and trans., Hermetica (repr.; Boston: Shambhala, 1993).

[40] As a sadder-but-wiser Croesus could attest after having "destroyed a mighty empire" by attacking the Persians. See Herodotus, *History*, 1.53.90–91.

[41] Dörrie, "Erotapokriseis," 347.

[42] Perkins, *Gnostic Dialogue*, 61, 69.

appeared in only three. Of these three, the first is a NT question,[43] the second is the mention of ascetical activity and the third is the reference to eschatological blessings (10.11–13). The first is problematic insofar as it is not certain that a NT passage is being referred to, let alone debated. The second and third are hardly uncommon topics for early Christian literature. Thus, a major problem arises with Perkins's inclusion of *ActsPet12Apost.* with gnostic revelation dialogues: the formal and topical content (by Perkins's own definition) is not gnostic. This is a serious issue. To this point Perkins's formal characteristics seemed to be present in our text. How does one explain such an important deviation in the area of formal content?

A REFINEMENT OF PERKINS'S THEORY:
A SLIGHT ADJUSTMENT

It is important to recognize what is the content of the questions and answers in *ActsPet12Apost.* Our text includes only two questions:[44] 1) Peter's question asking exactly how they will be able to provide for the needs of the poor in light of their own asceticism (10.13–21); and 2) John's question asking how they will know how to heal bodies since they lack medical training (11.6–13). In short, the questions and answers are exclusively focused upon ministry. The questions are not formalized (i.e., merely present to afford the revealer the opportunity to launch into a doctrinal sermon). They are practical and logical in light of the commission being given to the disciples. The commission element of the

---

[43] This is described by Perkins as "alluded to or barely mentioned." I can only assume that Perkins was referring to the "food for a single day" in 10.13–21, which may be alluding to the "daily bread" of Matt 6:11 and parallels. However, this is not a strong allusion.

[44] The fact that *ActsPet12Apost.* has only two questions is not at issue. *Ep. Pet. Phil.* also has two questions: 1) 134.18–135.2 (with 4 or 5 parts) and 2) 137.13–17; *Hyp. Arch.* has three: 1) 93.32–94.2 (4 parts); 2) 96.17–19; and 3) 96.31–32. The number of questions is dependent upon the length of the text and the author's stylistic tastes (e.g., the choice whether to ask a few questions which are many-faceted or to ask many questions which are easier to address).

revelation dialogue form has completely taken over the dialogue. The text is no longer a typical revelation dialogue. The revelation dialogue form is being employed to accomplish a different task.

While the focus of our text's revelation dialogue is ministry, this concern is not altogether foreign to the genre. In the *Epistula Apostolorum*, a mid-2nd century Christian revelation dialogue, a commission to preach and teach is given to the apostles which has a similar tone to that found in our text:

> And both preach and teach this to those who believe in me, and preach concerning the heavenly kingdom of my Father, and as my Father has given me the power that you may bring near the children of the heavenly Father. Preach, and they will believe. You it is whose duty is to lead his children into heaven. And we said to him, "O Lord, it is possible for you to do what you have told us; but how will we be able to do it?" (*Ep. Apost.* 19)

A similar passage is also found in chapter 30 as well as 41–42. In both of these examples, as with *ActsPet12Apost.*, a commission is followed by a question of the disciples that requests an explanation of the "how" of ministry. In both *Ep. Apost.* and *ActsPet12Apost.* the disciples are willing to do what they are asked. Yet they feel unqualified for their assignment and require further details.

This similarity with *ActsPet12Apost.* only goes so far. Unlike our text, the focus of *Ep. Apost.* is not exclusively ministerial. Issues of proper doctrine take the forefront (albeit with an 'orthodox' tone) just as they would in a gnostic revelation dialogue. Thus, while there are similarities, *ActsPet12Apost.* further demonstrates its uniqueness. Unlike other revelation dialogues it is unconcerned with doctrine. Proper explanation and execution of divinely imparted ministry is its sole purpose.

This concern with ministry leads me to consider yet another similar text. This time it is a text that lies within the genre of church order, *The Testament of Our Lord*. This text begins with the disciples questioning the risen Lord about the end times. Finally, after a rather lengthy description of the impending doom of the world the disciples ask Jesus the following question:

> O our Lord, truly thou hast spoken to us now also words of warning and of truth which we do not deserve. Thou hast bestowed upon us many things and hast given also to the generations, those which are to come, who are worthy to know Thy words and who shall escape from the snare of the evil one. But, O our Lord, we beseech Thee to make Thy perfect light shine upon us and upon those who are predestined and set apart to become Thine. *Because many times we have inquired of Thee, we also pray Thee to teach us in what way it is right to be for him who stands at the head of the church or leads the church, and by which rule one shall establish and order it.* For it is urgent that, when we are sent to the nations to proclaim the salvation which is from Thee, it should not escape us as to what is right in administering the mysteries of the church. Therefore, from Thine own mouth, O our Savior and perfecter, we wish to learn without omission what is right for the chief of the holy things to be pleasing before Thee and for all those who serve within Thy church.[45]

Again the same pattern is present. In the text immediately preceding these lines the disciples are commissioned to "rectify," "order well" and "regulate" the churches. Again the disciples feel unqualified to execute their assigned task and seek detailed instructions, which they receive — in this case, a full-blown church order which, among other things, details an episcopal ordination rite.

---

[45] Arthur Vööbus, trans., *The Synodicon in the West Syrian Tradition* (CSCO 368; Louvain: Secrétariat du CSCO, 1975) 31–32. The famous liturgical scholars R. C. D. Jasper and G. J. Cuming describe this text's provenance: "This work is a greatly expanded version of the Apostolic Tradition of Hippolytus, and has received much, perhaps too much, attention from the editors of that text. Extant only in Syriac, it is uncertain where or when the original Greek was written, though most scholars would accept the first half of the fifth century in Syria or Asia Minor" (*Prayers of the Eucharist: Early and Reformed* [3d ed.; New York: Pueblo, 1987] 138).

I conclude that while *ActsPet12Apost.* is not a church order it may be profitable to view it as located somewhere in the gray area between a revelation dialogue (not like the gnostic dialogues in emphasis) and a church order.[46] In short, it may be that the author of *ActsPet12Apost.* consciously used the form of revelation dialogue but then his or her pastoral concerns altered it, shifting its center of gravity toward that of a church order, without actually employing the genre. I do not envision this movement as necessarily intentional, rather I prefer to think of this movement as brought about by the gravitational pull of the redactor's pastoral concerns.

A NARRATIO FABULOSA:
ACCOUNTING FOR THE ALLEGORY

Some time after the actual composition of the Story of the Pearl Merchant, the final redactor of our text recognized its figurative or referential quality and labeled it as a "parable; ⲠⲀⲢⲀⲂⲞⲖⲎ" ("The Lord answered and said, 'O Peter, it was necessary that you understand the parable [παραβολή] that I told you! Do you not understand that my name, which you teach, surpasses all riches, and the wisdom of God surpasses gold and silver and precious stones?'" 10.22–30). These lines represent the redactor's attempt to interpret the significance of the pearl in the Story of the Pearl Merchant. Over the years many scholars who have commented upon *ActsPet12Apost.* have also recognized an element of allegory within its pages.[47] Certainly, the French-speaking scholars

---

[46] It may be this similarity to a church order that Schenke has in mind when he notes that the genre "played a part" in *ActsPet12Apost.* ("The Acts of Peter and the Twelve Apostles," 414).

[47] Perkins views the text as made up of two allegories (the Pearl merchant and the physician) and calls the text an "allegorical tale" (*Gnostic Dialogue*, 125, 128). Krause himself notes that "our text contains many images which are to be understood as parables by the hearers and readers. They therefore have a deeper meaning" ("Die Petrusakten," 53). Salvoni also views the story as symbolic and describes the pearl and wild animals as symbolizing salvation and the demons respectively ("Un nuovo Apocrifo," 39). Sell describes the text as "a

Guillamont[48] and Keller[49] see the text as symbolic and even attempt to interpret the symbolism. However, while these and other scholars use either the term "allegory" or some similar word to describe *ActsPet12Apost.*, no one as yet has attempted to delineate the formal characteristics in our text which show in what sense it is to be understood allegorically.

I propose, as does Schenke, that our text is "a hybrid which has come into being through the forced combination of individual texts."[50] In keeping with this view, I suggest that the various source divisions for which I have argued represent two major types of genres. Since I have already proposed above that 9.1 to 12.19 (Resurrection Appearance and the Author/ Redactor's Theology) contains a revelation dialogue with a church order-like focus, I must now turn my attention to the genre of 1.1 to 9.1 (The Story of the Pearl Merchant).

There are really two formal aspects that must be identified so as to fully grasp the allegorical character of the text. First, there are the symbolic elements of the story (e.g., the cities of Habitation and Nine Gates, the Pearl and the divisions of rich and poor within Habitation). These are story components which serve as one-to-one representations of perceived real-world realities or constructions of mythic reality. Second, there is the story which deals with the journey elements of the text. This includes both of the apostles's journeys: to Habitation and Nine Gates. Both of these formal aspects are important but it is the element of journey (the "how" of attaining the Pearl) that is the key focus of the story. I shall now attempt to designate the ancient forms for these two aspects.

---

text with a basically Christian purpose which often employs allegory" ("Simon Peter's 'Confession,'" 345). See also Schenke, "The Acts of Peter and the Twelve Apostles," 414.

[48] Guillamont, "De nouveaux Actes," 145–46.

[49] Keller, "De la Foi à la Connaissance," 134–35.

[50] Schenke, "The Acts of Peter and the Twelve Apostles," 414.

THE GRECO-ROMAN CONCEPTIONS OF ALLEGORY

What could it mean, then, to describe *The Story of the Pearl Merchant* as allegorical? By allegorical I do not mean that this story was subsequently interpreted by commentators in an allegorical fashion, as was Genesis by Philo in *Allegorical Interpretation* or as was the Isis and Osiris myth by Plutarch in *Isis and Osiris*. This is allegorical exposition and it occurs, as is noted by Friedrich Büchsel, "with a certain regularity where an authoritative tradition is outstripped by development but is neither discarded nor interpreted historically."[51] While this is one way of understanding the term, in this case by allegorical I mean that the story was composed with the intention of making veiled reference to something else.

The famous Roman theorist of rhetoric, Quintilian (1st century A.D.) describes the concept of allegory in his monumental work *Institutio Oratoria*. In discussing the trope "metaphor," Quintilian states, "If we introduce them in one continuous series, our language will become allegorical and enigmatic (*allegorias et aenigmata*)" (8.6.14). Later, Quintilian further expands upon this idea as he explains the trope "allegory:"

> Allegory, which is translated in Latin by *inversio*, either presents one thing in words and another in meaning, or else something absolutely opposed to the meaning of the words. The first type is generally produced by a series of metaphors. Take as an example: "O ship, new waves will bear thee back to sea. What dost thou? Make the haven, come what may," and the rest of the ode, in which Horace represents the state under the semblance of a ship, the civil wars as tempests, and peace and good-will as the haven. (8.6.44)[52]

---

[51] Büchsel, "ἀλληγορέω," *TDNT* 1 (1964) 260.

[52] H. E. Butler, trans., *The Institutio oratoria of Quintilian* (4 vols; LCL; London: Heinemann, 1921–22). Here Quintilian alludes to Horace, *Odes* 1.14, in which the Roman state is compared to a ship in the midst of storms: "On billows as these you will again be swept out to sea, O my ship! What are you doing! Make utmost effort to make the port! On your one side your oars are lost;

Quintilian proceeds to discuss the concept of allegory in detail (8.6.44–59). He offers as a further example the lines from Virgil's *Georgics* 2.541. In these lines Virgil allegorically compares his writing of Book 2 to a journey over a plain, which, now ended, requires the unhitching of his poetic horses from their implied chariot.

While Quintilian's description of the concept of allegory is helpful it is far from universally accepted. Even he mixes other concepts with allegory, such as simile, metaphor (8.6.49) and riddle (8.6.52). This confusion is sensed by Quintilian himself as he begins his discussion of tropes:

> This is a subject which has given rise to interminable disputes among the teachers of literature, who have quarreled no less violently with the philosophers than among themselves over the problem of the genera and species into which tropes may be divided, their number and their correct classification. (8.6.1)

For example, the anonymous rhetorical work, *Rhetorica ad Herennium* (1st century B.C.), does not even use the word "allegory." Rather, it uses the word *permutatio* ("a manner of speech denoting one thing by the letter of the words, but another by their meaning"; 4.34.46) and associates it with similitudes, arguments and comparisons.[53]

---

see, your mast has been split under the Southwind's gusts, yard-arms groan with the strain, and with its cables burst, not for long will the keel stand this implacably hurtling sea's force. Your sails are in shreds, battered and broken off stand the after-deck gods heedless of cries for help. Pontic pine though you are, still, famous daughter of forests green, it will do you no good boasting your race and name; daunted sailors do not pluck up their courage from painted prows. Have a care your fate is not to be a gale-wind's toy. Once my anxious concern and my most heartsick care, now the theme of my thoughts, O my beloved ship, shun the sea lanes where thick strewn lie the glittering Cyclades" (Charles E. Passage, trans., *The Complete Works of Horace* [New York: Ungar, 1983]).

[53] Harry Caplan, trans., *(Cicero) Ad C. Herrennium de ratione dicendi* (LCL; Cambridge: Harvard University Press, 1968).

In his study of the classical theories of allegory and their impact on Christianity, Philip Rollinson states that Plato himself, in *Republic* 2.378d, insisting that young people should not be exposed to "poetical tales" even if they have (often translated) "allegorical" meanings, does not use the word allegory but rather, *hyponoia* ("hidden underlying meaning").[54] Furthermore, Rollinson notes that both Philo and Plutarch use a variety of different terms, such as symbol, symbolic, enigma, sign and figurative to describe non-literal meanings.[55] Rollinson succinctly describes the Greco-Roman fluidity in understanding of allegory and its connection with such fanciful tales as our Story of the Pearl Merchant:

> The evolution of ideas about allegory and personification in Greek and Latin antiquity and their transmission in the Latin West are not, however, simple matters. The connection of fable or myth with personification and with allegory is gradual and occasional, and it involves many concepts which in our day are not thought of as involving allegory. Certainly Philo's explanation of God's creative embodying of incorporeal ideas in concrete, albeit verbal, symbols is a significant development, although Plato himself identified his story of the cave as an illustrative image or likeness (έίκών, Republic 7.517a, d). The concept of visualized idea is elaborated by the Greek Neoplatonists and becomes... central to their theory of symbolic representation.[56]

---

[54] Rollinson, *Classical Theories of Allegory and Christian Culture* (Pittsburgh: Duquesne University Press, 1981) 5. Rollinson's work describes systematically the ideas of many ancient theorists. His first chapter "The Classical Background" is a veritable gold mine of ancient bibliography. Also beneficial is Jon Whitman, *Allegory: The Dynamics of an Ancient and Medieval Technique* (Cambridge: Harvard University Press, 1987) 1–121; 263–68. Whitman was especially helpful in clarifying the difference between allegorical interpretation and allegorical composition.

[55] Rollinson, *Classical Theories*, 7–8.

[56] Ibid., 10.

THE ICON: ONE-TO-ONE REPRESENTATION OF REAL-WORLD OR
MYTHIC REALITY

The symbolic elements of the Story of the Pearl Merchant (e.g., the cities
of Habitation and Nine Gates, the Pearl and the divisions of rich and poor
within Habitation), as rather general categories, invite the reader to look
beyond their simple constructs to a more significant underlying reality.
Certainly, this is what the redactor did as he or she interpreted the "name"
of Jesus as the elusive "pearl" offered by the merchant (10.23–30). In
isolating these rather simple story components and their possible
referents, I am reminded of the powerful simplicity of Plato's image of the
Cave, mentioned by Rollinson. In this famous story Plato describes,
rather transparently, the attempts of Socrates to enlighten his fellow
Athenians. A short segment of Plato's interpretation of this story will
suffice in demonstrating the one-to-one references of such a story:

> This entire image, I said, you may now append, dear Glaucon, to the
> previous argument; the prisonhouse is the world of sight, the light of the
> fire is the sun, and you will not misapprehend me if you interpret the
> journey upwards to be the ascent of the soul into the intellectual world
> according to my poor belief, which, at your desire, I have expressed —
> whether rightly or wrongly God knows. But, whether true or false, my
> opinion is that in the world of knowledge the idea of good appears last
> of all, and is only seen with an effort; and, when seen, is also inferred
> to be the universal author of all things beautiful and right, parent of
> light and of the lord of light in this visible world, and the immediate
> source of reason and truth in the intellectual...." (*Republic* 7.517b,c)[57]

It is precisely this type of one-to-one referential quality that is present in
ActsPet12Apost.

---

[57] Here and elsewhere whenever the *Republic* is quoted I am using
Benjamin Jowett, trans., *The Works of Plato* (4 vols. in 1; New York: Tudor, n.d.).
The Greek is taken from Emile Chambry, trans., Platon: Oeuvres complétes, vols.
6–7/ 1,2 *La république* (Collection des universités de France; Paris: Les Belles
Lettres, 1947–49).

In his study of the classical theories of allegory Rollinson includes a translation of Diomedes, a late fourth-century (A.D.) grammarian, which is helpful in further understanding this one-to-one referential quality present in *ActsPet12Apost*. This section, entitled "Concerning Tropes," is from Diomedes' *Ars Grammatica*, which contains the most extensive systematic discussion of ancient literary genres in Latin.[58] In "Concerning Tropes" Diomedes describes twelve tropes[59] which he views as species of the universal trope, metaphor. Surprisingly, it is not the trope allegory, "speaking, saying one thing and signifying something else by means of similitude or antithesis," that best describes this one-to-one referential quality which is occurring in the Story of the Pearl Merchant (or for that matter in Plato's image of the cave). This is because Diomedes associates the aforementioned image of the horses from Virgil's *Georgics* 2.541 with allegory. While this is, no doubt, allegorical it lacks the one-to-one referential quality that is found on Plato's image of the cave and Horace's description of the ship of state. Rather, it is the trope *homoeosis*, that best captures this first formal aspect:

> Concerning *homoeosis*. *Homoeosis* is the vivid delineation [*demonstratio*] of something less known by its similitude to something which is better known and the representation [*descriptio*] of something unknown by its similitude to what is better known. It has three species: icon or characterization, parable, and paradigm. Icon is a representation portraying some figure or a mutual comparison [*comparatio*] of characters or of those things which happen to characters, as: "like a god in face and shoulders," (*Aeneid* 1.589) and, "in everything like Mercury" (*Aeneid* 4.558). Also, "Such, tamed by the reins of Pollux of Amyclae, was Cyllarus." (*Georgics* 3.89–90)

---

[58] Ibid., 87–98.

[59] The tropes are metaphor, catachresis, metalepsis, metonymy, antonomasia, synecdoche, onomatopoeia, periphrasis, hyperbaton, hyperbole, allegory and homoeosis.

In this quotation Diomedes describes *homoeosis* as having three species: icon (or characterization), parable and paradigm. The first of these three, icon, is of special interest here. Diomedes defined icon as "a representation...or a mutual comparison of characters or those things which happen to characters." This word (ἐἰκών) is of particular significance in that Plato uses it to describe both his famous image (commonly translated, "allegory" or even "parable") of the Cave[60] and the image of the Captain (the philosopher in relation to the State).[61] These images, with their almost one-to-one relationships between story and "reality," are excellent parallels to the first formal aspect of the Story of the Pearl Merchant. They illustrate how story components can be used to refer beyond themselves to perceived real-world realities or constructions of mythic reality. It is precisely this aspect of *homoeosis*/ icon that forms the foundation of the Story of the Pearl Merchant.

MACROBIUS'S NARRATIO FABULOSA

The second formal aspect of the Story of the Pearl Merchant, the "journeys" element, is related to the *homoeosis* aspect as a building is related to its foundation. The journeys and, most importantly, their "how" would not make sense without the reality created by the *homoeosis*.

A definition I have located in antiquity which is helpful in understanding this "journeys element" comes out of the late fourth or early fifth century (A.D.) in Macrobius's *Commentary on the Dream of Scipio*.[62] In this work, Macrobius defends Cicero's *Dream of Scipio* from the indirect attack implied by the Epicurean attack on Plato's vision of Er

---

[60] *Republic* 7.517b, 517d.

[61] *Republic* 6.488a–489a.

[62] The dating of Macrobius's *Commentary on the Dream of Scipio* is not uniform. Scholars have argued for both a late fourth century dating: Georg Wissowa, *De Macrobii Saturnaliorum fontibus capita tria* (Vratisslaviae: Koebnerum, 1880) 15; and an early fifth century dating: H. Georgii, "Zur Bestimmung der Zeit des Servius," *Philologus* 71 (1912) 518–26. Both are cited in Rollinson, *Classical Theories*, 11.

(*Republic* 10).[63] In defending the value of both Plato and Cicero's works, Macrobius describes these texts as *fabulae* (1.1) and then offers a new, more qualified term *figmentum* (1.2; something invented or made, especially a fictitious creation).[64]   The following is the heart of Macrobius's argument (2.6–14):

> Philosophy does not discountenance all stories nor does it accept all, and in order to distinguish between what it rejects as unfit to enter its sacred precincts and what it frequently and gladly admits, the points of division must needs be clarified. Fables — the very word acknowledges their falsity — serve two purposes: either merely to gratify the ear as do the comedies of Menander and his imitators, or the narratives replete with imaginary doings of lovers in which Petronius Arbiter so freely indulged and with which Apuleius, astonishingly, sometimes amused himself. This whole category of fables that promise only to gratify the ear a philosophical treatise avoids and regulates to children's nurseries. The other group, those that draw the reader's attention to certain kinds of virtue, are divided into two types. In the first both the setting and plot are fictitious, as in the fables of Aesop, famous for his exquisite imagination. *The second rests on a solid foundation of truth, which is treated in a fictitious style. This is called the fabulous narrative to distinguish it from the ordinary fable; examples of it are the performances of sacred rites, the stories of Hesiod and Orpheus that treat of the ancestry and deeds of the gods, and the mystic conceptions of the Pythagoreans.* Of the second main group, which we have just

---

[63] Rollinson, *Classical Theories*, 11.

[64] "The triad *historia, argumentum, fabula* had been introduced as early as the first century B.C. *Rhetorica ad Herennium* (1.8.13) as three basic kinds of narrative, and the definitions there generally remain standard. History recounts events which actually happened. Fiction recounts events which did not actually happen but could have (i.e., they are like real events), and, of course, fables recount events which did not and could not have happened. Cicero's *De inventione* offers the same distinction (1.19.27), as does Quintilian, *Institutio oratoria* (2.4.2) and another contemporary of Macrobius, the commentator Servius (in the note to *Commentary on the Aeneid* 1.235)" (Rollinson, *Classical Theories*, 12).

mentioned, the first type, with both setting and plot fictitious, is also inappropriate to philosophical treatises. *The second type is subdivided, for there is more than one way of telling the truth when the argument is real but is presented in the form of a fable. Either the presentation of the plot involves matters that are base and unworthy of divinities and are monstrosities of some sort* (as, for example, gods caught in adultery, Saturn cutting off the privy parts of his father Caelus and himself thrown into chains by his son and successor), *a type which philosophers prefer to disregard altogether; or else a decent and dignified conception of holy truths, with respectable events and characters, is presented beneath a modest veil of allegory.* This is the only type of fiction approved by the philosopher who is prudent in handling sacred matters.

Therefore, since the treatises of Plato and Cicero suffer no harm from Er's testimony or Scipio's dream, and the treatment of sacred subjects is accomplished without loss of dignity by using their names, let our critic at last hold his peace, taught to differentiate between the fable and the fabulous narrative.

We should not assume, however, that philosophers approve the use of fabulous narratives, even those of a proper sort, in all disputations. *It is their custom to employ them when speaking about the Soul, or about spirits having dominion in the lower and upper air, or about the gods in general.* But when the discussion aspires to treat of the Highest and Supreme of all gods, called by the Greeks the Good and the First Cause, or to treat of Mind or Intellect, which the Greeks call nous, born from and originating in the Supreme God and embracing the original concepts of things, which are called Ideas, when, I repeat, philosophers speak about these, the Supreme God and Mind, they shun the use of fabulous narratives.[65]

In the above section from *Commentary on the Dream of Scipio*, Macrobius argues that fables serve two purposes: to gratify the ear and to encourage the reader to good works. He offers examples of the first type

---

[65] William H. Stahl, trans., *Macrobius: Commentary on the Dream of Scipio* (Records of Civilization, Sources and Studies 48; New York: Columbia University Press, 1952).

of fable, listing such works as the comedies of Menander, the *Satyricon* of Petronius Arbiter and the *Metamorphoses* of Lucius Apuleius. This whole type of fable is declared useless to the philosophical treatise and relegated by Macrobius to children's nurseries (2.8). Rather, he focuses attention on the morally encouraging fable and distinguishes between its two species. The first type has both a setting and plot that are fictitious, as with Aesop's fables. The second has a solid foundation of truth which is treated in a fictitious style. This type of fable Macrobius calls a *narratio fabulosa*. He gives three examples of this type of literature: the performance of the sacred rites, the stories of Hesiod and Orpheus and the mystic conceptions of the Pythagoreans (2.9). Macrobius further divides the genre of *narratio fabulosa* into two subgroups: those that deal with base matters, unworthy of divinities (such as Saturn cutting off the privy parts of his father Caelus)[66] and those that present a decent and dignified conception of holy truths with respectable events and characters cloaked in a modest veil of allegory. The first of these is to be shunned by the philosopher. However, according to Macrobius, the second is the only type of fiction to be deemed acceptable and used by the prudent philosopher. Macrobius asserts that the vision of Er and *Scipio's Dream* were *narrationes fabulosae* of this latter type (2.12). According to Macrobius, philosophers use this second type of fabulous narrative when speaking about the soul, spirits having dominion in the lower and upper air and the gods in general. However, he notes that this type of literature

---

[66] Probably the story to which Macrobius is referring here is that recorded in Hesiod, *Theogony* 176–81: "Ouranos came dragging with him the night, longing for Gaia's love, and he embraced her and lay stretched out upon her. Then his son reached out from his hiding place and seized him with his left hand, while with his right he grasped the huge, long, and sharp-toothed sickle and swiftly hacked off his father's genitals and tossed them behind him" (Apostolos N. Athanassakis, trans., *Hesiod: Theogony, Works and Days, Shield* [Baltimore: Johns Hopkins University Press, 1983]). The point Macrobius is making is that such offensive (and by implication, overly anthropomorphic) images have no part in true philosophical discourse.

is not used to speak about the Good, the First Cause and the Mind (2.13–14).

I suggest that *ActsPet12Apost.* 1.1–9.1 is precisely this second, philosophically proper type of *narratio fabulosa.* To establish the viability of this theory I shall compare Macrobius's examples of *narrationes fabulosae* with *ActsPet12Apost.* (especially the Story of the Pearl Merchant) so as to demonstrate that formal similarities exist between the three texts. In both the vision of Er and *Scipio's Dream* (both described by Macrobius as *narrationes fabulosae*) it is the element of speaking about the soul that is central. In Plato's vision of Er, a soldier who is killed in battle witnesses the fates of the souls of the deceased and is sent back as a warning to the living. Awakening upon his own funeral pyre, Er speaks quite vividly about the punishments measured out to the souls of the deceased. While Er does note that virtue is rewarded in an abundant fashion, it is the punishments that are stressed.[67] The point of the tale is made at the end: "Wherefore my counsel is, that we hold fast ever to the heavenly way and follow after justice and virtue always, considering that the soul is immortal and able to endure every sort of good and every sort of evil" (*Republic* 10.621c–d). Thus, virtue is hailed as the "path" to a positive afterlife.

In *Scipio's Dream* a sleeping Publius Cornelius Scipio is, like Er, shown the heavenly realms and counseled how a soul may assure its speedy return to the celestial environs. Scipio is told by his father that virtue, especially preserving one's country, is a sure "path" to heaven:

Now for your encouragement, my dear Africanus, that you may be the readier to assume our country's defense, you must know that there is a

---

[67] "He said that for every wrong which they had done to any one they suffered tenfold; or once in a hundred years — such being reckoned to be the length of a man's life, and the penalty being thus paid ten times in a thousand years. If, for example, there were any who had been the cause of many deaths, or had betrayed or enslaved cities or armies, or had been guilty of any evil behavior, for each and all of their offenses they received punishment ten times over..." (*Republic* 10. 615a–b).

sure place in heaven for all who have preserved, defended, and enlarged their country; here they will enjoy eternal happiness. For nothing finds greater favor in the eyes of the supreme God who rules the universe than the orderly associations of men, founded upon law, which are called states. The rulers and preservers of states descend from this heavenly place and return hither.[68]

In the Story of the Pearl Merchant the Pearl merchant cries out to the poor of Habitation, appealing to them to "come to my city, so that I may not only show you it (i.e., the pearl), but give it to you for nothing" (4.32–34). He describes the "road" as passable only by a person who has "forsaken everything"[69] and has fasted from "stage to stage" (5.23–25). Furthermore, this route is infested with robbers and various semi-intelligent wild animals (5.26–6.8). Thus, if the merchant's city, Nine Gates, is a heavenly city, as several commentators have already suggested,[70] then the ascetical way of life advocated by the merchant is the "how" in the soul's journey or "path" to heaven. This element of presenting the heavenly realms and then encouraging a particular ethic so as to attain them is common to all three texts. In other words, all three texts speak of the soul's journey or "path" to heaven and present a "how"

---

[68] Cicero, *De republica* 6.13 (see also 6.16; 24).

[69] There is also an ascetic element in *Scipio's Dream*. In 6.26, Scipio is told: "Work, first of all, for your country's welfare and your soul will sooner return to this heavenly place. It will do so even more quickly if, while still enclosed in the body, it already makes itself independent, and succeeds as far as possible in separating itself from the body. As for the men who indulge in physical dissipations, whose souls have served as slaves of their bodies in their search for low pleasures, they have violated the laws of God and man. Once their souls are released from their bodies, they are forced to hover continually around the earth, and only after many centuries return to this heavenly place."

[70] For example, Schenke, "Die Taten des Petrus," 13; "The Acts of Peter and the Twelve Apostles," 416; Guillamont, "De nouveaux Actes," 146; and Keller, "De la Foi à la Connaissance," 134.

for the reader. This is the decisive aspect of similarity between the three texts.[71]

The second topic Macrobius claims to be typical of the *narratio fabulosa*, speaking about spirits that have dominion in the upper and lower air, is also present in all three texts. However, this is emphasized to a far lesser degree than the first topic. In the vision of Er, judges are described as inhabiting the intermediate space and handing out sentences to the souls (10.614c). Further, the souls of the truly wicked are described as being prevented from ascending by supernatural figures, "wild men of fiery aspect" (10.615e). In *Scipio's Dream* the emphasis is decidedly less. The stars are described as being endowed with reason (6.15).[72] In the Story of the Pearl Merchant the "stages" on the way to Nine Gates are inhabited by hostile entities described allegorically as robbers, wild beasts, black dogs, wolves, lions and bulls (5.26–6.8). Even the spacial

---

[71]At this juncture I must state that I do not imagine myself to be discovering a new genre for the study of the NT and early Christianity. The *narratio fabulosa* and the heavenly descent/ ascent literature, whose numerous samples are discussed so competently by Alan F. Segal ("Heavenly Ascent in Hellenistic Judaism, Early Christianity and their Environment," *ANRW* 2.23.2 [1980] 1333–94), Martha Himmelfarb (*Tours of Hell: An Apocalyptic Form in Jewish and Christian Literature* [Philadelphia: University of Pennsylvania Press, 1983] and *Ascent to Heaven in Jewish and Christian Apocalypses* [Oxford: Oxford University Press, 1993]) and James D. Tabor ("Ascent to Heaven," *ABD* 3.91–94), are surely two names for the same literary phenomenon. However, my goal in analyzing the genre of the Story of the Pearl Merchant is to find a definition of this phenomenon in the treatises of the ancient Greek and Roman grammaticians so as to better understand its literary characteristics from an ancient author's standpoint.

[72] "Aristotle assigned a spirit or separate motive force to each sphere within the heaven of fixed stars, in order to explain their motion in a direction contrary to that of the outer sphere as described in chapter 17 [referring to Cicero, *De republica* 6.17]; see *Metaph.* 1073 a 26–b 1; *De caelo*, 279 a 18–22. Plato (*Timaeus*, 41d) assigns a star to each created soul, and declares (*Laws*, 899b) that the souls of the stars are divine," (George H. Sabine and Stanley B. Smith, trans., *Cicero: On the Commonwealth* [Indianapolis: Bobbs-Merrill, 1976] 260 n. 30).

conceptions of the heavenly realms that these spirits inhabit are similar.[73] While this topic is present in all three texts it is not a major focus of these stories.

Macrobius's third and final formal element of the *narratio fabulosa* concerns speaking "about the gods in general." It is interesting to note that the three texts compared above only minimally take up this particular aspect of the *narratio fabulosa*. In both the vision of Er and the *Dream of Scipio* the gods are never really addressed in great detail. In both texts the gods are referred to indirectly by way of a description of their relative positions in the heavenly spheres. The following section from the *Dream of Scipio* aptly demonstrates this usage:

> As I stayed still gazing down on the earth, Africanus interrupted me. "How long, pray, will you keep your attention earth-bound? Look up and see the heavenly space to which you have come. Nine circles, or rather spheres, compose the universe, the outmost of which is heaven, that surrounds the rest. This heavenly sphere itself is the supreme God, who rules and controls all the others. Within it the fixed stars revolve in their unchanging course. Beneath it seven spheres rotate in a contrary direction. One of them contains the planet which on earth they call Saturn. Next comes Jupiter, whose brilliant ray is auspicious to mankind. Then follows Mars with his red gleam boding ill for the earth. The middle sphere is that of the Sun, the chief of the stars and their leader. On it depend the system and order of the universe; its size is so tremendous that it fills everything with its light. After the Sun come the spheres of Venus and of Mercury. The eighth and lowest sphere is that of the moon, which reflects the rays of the Sun. Below it is the region

---

[73] The vision of Er describes eight "whorls" or spheres which are home to the various stars and planets (*Republic* 10.616d–617b). *Scipio's Dream* details nine spheres (6.17). *ActsPet12Apost.* may well be envisioning a similar conception of the heavenly spheres. The statement in 6.22–26 may be a reference to the divine city as being located at the ninth sphere with the tenth sphere representing God himself. (He said to me, "This is the name of my city, 'Nine Gates.' Let us praise God as we are mindful that the tenth is the head"). Of course, in no way do I intend to imply that such a spatial conception of the universe is unique to these texts.

of mortality and decay, except for the human soul, which the gods gave as their gift to man; whereas above the moon's sphere eternity reigns. Last of all the Earth, the ninth sphere, lies in the center, immovable.[74]

In Plato,'s vision of Er, a similar passage is found and, in the lines immediately following, Er is shown the immortal Fates: Lachesis, Clotho and Atropos.[75] Turning to our text, it is obvious that such references to the gods would be out of place in a Christian text. However, it appears that, despite this, the Story of the Pearl Merchant accepts much of the same cosmology as described by Cicero (and implied in the vision of Er).[76] While the gods are not mentioned, their spheres of influence are still accepted as part of the heavenly landscape.

With these thoughts my consideration of the form of *ActsPet12Apost.* comes to an end. The similarities between the vision of Er, *Scipio's Dream* and our text lead me to conclude that *ActPet12Apost.* is the combination of two major forms: a *narratio fabulosa* (built upon the foundation provided by the *homoeosis*) and a unique revelation dialogue. Despite the above analysis, it may have been Schenke who came closest to articulating the difficulties a scholar encounters when attempting to identify *ActsPet12Apost.*'s form:

> Our tractate is an extremely curious text. If we attempt to classify it, we are immediately plunged into deep perplexity. It displays a manifold

---

[74] *De republica* 6.17.

[75] *Republic* 10.616c–617c.

[76] I would add here that the cosmology of the Story of the Pearl Merchant is slightly different from that described in *Scipio's Dream*. In Scipio's description the ninth sphere is the supreme God. However, in the Story of the Pearl Merchant the ninth sphere is the city (or dwelling place) of God but God is still to be differentiated from this sphere: "This is the name of my city, 'Nine Gates.' Let us praise God as we are mindful that the tenth is the head" (6.23–26). God is the tenth, and so, separate from the city.

variety of aspects. We are reminded of Lucian's "True Histories,"[77] and might also be tempted to think of our author as an early Christian Münchhausen. What is related appears to be half reality and half a dream, half history and half fable, half apostolic legend and half portrayal of a vision, or allegory; paraenesis and church order also play a part.... The problematic relationship to reality of what is reported in this document, its surrealism, may in fact be described as its most striking feature.[78]

---

[77] At first glance the main aspects of similarity between *ActsPet12Apost.* and Lucian's *A True Story* appear to be their travel motifs of journey by sea, storm at sea and visit to a peculiar island. However, if one reads Lucian more carefully he is actually satirizing the *narratio fabulosa* by presenting its typical concerns in an absurd manner. First, he makes fun of the heavenly powers by irreverently describing the ridiculous war between the sun and moon (1.9–26). Second, Lucian describes a visit to a mysterious island called "The Island of the Blest," a kind of heavenly home for the heroes of Greek culture (2.6–31). While alive on this island, properly reserved for those who are no longer living, Lucian is instructed by Rhadamanthus, the king of the island, as to exactly how one might act in this world so as to return to the island when one died. These ridiculous instructions are obviously offered in jest (2.31): "He also enjoined me, if ever I reached this world, not to poke fires with a sword, not to eat lupines, and not to associate with boys over eighteen; if I kept these things in mind, he said, I could have hopes of returning to the island." Furthermore, as in the Story of Er, a warning of what not to do so as to avoid punishment in the afterlife is given. This also is given tongue in cheek: "Our guides described for us the life of each of the victims and the reason for his punishment. The people who suffered the greatest torment were those who had told lies when they were alive and written mendacious histories; among them were Ctesias of Cnidos, Herodotus and many others. You may guess that, seeing them, I had high hopes for the next world — I knew very well I had never told a lie" (Bryan P. Reardon, trans., *Lucian: Selected Works* [Library of Liberal Arts; Indianapolis: Bobbs-Merrill, 1965]).

[78] Schenke, "The Acts of Peter and the Twelve Apostles," 414.

Chapter 3
The Shape of the Tradition

Having now differentiated between the *homoeosis* and the *narratio fabulosa*, I would like to take the next step in examining the allegorical nature of this text by considering the underlying mythical structure which drives and informs the *homoeosis*/ image (εἰκών). To do this it is crucial to reiterate my understanding of how these two forms interact in our text. The image, with its almost one-to-one relationships between story and "reality," illustrates how story components can be used to refer beyond themselves to perceived real-world realities or constructions of mythic reality. This aspect of *homoeosis* forms the foundation of the Story of the Pearl Merchant. The second formal aspect of the Story of the Pearl Merchant, the *narratio fabulosa* element, is related to the *homoeosis* aspect as a building is related to its foundation. The proposed journey to Nine Gates and, most importantly, its "how" would not make sense without the reality created by the *homoeosis*.

My purpose in the following pages will be to examine the "perceived real-world realities or constructions of mythic reality" (i.e., traditions) that are the referents of the text. I propose that these traditions are gnostic in their world-view and Christian in their type of gnosticism. My method will be to first lay out all the gnostic mythical referents underlying the image. Then, once this is accomplished, I will work through these same gnostic mythical referents and provide passages from gnostic documents which demonstrate the existence of this gnostic mythical structure.

THE BASIC STRUCTURE OF THE GNOSTIC MYTH

The gnostic myth referred to in the story of the Pearl Merchant does not seem to make reference to a primordial fall from grace by a heavenly power. It simply assumes a fallen or needy state for humanity. Its focus is upon gnostic soteriology (i.e., the process of attaining salvation). The following is the basic structure of the myth:

A part of the Pleroma, outside of earthly space and time, is described in which the Lord exists with the spirits of his companions. These companions are given a commission which is part of the divine plan of salvation. They are to journey, protected by angelic escorts, through a hostile realm to Earth. At the same time, whether known or unknown by the companions, the Lord himself also journeys to Earth so as to execute his role in the salvific plan.

When the companions arrive at Earth they have only the most basic concept of their ministry: "It is necessary for us to spread the word of God in every city harmoniously" (5.12–14). Their ministry is almost a latent ministry, in need of the Lord's activation and direction. It is at this point that the Lord makes his appearance on Earth and presents to humanity his invitation to join him in the Pleroma. The myth speaks of three groups of people to whom he extends his invitation: 1) *the material*, who ignore the invitation; 2) *the psychic*, who receive the invitation but require considerable assistance in their faith; and 3) *the spiritual*, who upon hearing the invitation never doubt but ask for specific directions and act upon them.

The journey to the Pleroma involves passage through a hostile realm. This realm is populated by archons or demonic entities whose goal is to "kill" or "eat" the soul. Thereby spiritual death is inflicted upon the journeying soul. Therefore the spiritual traveler must prepare for this journey by proper actions while on Earth. This preparation involves ascetical practices, i.e., renunciation of the world. Only through these actions can the soul successfully return to the Pleroma.

TESTING THE MYTH:
DEMONSTRATING THE GNOSTIC STRUCTURE

HABITATION AND NINE GATES
To begin to unravel the specifics of the underlying gnostic myth it is important to come to a basic understanding of the identities of the cities

of Habitation and Nine Gates. As early as 1973, Schenke argued that "we must look at the symbolic names of both the worldly and heavenly city, since the little city in the sea and the city of Lithargoel respectively symbolize the world and the kingdom of heaven."[1] Likewise, Guillamont views these two cities as symbolically referring to this world and the kingdom of heaven.[2] Perkins and Keller also view the cities as symbolic,[3] although Keller views Habitation as representative of the earthly church and not as the world in general.[4]

For the purposes of the following reconstruction of a possible gnostic myth I will assume with Schenke and Guillamont that the two cities represent earth and the kingdom of Heaven (in gnostic terms, the Pleroma). My reasons for viewing Habitation as symbolic of the world are these: 1) Habitation is the realm in which missionary activity takes

---

[1] Schenke, "Die Taten des Petrus," 13. Schenke remained true to this position in his 1992 introduction ("The Acts of Peter and the Twelve Apostles," 417).

[2] Guillamont, "De nouveaux Actes," 145–46.

[3] Perkins recognizes Habitation as related to the Gnostics's use of the expression "dwelling place" to refer to life in this world. However, she does not expressly link Nine Gates with Heaven (*Gnostic Dialogue*, 126).

[4] Keller writes: "Finally, the 'little city in the midst of the sea,' surrounded by walls and formidable waves, is identified by the Berlin translators as the world (or as the 'terrestrial city'). We hesitate to rally ourselves to this interpretation. The exact name of the city is not preserved (the least damaged form is found in 10.3–4), but it is certain that the name is characterized principally by the notion of *hypomone*. This is a city that is exposed to all the temptations and all the storms, but which is not herself the cause of temptations or storms. It is rather the symbol of perseverance (*hypomone*) in the temptations and in the midst of storms. Besides, the city is inhabited by believers (7.16; cf. also 10.7; 11.1), it is even a question of *ekklesiai* (12.6–7, 12–13). Finally, we underline that the city is small: all that suggests that the 'little city surrounded by storms' is to symbolize the Church" ("De la Foi à la Connaissance," 134–35). I have one problem with Keller's suggestion. If Habitation is the Church, why does Peter, the supposed "rock" of the Church, describe himself as a "stranger" in her midst? Note that Lithargoel also expresses this same foreignness, in that he also is a "stranger" (cf. 2.32–3.11).

place. Some reject Lithargoel's invitation (3.25–27), some accept it (4.35–5.1); 2) Lithargoel's invitation points away from Habitation as the ultimate place in which to receive the desired object, the pearl. (This is similar to the Christian emphasis on Heaven as the desired place, as opposed to this world, e.g., in John 14:1–7); 3) Habitation is the place of trials (7.9), apostasies and difficulties (7.14); and 4) the "precious kingdom" (ⲞⲨⲘⲚ̄ⲦⲢ̄Ⲣ̄Ⲟ ⲈⲦⲀⲈⲒⲎⲞⲨ) (undoubtedly referring to the "saved") comes out of Habitation (7.11–12). They are those who are to be "included in the Kingdom of Heaven" (7.18–19). As for Nine Gates, it is the desired object. Only those who respond to Lithargoel's invitation and then have the faith in Jesus' name to face the hardships on the road (6.9–19) can reach its gates. Therefore, heaven is the likely referent of the symbol, Nine Gates.

THE PRE-EXISTENCE OF THE DISCIPLES WITH THE LORD

Having said this, the first aspect of the above myth that needs to be addressed is the concept of the previous, heavenly existence of a redeemer figure and his companions. In *ActsPet12Apost.* 1.1–29, the apostles are described as receiving a commission from the Lord and traveling in "a ship moored at the shore" (1.17) to the city of Habitation. If one judges, as I have, that in the allegorical structure of this text the two cities of Habitation and Nine Gates are representative of Earth and Heaven (the Pleroma), then an interesting set of questions arises: If Habitation represents the world, then from what "shore" do the apostles depart? Could information suggesting a heavenly departure have been contained in the now destroyed introduction of the text (1.1–7)? Could the fragments in 1.6–7 that mention "sailing" and "the body" have originally referred to the soul's entrance into a body as part of a salvific journey to the world? While answers to the latter two questions must remain conjectural, an answer to the first may well be within our grasp.

Kurt Rudolph, quoting the 1966 Congress on the Origins of Gnosticism, defines the central myth of Gnosticism as follows:

the idea of the presence in man of a divine "spark"..., which has proceeded from the divine world and has fallen into this world of destiny, birth and death and which must be awakened through its own divine counterpart in order to be finally restored. This idea... is ontologically based upon the conception of a downward development of the divine whose periphery (often called Sophia or Ennoia) has fatally fallen victim to a crisis and must — even if only indirectly — produce this world, in which it then cannot be disinterested, in that it must once again recover the divine "spark."[5]

It is this principle, the salvific action of a divine counterpart, that is the premise behind the apostles's mission to Habitation (1.1–33). Important to this concept in *ActsPet12Apost.* is the mention of the Lord's commission of the apostles in an undefined time and place before the apostles set off on their journey, a journey which eventually leads them to Habitation. Logically, if Habitation is symbolic of the world, then this undefined "port" must be located outside the world. Further, this undefined "port" must be a place where the Lord dwells with a specific group (apostles, "those sent") who are to participate in ministry to Habitation.[6]

---

[5] Rudolph, *Gnosis: The Nature and History of Gnosticism* (San Francisco: Harper, 1977) 57. The quotation to which Rudolph is referring can be found in Ugo Bianchi, ed., *Le Origini dello Gnosticismo* (Studies in the History of Religions 12; Leiden: Brill, 1967) xxvi–xxvii.

[6] This is implied by the commission which is followed by the apostles's arrival in Habitation (1.1–2.4) and stated implicitly, albeit in a different source (The Author/ Redactor's Theology), in 10.1–14.

The *Tripartite Tractate* (I,5), a Valentinian treatise,[7] is an important text with which to compare *ActsPet12Apost.* because it is an example of a Christian-Gnostic document that also speaks about the pre-existence of the Savior and his companions in a realm outside of this world. *Tri. Trac.* presents the idea that "Not only did the Son exist from the beginning, but the Church, too, existed from the beginning" (57.34–35).[8] According to

---

[7] Harold W. Attridge and Elaine H. Pagels claim: "The heresiologists attest that Valentinian teachers disagreed on the interpretation of several fundamental issues, including the nature of the Father, the origin and structure of the Pleroma, the motives and results of the fall of Sophia, and the nature of the redemption offered by Christ. The *Tri. Trac.* engages each of these issues, taking positions which resemble the "Monadic" version of Valentinian ontology recounted by Hippolytus, the theology of *Val. Exp.*, and the soteriology of the western school, which held that Christ offered redemption to psychic as well as spiritual Christians. Yet the *Tri. Trac.* revises the major themes of Valentinian theology more radically than any other extant source and approximates more closely than any other Valentinian thinker the positions taken by more orthodox theologians of the third and fourth centuries" ("The Tripartite Tractate: Introduction," in Harold W. Attridge, ed., *Nag Hammadi Codex 1 [The Jung Codex]: Introductions, Texts, Translations, Indices* [NHS 22; Leiden: Brill, 1985] 177). This position is also upheld by Einar Thomassen who states, "All the specialists have agreed to say that the milieu from which the text has originated is Valentinian, and there does not exist any valid reason to put this in doubt. In the first place, the commentary that we are giving further provides sufficient elements to demonstrate that the *Tri. Trac.* belongs to a Valentinian literary tradition, tradition which concerns also the Valentinian sources of Irenaeus, Hippolytus and Epiphanius, and even the *Excerpts of Theodoto* of Clement of Alexandria and the *Val. Exp.* of NH XI.2. In the second place, the attention given by the author to the spiritual Church in general (principally in the last parts of the tractate to 114.30), and in particular the phrase 'we who are in the body amount to his Church,' 125.4–5, confirms the fact that the author was not only a Valentinian of the literary tradition, but also a practicing member of the spiritual Valentinian Church" (idem, ed., L. Painchaud and E. Thomassen, trans., *Le Traité Tripartite (NH 1,5)* (Bibliothèque Copte de Nag Hammadi Section Textes 19; Quebec: Les Presses de l'Université Laval, 1989) 11–12).

[8] This concept of the pre-existent Church is also found in orthodox texts, e.g., *2 Clem.* 14.1–3: "So then, brothers, if we do the will of God our Father we will belong to the first church, the spiritual one, which was created before the sun and moon.... Moreover, the Books and the Apostles declare that the church not only exists now, but has been in existence from the beginning. For she was

this text, the Church existed "forever in thought, for the Father was like a thought and a place for them" (60.1–5). For *Tri. Trac.*, the Church existed in the "manner of seed" (60.30–35), begotten like the word, existing in his thought as "mental substance."

This concept of the Church's pre-existence is further developed by *Tri. Trac.* in a manner that may shed some light upon the confusing existence of the Lord and the apostles in a place separate from the city assumed to symbolize the world in *ActsPet12Apost*. In *Tri. Trac.* 114.31–118.15, entitled in the NHLE "The Incarnate Savior and his Companions," the writer describes the taking on of flesh by the Savior and how his disciples followed him from their previous state of unity with him. This section strongly suggests that the disciples's coming to earth is very similar to the Savior's coming and for much the same purposes. The information in parentheses is my addition:

> When they (the disciples) thought of the Savior they came, and
> they came when he knew, they also came more exalted in the
> emanation according to the flesh than those who had been brought
> forth from a defect, because in this way they, too, received their
> bodily emanation along with the body of the Savior, through the
> revelation and the mingling with him. These others (the disciples)
> were those of one substance and it indeed is the spiritual
> substance. The organization is different. This is one thing, that is

---

spiritual, as was also our Jesus, but was revealed in the last days in order that she might save us." See also *Shepherd of Hermas*, Visions 2.4.1. Einar Thomassen suggests that this concept of the pre-existent Church is already present in the NT texts themselves: "The notion is also present in the New Testament: the existence of the ἐκκλησία πρωτοτόκων ἀπογεγραμμένων ἐν οὐρανοῖς of Hebrews 12:23, although not *ab aeterno*, precedes creation. As in Galatians 4:26 and Revelation 3:12; 21:2, the Church there is also identified with the heavenly Jerusalem. This doctrine originates from the notion of the heavenly assembly, which appeared in certain late currents of Judaism. In the Similitudes of 1 Enoch (particularly 39.4), the visionary sees in heaven an assembly formed of angels and just men; in this case, an eschatological condition is transformed into an ideal eternal existence. This assembly is made 'to appear' on the day of judgement (38.1); cf. *2 Clement* 14.3" (*Le Traité Tripartite*, 286).

another. Some come forth from passion and division, needing
healing. *Others are from prayer, so that they may heal the sick,
when they have been appointed to treat those who have fallen.
These are the apostles and the evangelists. They are the disciples
of the Savior, and teachers who need instruction* (ϨⲚ̄Ⲛ̄
ⲞⲨⲦⲰⲂϨ̄ ⲚⲈ ⲀⲦⲢⲞⲨⲦⲀϭⲰ Ⲛ̄ⲚⲈⲦϢⲰⲚⲈ·
ⲈⲀⲨⲔⲀⲀⲨ ⲀⲦⲢⲞⲨ Ⲣ̄ ⲐⲈⲢⲀⲠⲈⲨⲈ Ⲛ̄ⲚⲈⲦⲀϨⲈⲒ·
ⲈⲦⲈ ⲚⲒⲀⲠⲞⲤⲦⲞⲖⲞⲤ ⲚⲈ· ⲘⲚ̄ ⲚⲒⲢⲘ̄Ⲧ̄ ϢⲘ̄ ⲚⲞⲨϤⲈ·
Ⲛ̄ⲘⲀⲐⲎⲦⲎⲤ Ⲛ̄ⲀⲈ Ⲛ̄ⲦⲀⲨ Ⲙ̄ⲠⲤⲰⲦⲎⲢ· ⲚⲈ ϨⲚ̄ⲤⲀϨ
ⲀⲈ Ⲛ̄ⲦⲀⲨ {Ⲛ̄}ⲚⲈ ⲚⲈⲈⲒ· ⲈⲦⲢ̄ ⲬⲢⲈⲒⲀ Ⲛ̄ⲤⲂⲞⲨ ⲈⲒ·).
Why, then, did they, too, share in the passions in which those who
have been brought forth from passion share...?" (*Tri. Trac.*
115.34–116.24)

It is important to review the mythic elements presented in this text.
First, we are told of the pre-existence of the Church, a pre-existence in a
place with the One and *not* in this world. Then we are taught about a
Savior who enters the world and about his companions who come to earth
accepting the "smallness to which they had descended when they were
born in body and soul" (115.5–10). Further, these companions or
"disciples" are described as people who are spiritual in nature, yet in need
of the Savior's instruction and subject to the same passions as those who
"have been brought forth from passion." These disciples are called or
appointed to heal the sick and treat the fallen.

Within these mythic elements there are some striking parallels with
ActsPet12Apost. In both texts the disciples are presented as entering the
world from a realm where they have previously been with the Savior.[9]
The disciples (in the person of Peter) are in need of the Savior's
(Lithargoel's) instruction as to the hardships on the way to Nine Gates

---

[9] In the *Tri. Trac.* the Savior is presented as coming into the world with
his disciples. In *ActsPet12Apost.* the disciples enter the world (Habitation) and
then meet Lithargoel who is later identified as Jesus (9.1–15, part of the
resurrection appearance source).

(5.8–6.8) and the power available through the name of Jesus (6.14–7).[10]
It also bears noting that similar emphasis is present in *ActsPet12Apost.* on
the disciples's 1) healing the sick (10.33–11.17); 2) healing of the "illness
of the heart" (11.18–26); and 3) vulnerability to passions, hence the need
for fasting and renunciation of the world (5.21–6.12). The similarities are
indeed striking but this is not the only material that can illuminate our
discussion.

Another text which bears witness to my proposed gnostic myth of a
previous, heavenly existence of Jesus and his disciples is the revelation
dialogue (books 1–3), *Pistis Sophia*.[11] This Sahidic Coptic translation of
a Greek original, probably Egyptian in origin, is a composite of at least
two different sources (books 1–3 and book 4). Dated variously from the
second to the third century, with a preference for the last half of the third
century currently holding sway, this text has been associated with both

---

[10] Later, in 8.3–32, the disciples as a group are taught about Lithargoel's
sonship and about their eventual ministry to Habitation.

[11] In this study I am using the translation found in G. R. S. Mead, trans.,
Pistis Sophia (1921; repr. London: Watkins, 1947). Mead includes an annotated
bibliography which provides a detailed summary of past scholarly positions on *PS*
from its appearance in 1770 to 1920. This summary is essential to anyone
beginning a detailed investigation into this text. At this time the most readily
available and authoritative study on *PS* is Carl Schmidt, ed. and trans., *Koptisch-
gnostische Schriften*, vol. 1: *Die Pistis Sophia, Die beiden Bücher des Jeû,
Unbekanntes altgnostisches Werk* (GCS 45: Berlin: Akademie-Verlag, 1954).
Actually this is Schmidt's translation of the text with a summary, by Walter Till,
of his earlier textual comments found in idem, ed. and trans., *Koptisch-gnostische
Schriften*; vol. 1: *Die Pistis Sophia, Die beiden Bücher des Jeû, Unbekanntes
altgnostisches Werk* (GCS 13; Leipzig: Hinrichs, 1905); see also idem, ed. and
trans., *Pistis Sophia; Ein gnostisches Originalwerk des 3 Jahrhunderts aus dem
Koptischen übersetzt* (Leipzig: Hinrichs, 1925). There is another, more recent,
translation available in Carl Schmidt ed. and trans., and Violet MacDermot trans.,
Pistis Sophia (NHS 9; Leiden: Brill, 1978). However, the last of these works is
disappointing in that it provides only the briefest of introductions with virtually
no scholarly discussion.

Valentian and Ophitic beliefs.[12] In Book 1, chapter 7, in rather elongated fashion, the risen Jesus explains to his disciples their heavenly origins:

> For this cause have I chosen you verily from the beginning through the First Mystery. *Rejoice then and exult, for when I set out for the world, I brought from the beginning with me twelve powers, as I have told you from the beginning, which I have taken from the twelve saviors of the Treasury of the Light, according to the command of the First Mystery. These then I cast into the womb of your mothers, when I came into the world, that is those which are in your bodies today.* (ⲢⲀϢⲈ ϬⲈ ⲚⲦⲈⲦⲚⲦⲈⲖⲎⲖ ⲬⲈ ⲚⲦⲈⲢⲒⲈⲒ ⲈⲒⲚⲎⲨ ⲈⲂⲞⲖ ⲈⲠⲔⲞⲤⲘⲞⲤ ⲬⲒⲚ ⲚϢⲞⲢⲠ ⲀⲒⲈⲒⲚⲈ ⲘⲘⲚⲦⲤⲚⲞⲞⲨⲤ ⲚϬⲞⲘ ⲚⲘⲘⲀⲒ ⲔⲀⲦⲀ ⲐⲈ ⲈⲚⲦⲀⲒⲬⲞⲞⲤ ⲈⲢⲰⲦⲚ ⲬⲒⲚ ⲚϢⲞⲢⲠ· ⲈⲚⲦⲀⲒⲬⲒⲦⲞⲨ ⲚⲦⲞⲞⲦⲞⲨ ⲘⲘⲚⲦⲤⲚⲞⲞⲨⲤ ⲚⲤⲰⲦⲎⲢ ⲚⲦⲈ ⲠⲈⲐⲎⲤⲀⲨⲢⲞⲤ ⲚⲞⲨⲞⲈⲒⲚ ⲔⲀⲦⲀ ⲦⲔⲈⲖⲈⲨⲤⲒⲤ ⲘⲠϢⲞⲢⲠ ⲘⲘⲨⲤⲦⲎⲢⲒⲞⲚ· ⲚⲀⲒ ϬⲈ ⲀⲒⲚⲞⲬⲞⲨ ⲈⲦⲔⲀⲖⲀϨⲎ ⲚⲦⲈⲦⲚⲘⲀⲀⲨ ⲬⲒⲚ ⲈⲒⲚⲎⲨ ⲈⲠⲔⲞⲤⲘⲞⲤ ⲈⲦⲈ ⲚⲀⲒ ⲚⲈⲦϨⲚ ⲠⲈⲦⲚⲤⲰⲘⲀ ⲘⲠⲞⲞⲨ·) For these powers have been given unto you before the whole world, *because you are they who will save the whole world, and that you may be able to endure the threat of the rulers of the world and the pains of the world and its dangers and all its persecutions, which the rulers of the height will bring upon you.* For many times have I said unto you that I have brought the power

---

[12] Mead suggests a Valentinian connection (*Pistis Sophia*, xxvi–xxxiv). Schmidt's positions on these matters are as follows: 1) the work, especially the fourth book, is of Egyptian provenance; 2) it dates from two periods (books 1–3 from the second half of the 3rd century and book 4 from the first half of the 3rd century); 3) it has no trace of Valentinian thought as it lacks the typically Valentinian philosophical ideas and profound speculation; and 4) it may well be associated with the Sethians or some other sect (*Koptisch-gnostische Schriften* [1954], xxiii–xxv). Pheme Perkins recognizes that *PS* is not representative of just one school of thought stating, "Pistis Sophia is a late compendium of gnostic lore complied from earlier writings" ("Pistis Sophia," *ABD* 5.376).

in you out of the twelve saviors who are in the Treasury of the Light. For which cause I have said unto you indeed from the beginning that you are not of the world. I also am not of it. For all men who are in the world have gotten their souls out of the power of the rulers of the aeons. *But the power which is in you is from me; your souls belong to the height.*[13]

Once again we are presented with the concepts of the pre-existence of the disciples with the savior and their pre-ordained role in a salvific mission. In both *PS* and *ActsPet12Apost.* there is also a sense of perceived threat imposed upon the disciples by the "rulers of the height" (envisioned as robbers and wild beasts by our text). Certainly, powers hostile to the elect are nothing out of the ordinary in gnostic conceptions. However, there is a crucial similarity between *Tri. Trac.*, *PS* and *ActsPet12Apost.* that is important to our comparison. In addition to being from the heavenly realm (having a pre-existence with the savior), the disciples are fundamentally different in nature when compared to all other people as well. In *Tri. Trac.* 116.5–14, the disciples are declared to be of "spiritual" substance and "from prayer." Likewise, in *PS* 1.7 the disciples are described as "not of this world" and possessors of souls which "belong to the height." This may shed some light on why in *ActsPet12Apost.* 3.5–11 both Peter and Lithargoel describe themselves as "strangers" (ⲩⲘⲘⲞ) to Habitation. They are from another realm, outsiders to this world.

This concept of a savior who descends in the company of other heavenly beings who are not merely ordinary humans is not unfamiliar to the heresiologists. In addition to the material we have examined from *Tri. Trac.* and *PS*, important corroborating witnesses to this conception are found also in Irenaeus, Clement of Alexandria[14] and Origen[15] — although

---

[13] Mead, *Pistis Sophia*, 8–9.

[14] Similar conceptions are found in Clement of Alexandria, *Excerpta ex Theodoto* (Theodoto's original work can be dated ca. mid-second century), which Robert Pierce Casey describes as consisting "mainly of quotations from

for our purposes we shall focus our discussion on the material available to us from Irenaeus.

As part of his description of the ideas of the disciples of Ptolemaeus, who was himself a disciple of the great gnostic teacher, Valentinus, Irenaeus reports that as a response to the supplications of the fallen mother, Achamoth, the Father sent the Savior in order to heal her passions. On this journey to the middle realm (i.e., the domain of the

---

Valentinian works, to which some criticism and theological speculation has been added." Particularly helpful for our discussion is the material found in chapter 35:

"Jesus our light" "having emptied himself," as the Apostle says, that is, according to Theodotus, having passed beyond the Boundary, since he was an angel of the Pleroma, *led out the angels of the superior seed with him.* And he himself had the redemption inasmuch as he proceeded from the Pleroma, *but he led the angels for the correction of the seed.* For, inasmuch as they are bound for the sake of the parts, and plead and being restrained for our sakes in their zeal to enter, they beg remission for us, that we may enter with them. *For since they may almost be said to need us in order to enter,* for without us they are not permitted (therefore not even the Mother has entered with them without us, they say), they are obviously bound for our sake.

Ὁ Ἰησοῦς "τὸ φῶς" ἡμῶν, ὡς λέγει ὁ ἀπόστολος, ἑαυτὸν "κενώσας," τουτέστιν ἐκτὸς τοῦ Ὅρου γενόμενος κατὰ Θεόδοτον, ἐπεὶ ἄγγελος ἦν τοῦ πληρώματος, τοὺς ἀγγέλους τοῦ διαφέροντος σπέρματος συνεξήγεν ἑαυτῷ. καὶ αὐτὸς μὲν τὴν λύτρωσιν ὡς ἀπὸ πληρώματος προελθὼν εἶχεν, τοὺς δὲ ἀγγέλους εἰς διόρθωσιν τοῦ σπέρματος ἤγαγεν. ὡς γὰρ ὑπὲρ μέρους δέονται καὶ παρακαλοῦσι, καὶ δι᾽ ἡμᾶς κατεχόμενοι σπεύδοντες εἰσελθεῖν, ἄφεσιν ἡμῖν αἰτοῦνται, ἵνα συνεισέλθωμεν αὐτοῖς. σχεδὸν γὰρ ἡμῶν χρείαν ἔχοντες, ἵνα εἰσέλθωσιν, ἐπεὶ ἄνευ ἡμῶν οὐκ ἐπιτρέπεται αὐτοῖς (διὰ τοῦτο γὰρ οὐδὲ ἡ μήτηρ συνελήλυθεν ἄνευ ἡμῶν, φασίν), εἰκότως ὑπὲρ ἡμῶν δέονται.

It should be stressed here that any analysis of the *Excerpta ex Theodoto* is complicated by the fact that ideas exist within it in a more fragmentary form than we would like. The Greek text cited in this study is taken from Casey (*The Excerpta ex Theodoto of Clement of Alexandria* [London: Christophers, 1934]). The text with a substantial introduction is also available in François L. Sagnard, *Extraits de Théodote / Clément d'Alexandrie* (SC 23; Paris: Éditions du Cerf, 1948).

[15] See Heracleon, Fragment 22, in *Commentary on John* 13.19.

mother), the Savior is expressly described as being accompanied by angelic beings. Irenaeus then proceeds to relate Achamoth's response:

"But when Achamoth was freed from her passion, she gazed with rapture on the dazzling vision of the angels that were with him; and in her ecstasy, conceiving by them, they tell us that she brought forth new beings, partly after her own image, and partly a spiritual progeny after the image of the Savior's attendants" *Hanc autem Achamoth extra passionem factam concepisse de gratulatione eorum quae cum eo sunt luminum uisionem, hoc est Angelorum qui erant cum eo, et delectatam in conceptu eorum peperisse fructus secundum illius imaginem docent, partum spiritalem secundum similitudinem factum satellitum Saluatoris.* (*Adv. haer.* 1.4.5)[16]

Later, Irenaeus, after digressing by explaining other aspects of the Valentinian myth, restates that it was on account of Achamoth's contemplation of the angels who were with the Savior that a special offspring was brought forth. According to Irenaeus, this offspring is claimed by the Valentinians to be the Ecclesia, an earthly "emblem of the heavenly Ecclesia" (*exemplum superioris Ecclesiae*; 1.5.6). While Irenaeus does not indicate that those angelic companions who accompany the Savior descend to earth with him, their incarnated seed is described as greatly loved by the Demiurge.[17]   It is also said that this seed was

---

[16] Τὴν δὲ ᾿Αχαμὼθ ἐκτὸς τοῦ πάθους γενομένην, [καὶ] συλλαβοῦσαν τῇ χαρᾷ τῶν σὺν αὐτῷ φώτων τὴν θεωρίαν, τουτέσιν τῶν ᾿Αγγέλων τῶν μετ᾿ αὐτοῦ, καὶ ἐγκισσήσασαν <εἰς> αὐτούς, κεκυηκέναι καρποὺς κατὰ τὴν <ἐκείνων> εἰκόνα διδάσκουσι, κύημα πνευματικὸν καθ᾿ ὁμοίωσιν γεγονὸς τῶν δορυφόρων τοῦ Σωτῆρος. The Greek and Latin texts are taken from Adelin Rousseau and Louis Doutreleau, *Irénée de Lyon; Contre les Hérésies* (SC 264; Paris: Les Éditions du Cerf, 1979); and idem, *Irénée de Lyon; Contre les Hérésies* (SC 294; Paris: Les Éditions du Cerf, 1982).

[17] Here the Demiurge is not the evil being that is typical of some gnostic systems. In this construct the Demiurge only remains ignorant until the advent of the Savior at which time it gladly joins itself to the Savior (1.7.4).

distributed in the prophets, priests and kings (1.7.3). In reality it appears that while this seed is spiritual, we are not dealing with the straightforward incarnation of Pleromatic entities. Rather, these spiritual beings are a kind of mixed bag with parts from several different sources: 1) their animal soul comes from the Demiurge; 2) their body from earth; 3) their flesh from matter and 4) their spiritual man from the Mother Achamoth (who conceived by the angels) (1.5.6). This mixed character actually affects their prophecies which are drawn from three separate sources — the mother, the seed and the Demiurge (1.7.3).[18] Still, there is a very strong connection between these angels and their spiritual offspring that acts as a magnet, drawing the separated together again. Irenaeus explains that when all the seed comes to perfection (i.e., presumably at some eschatological moment in the future) the spiritual seed will be given as brides to the self-same angels who descended with the Savior (1.7.1; see also 1.7.5).

There is a further point of comparison upon which we have only briefly touched. Irenaeus claims that this seed was distributed in the prophets, priest and kings (1.7.3) while in both *Tri. Trac.* and *PS* the companions of the Savior have their earthly expression in the apostles. Certainly, the general point here is that those beings endowed with the seed of Achamoth/ the angels are incarnated in those beings who become spiritual leaders. However, the Valentinians whose system(s) is (are) reported by Irenaeus may have also included this understanding of the apostles as imbued with spiritual seed and reflecting heavenly realities. In *Adv. haer.* 2.19–20, Irenaeus launches into an extended critical response to the Valentinian theories previously discussed (note the

---

[18] Likewise, the Christ is a compound of four substances 1) a spiritual part which, like the other spiritual people, is drawn from Achamoth; 2) the animal soul from the Demiurge; 3) the corporeal part and 4) the Savior who is said to have descended upon him as a dove (1.7.2). In keeping with this parallelism, the sayings of Jesus are also drawn from three sources — the Savior, the Mother and the Demiurge (1.7.3). Presumably, this tripartite character of the prophecies and the sayings of Jesus demand careful and qualified interpretation — no doubt only fully available to the Valentinians themselves.

specific claim he makes that the system he is criticizing is, in fact, Valentinian; 2.19.8). His criticisms are certainly interesting in themselves but for our purposes (discussion of the apostles role in the salvific drama) it is the remarks he makes in 2.20–21 that are most pertinent. In this passage Irenaeus challenges the Valentinian position as to the connection between the apostles and the highest realm: "*If, again, they maintain that the twelve apostles were a type only of that group of twelve Aeons which Anthropos in conjunction with Ecclesia produced*, then let them produce ten other apostles as a type of those ten remaining Aeons, who, as they declare, were produced by Logos and Zoe" (*Si autem doudecim apostolos dicunt typum esse illius solius duodeim Aeonum prolationis quam Homo cum Ecclesia protulit*; 2.21.1). It must be granted that this is not precisely the same concept as described by Irenaeus in the texts we have previously examined but it does have a rather interesting similarity with *PS* 1.7. In both these texts the apostles are reflections of the highest Pleromatic entities. It would be untrue to claim that the systems expounded in *Tri. Trac.*, *PS* and Irenaeus are the same.[19] However, there is a general similarity of thought that bespeaks an overall Valentinian trajectory, despite what might be termed "denominational differences."

One final point that all three texts do have in common — the incompleteness of the spiritual seed (i.e., the apostles/ disciples) and their need for perfection/ instruction . First, *Tri. Trac.* describes the disciples as "teachers who need instruction" who also "share in the passions" (116.19–21). Likewise, *PS* 1.7 presumes this need by its very form, the revelation dialogue, in which the disciples pose questions and are given

---

[19] It is important here to weigh Irenaeus' comments as we compare them with the systems found in *Tri. Trac.* and *PS*. The latter two texts represent primary sources, presumably either written by Valentinians or, in the case of *PS*, at least containing some Valentinian material. The former is the summary of an unsympathetic, albeit well-meaning, critic, which may well reflect misunderstandings, oversimplifications and/ or mistakes. Therefore, the primary texts must be given priority as representative of authentic Valentinian systems.

systematic instruction in the nature of things.[20] As for Irenaeus' account, he states that the Valentinians claim: "The consummation of all things will take place when all that is spiritual has been formed and perfected by Gnosis; and by this they mean spiritual men who have attained to the perfect knowledge of God, and been initiated into these mysteries by Achamoth.   And they represent themselves to be these persons" (*Consummationem uero futuram, cum formatum et perfectum fuerit scientia omne spiritale, hoc est homines qui perfectam agnitionem habent de Deo et hi qui ab Achamoth initiati sunt mysteria: esse autem hos semetipsos dicunt*; 1.6.1). Along these same lines we might also consider Irenaeus' critique of the imperfection of the angels who sired the spiritual seed (2.19.1).

In summary, we are confronted, once again, with a Valentinian myth that views the Savior as accompanied by angelic escorts who, through an incarnation, become an elite, spiritual corps. While these spiritual beings are described as imperfect and in need of knowledge, they are able to respond to the Savior's advent and participate in the salvific drama so as to facilitate the redemption of the psychics.

RICH, POOR AND DISCIPLES: THREE TYPES OF PEOPLE

Among the ideas discussed above, the concept of the disciples being fundamentally different from the other inhabitants of Habitation leads us to consider the mythic identities of the "rich" and "poor" in Habitation. As I noted above, I propose that in the underlying mythic structure of *ActsPet12Apost.* there are three groups of people to whom Lithargoel extends his invitation: 1) *the material* (the Rich), who ignore the invitation; 2) *the psychic* (the Poor), who receive the invitation but require considerable assistance in their faith; and 3) *the spiritual* (the disciples),

---

[20] Note the repeated references to the disciples in 1.2; 1.4; 1.5.

who upon hearing the invitation never doubt but ask for specific directions and act upon them.[21]

Once again *Tri. Trac.* supplies a text which further clarifies the underlying gnostic myth:

> Mankind came to be in three essential types, the spiritual, the psychic and the material.... *The spiritual race*, being light from light and spirit from spirit, *when its head appeared, it ran toward him immediately.* It immediately became a body of its head.... *The psychic race* is like light from fire, since *it hesitated to accept knowledge of him who appeared to it.* It hesitated even more to run to him in faith. *Rather, through a voice it was instructed and this was sufficient,* since it received, so to speak as a pledge, the assurance of things which were to be. *The material race,* however, is alien in every way; since it is dark, it *shuns the shining of the light because its appearance destroys it.* (118.14–119.13)

When one compares the descriptions of the three races of *Tri. Trac.* with the actions of the rich, poor and disciples of *ActsPet12Apost.* the similarities are striking. The rich are the material people of *Tri. Trac.*, shunning Lithargoel, "the light, gazelle-like stone" (3.25–27). The poor are the psychics of *Tri. Trac.*, hesitating in their acceptance, doubting the reality of Lithargoel's invitation (4.17–29). However, after being assured by Lithargoel of his offer's validity, they rejoice (4.29–5.1) — but, unlike Peter, take no direct action to get to Nine Gates ("Rather, through a voice it was instructed..."). Lastly, the disciples and particularly Peter are the

---

[21] Although Keller sees Habitation as representative of the Church and not the world, he contributes much to the discussion of the rich and poor in Habitation. Keller views "rich" and "poor" as "spiritual categories, that is to say two attitudes or mentalities.... The rich believe they know all and have need of nothing whereas the poor admit to having never seen the 'pearl' and recognize having need of being healed. These poor symbolize, in the bosom of the Church, those who confess ignorance and sickness" ("De la Foi à la Connaissance," 135). On the other hand, Perkins is unconvinced that the categories of rich and poor have any allegorical significance: "There is no indication in the story that we are to understand rich and poor as allegorical expressions" (*Gnostic Dialogue*, 128).

spiritual, who recognize the beauty in Lithargoel (2.17–19), accept his offer and desire to journey to his city (5.7–14).

This discussion of *Tri. Trac.* and the three classes of people necessarily evokes the question as to the relationship between this proposed Story of the Pearl Merchant and Valentinianism. In *Adv. haer.* 1.7.5, Irenaeus also describes three types of people, attributing this teaching to the disciples of Valentinus:

> They conceive then of three kinds of men, spiritual, material, and animal, represented by Cain, Abel and Seth.... The material goes, as a matter of course, into corruption. The animal, if it make choice of the better part, finds repose in the intermediate place; but if the worse, it too shall pass into destruction. But they assert that the spiritual principles which have been sown by Achamoth, being disciplined and nourished here from that time until now in righteous souls (because when given forth by her they were yet but weak), at last attaining to perfection, shall be given as brides to the angels of the Savior, while their animal souls of necessity rest for ever with the Demiurge in the intermediate place.[22]

Actually, this concept of three classes of people should be considered primarily in terms of Platonism and not necessarily as Valentinian. In the *Phaedo* 80–83, Socrates, expanding upon his theory of reincarnation, describes three categories of people. The first he describes as "wicked." These people, "through craving for the corporeal, which unceasingly pursues them, ...are imprisoned once more in a body." They are corporeal, heavy, earthly and visible and because of this their souls are "tainted by its [the body] presence...weighed down and dragged back into the visible world." According to Socrates, they will come back to this earth as animals such as donkeys, wolves and hawks, animals that reflect their perverse attachments to this world. The second group Socrates

---

[22] See also *Adv. haer.* 1.8.3, for Valentinian eisogesis of the gospels in an attempt to prove this teaching.

describes as "the ones who have cultivated the goodness of the ordinary citizen — what is called self-control and integrity — which is acquired by habit and practice, without the help of philosophy and reason." These people will come back as social and disciplined animals such as ants or bees or even as people again, as decent citizens. The third and final group is the only group to which Socrates affords a chance to escape the vicious cycle of reincarnation. They alone "may attain the divine nature." These are the "lovers of wisdom," the "true philosophers."

This is not to rule out a Valentinian background for the Story of the Pearl Merchant. On the contrary, it is well attested by Irenaeus and Hippolytus that Valentinus drew upon (or merely plagiarized, as Hippolytus would have it) Platonic ideas as the basis for his teaching.[23] However, as G. C. Stead states, there were other groups that were also using this Platonic concept of the three classes of people:

> The gnostic Basilides also presents a radically optimistic view. He takes over a Platonic myth of a choice of lives by three classes of rational beings, which can also be found in Philo. In the usual form of the myth, the three classes are distinguished by the varying degrees in which they yield to the attractions of the body and of earthly things, and the lowest class is represented as entirely given over to bodily concerns, like the *hylikoi* in Valentinian anthropology. In Basilides' version, however, the highest class of the three reverts immediately to the heavenly world (Hippolytus, *Haer.* 7.22.8) and the second follows with some difficulty, aided by the Holy Spirit (ibid. 9–16); it is only the third class that remains within the germinating lower world, and even this apparently has the respectable motive of "conferring and receiving benefits" (ibid. 16, cf. 10–11). All these classes indeed share the dignity of "sonship," υἱότης, which is withheld even from the Holy Spirit (ibid. 12–13).
>
> Philo reproduces the same myth in a less optimistic and more typical form. The version given in *Gig.* 12–15 has some features

---

[23] Irenaeus, *Adv. haer.* 2.14; Hippolytus *Ref.* 6.16–24.

in common with Basilides. All three classes share the common
denominator of souls, but those of the first class refuse all dealings
with the earth, and are appointed to wait upon their creator. A
second group emerge with difficulty from the whirlpool of bodily
passions and return to their source; these are the souls of genuine
philosophers who follow Plato's advice by meditating upon death
(*Phaedo* 64a, 67e, 81a, often quoted by Philo and the Fathers).
The third class are completely overwhelmed by the body and
worldly concerns.[24]

From these examples of other versions of the basic Platonic teaching of
the three classes of people, it is difficult to conclusively link the Story of
the Pearl Merchant with Valentinianism. One turns to the pre-existence
of the Church as an indicator of Valentinian influence, but, as I have
noted above, this is not an exclusively Valentinian teaching either. Still,
the similarities with the mythical structure in *Tri. Trac.*, a clearly
Valentinian text, forbid me to rule out this possibility.

THE JOURNEYS THROUGH THE HOSTILE REALMS
ActsPet12Apost. describes Habitation as "a small city in the midst of the
sea" (ⲈⲨⲔⲞⲨⲈⲒ ⲘⲠⲞⲖⲒⲤ ⲈⲤⲈⲚ ⲦⲘⲎⲦⲈ ⲚⲐⲀⲖⲀⲤⲤⲀ;
1.28–29). It is essentially an island, with "waves and large high walls
surrounding the bounds of the city" (ⲀⲈⲒⲚⲀⲨ ⲈⲈⲈⲚⲞⲞⲈⲒⲚ ⲘⲚ
ⲈⲚⲚⲞⲞ ⲚⲬⲞⲖⲬⲖ ⲈⲨⲬⲞⲤⲈ ⲈⲨⲔⲰⲦⲈ ⲈⲚⲒⲔⲢⲞ ⲚⲦⲈ
ⲦⲠⲞⲖⲒⲤ; 6.29–31). The apostles can only arrive at its dock after a
journey by boat. This image would really present no problem except for
the peculiar instructions that are given by Lithargoel to Peter as to how the
apostles are to reach Nine Gates. When questioned by Peter as to the way
to Lithargoel's city, Peter is told of a "road" (5.19, 23) that is populated
by robbers, killer animals and man-eating lions and bulls. The question

[24] Stead, "In Search of Valentinus," in Bentley Layton ed., *The
Rediscovery of Gnosticism*, vol. 1: *The School of Valentinus* (Studies in the
History of Religions 41; Leiden: Brill, 1980) 93–94.

arises: How can an island city (surrounded by waves) have a road which leads to another city? Furthermore, the traveling instructions given to Peter by Lithargoel are peculiar. Peter is told that the traveler must forsake everything and "fast daily from stage to stage" (5.23–25). Presumably one should take provisions for a journey. Yet the text not only forbids possessions but even refuses the traveler physical sustenance along the way. These are all important aspects that have direct relation to the underlying mythic structure. There are three distinct allegorical elements to the journey aspect of the gnostic myth: 1) the geographical setting of Habitation and its relation to gnostic cosmology; 2) the presence of hostile entities; and 3) the method of travel through these realms.

The text makes it clear that the city of Habitation is an island and must be reached by boat. If Habitation itself is viewed as representative of this world, then the image of water separating the realm from which the Lord and the apostles launch their mission and the world takes on a special significance to the gnostic mind as influenced by the ancient world. Within the ancient world in general there are other examples of the realm between this world and the next as being separated by water, such as Plutarch's myth of the libertine man from Soli who died from a fall and came back from the dead, a changed man, after three days. Plutarch states:

> He said that when his intelligence was driven from his body, the change made him feel as a pilot might at first on being flung into the depths of the sea; his next impression was that he had risen somewhat and was breathing with his whole being and was seeing on all sides, his soul having opened wide as if it were a single eye. But nothing that he saw was familiar except the stars, which appeared very great in size and at vast distances apart, sending forth a marvelously colored radiance possessed of a certain cohesion, *so that his soul, riding smoothly in the light like a ship on a calm sea, could move easily and rapidly in all directions*

(ὥστε τὴν ψυχὴν ἐποχουμένην λείως πλοῖον ὥσπερ ἐν
γαλήνῃ τῷ φωτὶ ῥᾳδίως πάντῃ καὶ ταχὺ διαφέρεσθαι).[25]

Ultimately, it is this same idea that is present in the ancient Greek image
of the river Styx, separating the world of the living from that otherworldly
sphere. In this conception, the soul is transported across the waters of the
Styx by the ferryman, Charon, without whom there simply is no passage.[26]

In the gnostic text *On the Origin of the World* the chaos out of which
the intermediate ruler, Yaldabaoth, emerges is described as "limitless
darkness and bottomless water" (99.37–38). The realm of this ruler was
originally only "water and darkness" (100.32) before the ruler separated
matter into heaven and earth. It is through these waters that this prime
parent sees the likeness of Pistis and is ashamed because of its own
brashness (107.18–25).   A similar scenario is described in the

---

[25] *Moralia* 7, ("On the Delays of Divine Vengeance," 563). Greek text
available in Phillip H. De Lacy and Benedict Einarson, trans., *Plutarch's Moralia
VII 523c–612b* (Cambridge: Harvard University Press, 1959).   In Philo's
description of his own philosophical ascent and how the political cares of this
world hindered it he compares these cares with a tumultuous sea: "Nevertheless,
the most grievous of all evils was lying in wait for me, namely, envy, that hates
every thing that is good, and which, suddenly attacking me, did not cease from
dragging me after it by force till it had taken me and thrown me into the vast sea
of the cares of public politics, in which I was and still am tossed about without
being able to keep myself swimming at the top" (*Special Laws* 3.1.3). This is
certainly a more literal application of this image but, nonetheless, water (seas) is
the chosen image for that which hinders the soul's progression or that which
separates the soul from the heavenly realm.

[26] See the description of the Styx and Charon (as well as a picture of the
other side) in Virgil's *Aeneid* 6.289–346, 538–669. Furthermore, this concept of
water as representing the intermediate realms may have some relationship with the
ancient Hebrew cosmological belief in waters above the heavens: "And God made
the firmament and separated the waters which were under the firmament from the
waters which were above the firmament...And God called the firmament heaven"
(Gen. 1:7–8a; see also 7:11; 8:2). This in turn may have been influenced by the
ancient Egyptian belief in the sun god Rā's journeys by day across the sky in his
heavenly bark. Here again the heavens are thought of in terms of water (E. A.
Wallis Budge, trans., *Book of the Dead* [London: Routledge and Kegan, 1956]
292–308).

Apocryphon of John. In 14.24–34, the "waters which are above matter" are illuminated and the chief archon and all the authorities see the form of the image of "the first Man" in the water.

This image of water as representing the intermediate realm is present in other Nag Hammadi texts. In *Second Treatise of the Great Seth* 50.16–17, the Redeemer figure speaks of a "descent upon the water, that is, the regions below." Further, in *PS* 1.41.17, in her fifth repentance Pistis Sophia, in the midst of the realm of chaos, describes her oppressions at the hands of the emanations of Self-Willed. She cries out: "And they have surrounded me, in numbers as water, they have laid hold on me together all my time" (ⲁⲩⲱ ⲁⲩⲕⲱⲧⲉ ⲉⲣⲟⲓ ⲉⲩⲟⲩ ⲛ̄ⲑⲉ ⲛ̄ⲟⲩⲙⲟⲟⲩ ⲁⲩⲁⲙⲁϩⲧⲉ ⲙ̄ⲙⲟⲓ ϩⲓ ⲟⲩⲥⲟⲡ ⲙ̄ⲡⲁⲟⲩⲟⲓⲩ ⲧⲏⲣϥ̄). Another text that is comparable with my theoretical mythic structure is found in *Authoritative Teaching* 29.3–21. This text presents a simile which refers to evil powers and their attempts to kill the spirit. The document compares the spirit to a fish and the "man-eaters" to fishermen attempting to catch and kill the fish:

> For this reason, then, we do not sleep, nor do we forget the nets
> that are spread out in hiding, lying in wait for us to catch us. For
> if we are caught in a single net, it will suck us down into its mouth,
> while the water flows over us, striking our face. And we will not
> be able to come up from it because the waters are high over us,
> flowing from above downward, submerging our heart down in the
> filthy mud. And we will not be able to escape them. For man-
> eaters will seize us and swallow us like a fisherman casting a hook
> into the water.

Here again we find the analogy of water. It is the realm where the spirit is in jeopardy, the realm of power for the "man-eaters" or archons. The water is a realm that must be carefully passed through. The mystic traveler must be aware of its hazards.[27] This reference to hostile forces that populate this intermediate realm leads us to examine the second allegorical element of the journey aspect of the gnostic myth: the presence of hostile entities.

In *ActsPet12Apost.* 5.19–6.8, Lithargoel describes the various robbers and animals that infest the road to his city. It is a surreal image that Lithargoel presents. He speaks of a road with black dogs that seek out and kill travelers for bread, wolves that kill travelers for water, and lions and bulls that eat travelers because they possess meat and green vegetables respectively, as if animals could be cognizant of a traveler's belongings and selectively kill on the basis of that cognition. Obviously, real animals do not have this selective cognition. In a symbolic text one is invited to look for the allegorical object. That object is the archons that populate the intermediate realms.

Probably the best examples that can be used for illustrating the gnostic tendency to attribute animal or even monster-like features to the archons are found in *PS*. In 1.30–31, Pistis Sophia is described as being oppressed by a hostile lion-faced power and a host of malevolent material emanations.[28] Again in 1.66, the emanations of the lion-faced Self-Willed are once again described as oppressing Pistis Sophia in the intermediate realms of chaos. The appearance of these emanations is described as "a great serpent," "a seven-headed basilisk," "a dragon" and "all the other very numerous emanations." While these statements support the general point of my argument, they cannot compare to 4.126, where the intermediate realms (the "regions of chastisement") are described. The regions of chastisement are viewed as being outside the world and surrounding the world. Within these regions there are twelve dungeons, each with an archon with an animal face. The list of animal-faced archons

---

[27] Note also the role played by water in *Paraphrase of Shem*. In this gnostic text water, described as below the clouds (15.25–26), is associated with darkness (2.23, 30), harm (5.35) and fright (7.22–23; 9.17; 14.11).

[28] This same creature is also mentioned in 1.39, 48 and 75.

includes a crocodile, a cat, a dog, a serpent, a black bull, a wild boar, a bear, a vulture and a basilisk (a mythical seven-headed dragon) as well as seven-headed variations on the cat and dog.

The conceptualization of the archons as animals is also present in the Nag Hammadi corpus. *Marsanes* includes statements to document this phenomenon. In 25.1–8, the author states: "But their powers, which are the angels, are in the form of beasts and animals." Likewise, in *Orig. World* 119.16–18, Adam and Eve are horrified to realize that the archons who modeled them have the form of beasts. Lastly, in *Exegesis on the Soul* 127.25–8, the original soul is described as falling "into the hands of many robbers" and "wanton creatures" when she comes into a body.[29]

---

[29] The *Apocryphon of John* (NHC 2.1) describes a series of animal-headed planetary spirits: "And the archons created seven powers for themselves, and the powers created for themselves six angels for each one until they became angels. And these are the bodies belonging with the names: the first is Athoth, he has a sheep's face; the second is Eloaiou, he has a donkey's face; the third is Astaphaios, he has a [hyena's] face; the fourth is Yao, he has a [serpent's] face with seven heads; the fifth is Sabaoth, he has a dragon's face; the sixth is Adonin, he had a monkey's face; the seventh is Sabbede, he has a shining fire-face" (11.22–34). Origen, in discussing Celsus's description of the Seven ruling Demons, describes a similar conceptualization of the archons (*Contra Celsum* 6.30; cf. also 6.33, "Celsus next relates other fables, to the effect that 'certain persons return to the shapes of the archontics, so that some are called lions, others bulls, others dragons, or eagles, or bears, or dogs'"). Another text that provides an interesting comparison is Clement of Alexandria, *Excerpta ex Theodoto*. In 70.1–73.3, the Valentinian commentator describes the realm of the stars and planets in which exist "an array of powers and angels" (some beneficent, some maleficent; 71.2). The evil elements of these powers and angels are described as brigands (οἱ δὲ λῃσταῖς) and as being "opponents who attack the soul *through the body and outward things* and pledge it to slavery" (τοὺς ἀντικειμένους, οἳ διὰ τοῦ σώματος καὶ τῶν ἐκτὸς ἐπιβατεύουσι τῆς ψυχῆς καὶ ἐνεχυράζουσιν εἰς δουλείαν). The conception is similar, though not identical, to the perilous situation faced by the would-be traveler to Nine Gates as described by Lithargoel (*ActsPet12Apost.* 5.21–6.8). In both cases "the body and outward things" become the target for hostile powers. While *Exc. Theod.* 73.1 does not delineate specifically what is included in "the body and outward things," *ActsPet12Apost.* explains that the hostile powers are drawn to one's possessions (e.g., bread, garments, water, meat, vegetables). Faced with this threat, the only hope the traveler has is to fast (i.e., keep the body under strict control) and

Certainly there are other ways in which the enigmatic archons can be interpreted. One such way is proposed by Walter Wink. According to Wink, the mythological images of the archons represented the spirituality of the oppressive power structures (not the actual powers themselves) of the Roman Empire: "What they [the Gnostics] called principalities, powers, authorities, dominions, thrones, forces, angels, archangels, elements, and so forth were, on my hypothesis, the real experiences of the spirituality of the monolithic political, economic and social forces that dominated and often tyrannized their daily lives."[30] However, in the

---

renounce the world (i.e., divorce oneself from "outward things"). As a further point of comparison we can note that both texts characterize the enemies as brigands "ληστής" (*Exc. Theod.* 72.2/; *Acts Pet12Apost.* 5.33) and wolves (*Exc. Theod.* 72.2/ *Acts Pet12Apost.* 6.2; more securely 7.29–30), as well as other frightening and deadly animals (*Exc. Thdot.* 76.2–3/ *Acts Pet12Apost.* 5.28–6.8). Lastly, the final intentions of these powers, while not the same, are far from positive — in *ActsPet12Apost.* the creatures intend to kill the traveler and in the *Exc. Theod.* they intend to enslave the soul (*Exc. Theod.* 73.1). For further discussion of the archons as animals see Robert M. Grant, *Gnosticism and Early Christianity* (2d ed.; New York: Columbia University Press, 1966) 48–51. Certainly, spiritual powers that are hostile to the soul and envisioned as animal-like are not unknown in the Mediterranean (e.g., the Greek had Cereberus, the multi-headed guard dog of Hades, and the ancient Egyptians had A'mut, the "devourer of souls").

[30] Wink, *Cracking the Gnostic Code: The Powers in Gnosticism* (SBLMS 46; Atlanta: Scholars Press, 1993) 4. Wink elaborates, stating: "This thesis avoids the reductionism of certain sociological or psychological approaches, in that it regards the spiritual beings of Gnostic mythology not as a mystification of the material forces at work in the institutions and systems of that day, but as the actual spirituality of those material forces and systems. The demonic spirits, whose hegemony over that world these Gnostics discerned, were real. But they were not disembodied phantoms flapping in the sky. They were the interiority or withinness — the essence, ethos, corporate personality, driving spirit — of the institutions and social arrangements that were the source of the Gnostic protest" (ibid., 13). For further discussion of the powers in the NT world see Wink's trilogy: *Naming the Powers: The Language of Power in the New Testament* (Philadelphia: Fortress, 1984); *Unmasking the Powers: The Invisible Forces That Determine Human Existence* (Philadelphia: Fortress, 1986); *Engaging the Powers: Discernment and Resistance in a World of Domination* (Minneapolis: Fortress, 1992).

interests of precision, it should be stressed here that Wink is referring to an interpretation of the archons in general and not these powers in their specifically animal forms.

Another way of interpreting the archontic powers which is more directly applicable to our situation is to understand them in terms of the attacks mounted by the passions against the human soul. Evidence is provided by the *Apocryphon of John* (NHC 2.1), which describes in ponderous detail the creation of the human body by the archons. In 15.1–19.12, one by one the parts of the body are assembled in a repetitive formula: "X (name of archon) created Y (body part)." Finally, the four chief demons that are associated with the human body are specifically identified with human passions:

> The four chief demons are: Ephememphi who belongs to pleasure, Yoko who belongs to desire, Nenentophni who belongs to grief, Blaomen who belongs to fear. And the mother of them all is Aesthesis-Ouch-Epi-Ptoe. And from the four demons passions came forth. And from grief (came) envy, jealousy, distress, trouble, pain, callousness, anxiety, mourning, etc. And from pleasure much wickedness arises, and empty pride, and similar things. And from desire (comes) anger, wrath, and bitterness, and bitter passion, and unsatedness, and similar things. And from fear (comes) dread, fawning, agony, and shame. (18.14b–31)

The writer of *Ap. John* makes it clear that these four demons are not the only heavenly powers to be associated with passions stating in 19.6–10: "Now there are other ones in charge over the remaining passions whom I did not mention to you. But if you wish to know them, it is written in the book of Zoroaster."

This understanding of the gnostic beasts as passions is encouraged in a recent dissertation on Logion 7 from the *Gospel of Thomas*. Howard M. Jackson suggests that this enigmatic saying ("Blessed is the lion which becomes man when consumed by man; and cursed is the man whom the lion consumes, and the lion becomes man") has an anthropological dimension.[31] In short, Jackson argues that the beasts (e.g., the lion in Logion 7) should be understood as referring to human passions. Jackson further asserts that a famous metaphor found in *Republic* 588b–589b provides the catalyst which stimulated the Gnostics to understand the passions as beasts besetting the soul. In this metaphor Socrates compares the human soul to the mythical creatures of ancient lore in which two or more animals are merged into one entity:

> Let us make an image of the soul, that he may have his own words presented before his eyes.
> Of what sort?
> An ideal image of the soul, like the composite creations of ancient mythology, such as the Chimera or Scylla or Cerberus, and there are many others in which two or more different natures are said to grow into one.
> There are said to have been such unions.
> Then do you now model the form of the multitudinous, many-headed monster, having a ring of heads of all manner of beasts, tame and wild, which he is able to generate and metamorphose at will.
> You suppose marvelous powers in the artist; but as language is more pliable than wax or any similar substance, let there be such a model as you propose.
> Suppose now that you make a second form as of a lion, and a third of a man, the second smaller than the first, and the third smaller than the second.
> That, he said, is an easier task; and I have made them as you say.
> And now join them, and let the three go into one.
> That has been accomplished.
> Next fashion the outside of them into a single image, as of a man, so that he who is not able to look within, and sees only the outer hull, may believe the beast to be a single human creature.

---

[31] Jackson, *The Lion Becomes Man: The Gnostic Leontomorphic Creator and the Platonic Tradition* (SBLDS 81; Atlanta: Scholars Press, 1985) 175.

Socrates goes on to describe the battle for dominance that is waged within the human soul. The many-headed monster represents the appetitive part of the soul which is a lover of gain, the lion represents the ambitious and pugnacious part of the soul which is a lover of honor and the man represents the learned aspect of the soul which is a lover of wisdom. Jackson argues, "The interest that Socrates' parable had for Gnosticism was not, however, primarily mythological; it was anthropological, for this passage from the *Republic*, along with others in Plato, was the ultimate and principal source of the Gnostic tradition making beasts into the symbols of passion and theriomorphic planetary powers the donors of passionate soul to the human amalgam."[32]

Another, more "orthodox" source, which also takes up the idea of the archons (demons) as beasts and which also links these demons to passions is Athanasius, *The Life of Saint Anthony*. Although written ca. A.D. 357, this account of the "Father of Monasticism" reflects elements current in Egypt during the lifetime of Anthony (ca. A.D. 250–356).[33] Using the term demons in the more traditional NT sense, the text depicts these powers as hostile animals:

> Well, the role of the evildoer is easy for the Devil. That night, therefore, they made such a din that the whole place seemed to be

---

[32] Ibid., 186–87. Clement of Alexandria provides further verification of this tendency to view the passions as beasts. He quotes a Basilidean source which, like Plato, links the passions to the soul — although for this source the passions are appendages "attached to the rational soul" and not necessarily part of the soul itself: "The adherents of Basilides are in the habit of calling the passions appendages: saying that these are in essence certain spirits attached to the rational soul, through some original perturbation and confusion; and that, again, other bastard and heterogeneous natures of spirits grow on to them, like that of the wolf, the ape, the lion, the goat, whose properties showing themselves around the soul, they say, assimilate the lusts of the soul to the likeness of the animals. For they imitate the actions of those whose properties they bear" (*Stromata* 2.20). Cf. Irenaeus, *Adv. haer.* 1.5.4.

[33] Robert T. Meyer, trans., *St. Athanasius: The Life of Saint Anthony* (ACW 10; Westminster, MD: Newman, 1950) 3–15.

shaken by an earthquake. It was as though demons were breaking through the four walls of the little chamber and bursting through them in the forms of beasts and reptiles. All at once the place was filled with the phantoms of lions, bears, leopards, bulls, and of serpents, asps, and scorpions, and of wolves; and each moved according to the shape it assumed. The lion roared, ready to spring upon him, the bull appeared about to gore him through, the serpent writhed without quite reaching him, the wolf was rushing straight at him; and the noises emitted simultaneously by all the apparitions were frightful and the fury shown was fierce." (chap. 9)[34]

Similar to the Gnostic sources mentioned above, the demons [archons] are associated with passions. In this case the attacks of the demons are directly connected with the arousal of manifold passions and emotions (chap. 36).

These considerations force me to acknowledge that the exact meaning of the mysterious beasts in *ActsPet12Apost.* may have a variety of levels and that these connotations may differ depending on which level of composition we are discussing. In short, the meaning these animals may have had for the author of the Story of the Pearl Merchant may not be the same for the redactor. In my final chapter I will propose a possible "new" significance that these animals might have for the redactor but for now I will concern myself with their sense for the author of the Story of the Pearl Merchant.

Understanding the animals as archons or demonic forces demands that we respect the power of mythological conceptions to be accepted as real. Before we can go the route of Wink or Jackson it is absolutely

---

[34] Cf. chapters 23 and 51. In light of the fact that both *Life of Saint Anthony* and *ActsPet12Apost.* 6.1–9 both refer to bulls, lions and wolves, it is interesting to note that chapter 36 calls the demons "robbers," a term used in *ActsPet12Apost.* 5.26, 33 and 7.26. Furthermore, just as Peter is advised by Lithargoel to forsake everything and fast daily from stage to stage (5.23–25), the reader of *Life of Saint Anthony* is told that the demons are "promptly thwarted" by "prayers and fastings and confidence in the Lord" (chap 23) for "indeed they [the demons] dread ascetics for their fasting, their vigils, their prayers" (chap. 30).

necessary to recognize that for many people, in antiquity as well as today, such mythological beings as archons/ demons do not suggest underlying spiritualities or refer to anthropological conditions. Rather, these entities simply are what they appear to be — malevolent creatures who hate humanity and seek every opportunity to bring about our destruction. One has only to set foot in virtually any evangelical Christian church to hear sermons that discuss this very "reality." For a great number of modern Christians this is the only meaning for such creatures. We have only to read the NT to realize that such a conception was also prevalent in the early Church. (The same holds true for the story of Adam and Eve as our original parents. Many modern Christians accept this as a historical fact without hesitation despite the frightening genetic repercussions of such an occurrence.) This is not to discount or refute the findings of Wink and Jackson but only to point out that they may well represent the views of the intellectual elite and not the ordinary Christian of antiquity (or, for that matter, today).

In light of these thoughts, it remains to examine the Story of the Pearl Merchant and determine which interpretation best fits the conceptual framework suggested by the allegory: 1) beasts as malignant archons/ demons (concretized myth) or 2) beasts = archons = passions (theoretical myth). To begin it is crucial to highlight the main spacial locations suggested by the Story of the Pearl Merchant: 1) Habitation = the earth; 2) Nine Gates = heaven/ the pleroma and 3) the "road to the city" (5.19) = a passage through an intermediate area that separates the two cities. The animals of the Story of the Pearl Merchant are neither occupants of Habitation, nor are they attached in some way to the individual traveler — as if they were within the soul (i.e., demonic possession). The threat of the animals is exterior not interior, the animals prey on possessions not the person (or the person's soul). In short, the traveler's death is almost incidental to the desires of the animals. The traveler's act of holding on to worldly possessions leads to his or her own death.

The animals are described as populating the "road" to Nine Gates. In the spacial (allegorical) universe created by the Story of the Pearl

Merchant the animals are those beings that inhabit the intermediate zone. Peter's lack of awareness of the animals's existence is evidence that they do not kill or eat in Habitation. Further, it is directly stated that the traveler is safe or "at rest" in Nine Gates (8.4–11). The danger zone is only along the way to Nine Gates. These considerations lead me to believe that the best way to understand the animals, at least as they were understood by the author of the Story of the Pearl Merchant, is as concrete beings that are hostile to the faithful Christian, i.e., archons/ demons.

Since *ActsPet12Apost.* assumes the presence of hostile forces in the intermediate regions separating the world from the Pleroma, it must also present some method of travel through these realms. It is really these two aspects, the suggestion of the possibility of journeying to heaven and the "how" of going about it, that are the key elements of the *narratio fabulosa*. These elements are no longer the simple one-to-one referents of the image (ἐἰκών) such as the undefined port from which the apostles embark, the water surrounding the city, Habitation and Nine Gates. Rather, these elements of the *narratio fabulosa* make all further revelatory information possible.

In *ActsPet12Apost.* the "how" of the journey is presented as renunciation of the world coupled with daily fasting (5.21–25). Renunciation of the world is familiar to both the NT,[35] the Nag Hammadi corpus[36] and to the Greco-Roman world in general.[37] However, there are

---

[35] E.g., Matt 19:21, 28–29; Mark 10:29–31.

[36] *Apocryphon of James* 4.24–28; *Gospel of the Egyptians* 63.17; *Dialogue of the Savior* 141.3–11; *2 Apocalypse of James* 63.21–22; *Apocalypse of Peter* 76.4–5; *Testimony of Truth* 69.23–24.

[37] There are many fine works available on asceticism in Greco-Roman antiquity. However, most of them deal with this issue from a primarily Christian standpoint, e.g., Peter Brown, *The Body and Society: Men, Women, and Sexual Renunciation in Early Christianity* (Lectures on the History of Religions 13; New York: Columbia University Press, 1988); Gilles Quispel, "The Study of Encratism: A Historical Survey," in Ugo Bianchi, ed., *La Tradizione Dell'Enkrateia: Motivazioni Ontologiche e Protologiche* (Rome: Dell'Ateneo, 1985) 35–81; and Vincent L. Wimbush, ed., *Ascetic Behavior in Greco-Roman Antiquity: A*

two important gnostic texts that link renunciation of the world to safe passage through hostile realms as I have proposed is suggested by our text.

The first example is found, once again, in *PS* 3.102. In this text Jesus instructs his disciples as to the content of their preaching to those in the world. He begins by urging his disciples, "Say unto them: Renounce the whole world and the whole matter therein and all its cares and all its sins, in a word all its associations which are in it, that you may be worthy of the mysteries of the Light and be saved from all the chastisements which are in the judgments." Following this statement are thirty-three warnings to be directed to the disciples's audience. They all are similar in form beginning with the phrase, "Say unto them," and followed by a command to renounce a particular sinful action so as to be "worthy of the mysteries of the Light" and to be saved from X. The X referred to is, in most cases, an animal-faced archon or its method of torture. The following is an example: "Say unto them: Renounce false witness, that you may be worthy of the mysteries of the Light and that you may escape and be saved from the fire-rivers of the dog-faced one." This pattern is somewhat different from that found in *ActsPet12Apost.* in that its focus is upon renunciation of worldly *actions* (moral conduct) rather than worldly *possessions*. However, the similarity remains in that renunciation of the world is linked to safe passage through the hostile realms populated by animal-like creatures.

Another, perhaps more similar, example is found in *Auth. Teach.* In 26.20–27.21, there is a passage that not only links renunciation of the world to safe passage through the hostile realms but also stresses the importance of fasting to this endeavor:

Sourcebook (Studies in Antiquity & Christianity; Minneapolis: Fortress, 1990). Thankfully, the recent work of James A. Francis is a notable exception to this trend (*Subversive Virtue: Asceticism and Authority in the Second-Century Pagan World* [University Park, PA: Pennsylvania State University Press, 1995]).

And as for those who contend with us, being adversaries who contend against us, we are to be victorious over their ignorance through our knowledge, since we have already known the Inscrutable One from whom we have come forth. *We have nothing in this world, lest the authority of the world that has come into being should detain us in the worlds that are in the heavens, those in which universal death exists,* (ЄMMN̄TАN ΛААΥ ҆M ΠЄ҆КОСМОС· МНΠШС N̄TЄ TЄ҅ОΥСІА M̄ΠКОСМОС ЄNTАСШШΠЄ N̄СP̄КАTЄХЄ M̄MОN ҆N N̄КОСМОС ЄT҆N̄ M̄ΠНΥЄ· NА҆ ЄTЄ ΠMОΥ N̄КАѲОΛІКОN ШООΠ ҆PА҆ N̄҆НTОΥ·) surrounded by the individual [...] worldly. We have also become ashamed of the worlds, though we take no interest in them when they malign us. And we ignore them when they curse us. When they cast shame in our face, we look at them and do not speak. For they work at their business, but *we go about in hunger and thirst, looking toward our dwelling place, the place which our conduct and our conscience look toward, not clinging to the things which have come into being, but withdrawing from them* (АNОN ΔЄ ЄNMООΥШЄ ҆А Π҆КО ҆А ΠІВЄ· ЄN҆АШT ЄВОΛ ҆НT҅ M̄ΠЄNMА N̄ШШΠЄ· ΠMА ЄTЄ TN̄ΠОΛЄІTЄІА MN̄ TN̄СΥNЄІΔНСІС ҆АШT ЄВОΛ ҆НT҅ ЄNTШ҆Є M̄MОN АN Є҆ОΥN ЄNЄNTАΥШШΠЄ· АΛΛА ЄNСІ҆Є M̄MОN M̄MООΥ·).

This idea of renunciation of the world's temptations as an integral part of the soul's ascent is strong in *Auth. Teach.* In fact, *Auth. Teach.* 26.8–20, explains that continence was a vital part of the Father's will from the very beginning:

He, then, the Father, wishing to reveal his [wealth] and his glory, brought about this great contest in this world, *wishing to make the contestants appear, and make all those who contend leave behind the things that had come into being* (Є҅ОΥШШЄ ЄTPЄNΔ̄ГШNІСTНС ОΥШN҆ ЄВОΛ·

N̄TENETⲰϢⲬΕ   THⲢOY   N̄CEKⲰ   N̄CⲰOY
N̄NENTⲀYⲰϢⲠE·), and despise them with a lofty,
incomprehensible knowledge, and to flee to the one who exists.

Once again, we are instructed that one must "leave behind" the things of
this world so as to be capable of reaching "the one who exists,"
representing much the same idea as is contained in the instructions of
Lithargoel.

However, this material has more in common with *ActsPet12Apost.*
than just an understanding that one must separate oneself from the world
to be able to make the journey to the heavenly realm. Both texts also
recognize that the journey is threatened by hostile forces that seek to kill
the traveler. In *Auth. Teach.* 26.8–20, the idea is straightforward enough
and the language used has a violence about it that is far from subtle. The
"great contest" (NOϭ N̄ⲀⲦⲰN) and "contestants" (NⲀⲦⲰNⲒCTHC)
are Greek loanwords — terms often used to refer to the arena and its
bloody entertainers, the gladiators. It is a peculiar image. The Father is
here compared with a wealthy citizen who, in an attempt to demonstrate
his social status, puts on a gladiatorial or boxing show for the populace —
fine if one is merely a spectator but another story entirely if one a
participant! Yet, with this image a new light is shown on the role of
renunciation of the world. Like the ⲀⲦⲰNⲒCTHC in the arena, the soul
must train and prepare (i.e., practice a regimen of asceticism) for the
contest so as to give glory (EOOY; 26.10) to the Father.[38] In this image,
when specific enemies are mentioned only a few lines later (26.20–32) the
terms used clearly indicate that the adversaries pose a deadly opposition
to the soul (see the text cited above).

We must not make the mistake of imagining that the author uses this
image of the gladiators casually, as if simply waxing poetic about the
violent intentions of the enemy. Later, in *Auth. Teach.* 29.21–31.24a, the
deadly seriousness with which the author speaks of the role of

---

[38] Cf. *Mart. of Perpetua and Felicitas* 10.

renunciation of the world is driven home by the allegory of the
fisherman.[39] (The initial part of this material was presented earlier in my
argument , i.e., the description of man-eating enemies of the soul who lie
in wait with their dragnet). This allegory of the soul (the fish) and the
fisherman (the spiritual adversaries) is drawn out with an almost
diabolical delight on the part of the author who describes how the
fisherman uses many different kinds of bait — each aimed at catching a
particular type of fish. The various baits are then plainly interpreted for
the reader as representing the desires of this world:

> In this very way we exist in this world like fish. The adversary
> spies on us, lying in wait for us like a fisherman, wishing to seize
> us, rejoicing that he might swallow us. For [he places] many foods
> before our eyes, (things) which belong to this world. He wishes to
> make us desire one of them and to taste only a little, so that he may
> seize us with his hidden poison and bring us out of freedom and
> take us into slavery. For whenever he catches us with a single
> food, it is indeed necessary for <us> to desire the rest. Finally,
> then, such things become the food of death. Now these are the
> foods with which the devil lies in wait for us. First he injects a
> pain into your heart until you have a heartache on account of a
> small thing of this life, and he seizes <you> with his poisons. And
> afterwards (he injects) the desire of a tunic so that you will pride
> yourself in it, and love of money, pride, vanity, envy that rivals
> another envy, beauty of body, fraudulence. The greatest of all
> these are ignorance and ease. Now all such things the adversary
> prepares beautifully and spreads out before the body, wishing to
> make the mind of the soul incline her toward one of them and
> overwhelm her, like a hook drawing her in by force in ignorance,

---

[39] Roelof Van den Broek discusses the background of this allegory of the
fisherman and suggests that it has Platonic roots ("The Authentikos Logos: A New
Document of Christian Platonism," *VC* 33 [1979] 266–69). Cf. this with the
position of George W. MacRae who suggests that it is a unique metaphor ("A Nag
Hammadi Tractate on the Soul," in C.J. Bleeker, ed., *Ex orbe religionum: Studia
Geo Widengren oblata* [Supplements to Numen 21; 2 vols.; Leiden: Brill, 1972]
1.473–75).

deceiving her until she conceives evil and bears fruit of matter and conducts herself in uncleanness, pursuing many desires, covetousnesses, while fleshly pleasure draws her in ignorance. (30.4b–31.24a)[40]

Thus we learn that renunciation of the world is really a matter of spiritual life or death — just as the gladiator's combat training gives him or her a better chance at survival. It makes it possible for the soul to breech the hostile ranks of the adversary so as to return to the Father, escape the fisherman's nets and, in the case of *ActsPet12Apost.*, successfully make the trip to Nine Gates. There is further similarity between these thoughts and those found in *ActsPet12Apost.*, particularly in regard to the importance of fasting. In *ActsPet12Apost.* 5.19–6.8, renunciation of the world and fasting prevent the traveler from being killed or eaten by the hostile forces. Likewise, in *Auth. Teach.* renunciation of the world helps the traveler avoid being detained in the region of death, i.e., being killed. Also, fasting is a way of letting go of the things of the world so as draw near to the ultimate "dwelling place."

This comparative study of the underlying gnostic structure of *ActsPet12Apost.* is concluded. The "perceived real-world realities or constructions of mythic reality" that are the referents of the text have become more clear. The underlying mythical structure which drives and informs the *homoeosis*/ image (ἐἰκών) involves a pre-existent Savior and disciples that come down to Earth on a salvific mission. It involves an intermediate realm populated by hostile forces that separates this world from the Pleroma. It also assumes the existence of three separate classes of people: material, psychic and spiritual. These aspects of the image, with their one-to-one relationships between story and "reality," illustrate how story components can be used to refer beyond themselves to

---

[40] For further commentary on this passage and a fine array of comparison texts see Jacques É. Ménard, *L'Authentikos Logos* (Bibliothèque Copte de Nag Hammadi Section Textes 1; Quebec: Les Presses de l'Université Laval, 1977) 53–57.

perceived real-world realities or constructions of mythic reality. This aspect of *homoeosis* forms the foundation of the Story of the Pearl Merchant.

The second formal aspect of the Story of the Pearl Merchant, the *narratio fabulosa*, is related to the *homoeosis* aspect as a building is related to its foundation. The proposed journey (Lithargoel's invitation to Nine Gates) and, most importantly, its "how" (renunciation of the world and daily fasting) could not make sense without the "reality" created by the *homoeosis*.

Chapter 4
A Theory of Composition

In the following pages I shall re-open the discussion of the three constituent parts of *ActsPet12Apost.* and attempt to separate the redactional material from the previous tradition. As the reader will recall, I have already identified three primary divisions in the text:

1) *The Story of the Pearl Merchant* (1.1 to 9.1, except for redactional additions): A first-person narrative, parable-like or allegorical in nature, involving a mysterious pearl merchant and two symbolic cities. A mystical journey must be undertaken to one of these cities so as to attain "the pearl," which is most likely salvation of the soul (i.e., heaven, oneness with God). There was probably a return from the heavenly city so as to pass on the knowledge of how to make the journey and any other knowledge that might have been revealed at "Nine Gates."

2) *A Resurrection Appearance* (9.1 to 9.29): This is told from the perspective of one of the followers of Jesus, but not Peter. It is written in the first person yet employs third person within its overall structure. It is possibly docetic or gnostic in tone and its reference to the "eleven disciples" associates it with a post-crucifixion period and with the traditions such as those recorded in the canonical gospels.

3) *The Author/Redactor's Theology* (9.30–12.19): A third person narration, didactic or hortatory in tone, that attempts to echo themes from the pearl merchant source. It shifts the emphasis of the first source from a heavenly hereafter to an earthly or pastoral focus.

THE AUTHOR/ REDACTOR'S THEOLOGY
Before considering in detail the complexion of the two sources used by the redactor it is necessary to discuss the actual process of redaction insofar as it can be reconstructed from textual clues. First, the redactor took over the Story of the Pearl Merchant. This story, as a *narratio*

fabulosa, included a journey to the heavenly sphere and explanations of both the journey process and other important details about how earthly conduct affects heavenly existence. The redactor next eliminated the heavenly explanation (and most of whatever material referred to Nine Gates) and replaced it with revelation dialogue material which reflected his or her own concerns.[1] However, there was still a "loose end," i.e., the

---

[1] It is important at this juncture to clarify the main differences in emphasis between the original *narratio fabulosa* (the Story of the Pearl Merchant) and the redactor's material. The Story of the Pearl merchant, like the other *narratio fabulosae* we have examined, turned on the axis of successful completion of the soul's journey to the heavenly realm. Like other pieces of literature of its genre it offered heavenly instruction (in this case, at the very gates of Nine Gates) which was intended to suggest earthly conduct that would secure a successful passage. However, in the case of the Story of the Pearl Merchant, this information is already made available to the travelers in the form of Lithargoel's instructions concerning the treacherous road to Nine Gates. In short, Lithargoel, a heavenly guide, comes to earth to make his revelation known, thus, apparently circumventing the usual purpose for the initial heavenly journey. Therefore it seems unlikely that the dialogue and instruction that took place at nine gates in the original story was concerned with the "how to" of making the journey. Its emphasis lay elsewhere. While we may never know the exact nature of its contents, the very fact that the redactor used a portion of this story in his or her new creation suggests that he or she did not find it terribly offensive. It is likely, based on our observation of other *narratio fabulosae*, that the events at Nine Gates involved some kind of tour of the city with an accompanying explanation of the universe's structure (both moral and geographical). Regardless of the exact material that the redactor left out, a change was made. Again, by re-examining the focus of the Author/ Redactor's Theology we are given a clue as to why the material was left out. The most basic of readings reveals that the redactor was nothing if not highly practical (pastoral) in his or her concerns, focusing in on issues of ministry, church membership and the quality of ecclesiastical leadership. Based on our knowledge of other *narratio fabulosae*/ heavenly journeys we can imagine that the original Story of the Pearl merchant was very speculative in tone — including description and discussion of things such as 1) various fantastic heavenly creatures; 2) the heavenly throne room; 3) the blissful lifestyle of the "saved"; and 4) a glimpse of the sufferings of the damned. While these things make for good literature and were probably not too different from the material found in other such literature of the day, they served little practical (pastoral) purpose. Thus, the redactor replaced them with something more pastorally efficient which would help address the needs of the moment.

matter of identifying or explaining the pearl. Therefore the redactor, seeking to alter the meaning of the pearl from what was found in the Story of the Pearl Merchant (i.e., from salvation in the Story of the Pearl Merchant to the "name of Jesus"), inserted the name Lithargoel so as to associate the pearl with Jesus. Third, the redactor, familiar with the form and function of the revelation dialogue, used an originally separate resurrection appearance source to introduce his or her new revelation. However, the redactional "seam" between the first and second sources was not left without trace. Not only did the redactor edit out a body of text of undeterminable size between 8.20 and 8.21 (cf. my previous comments on the use of ⲞⲨⲰⲰⲂⲈ), he or she also complicated the desired association between Lithargoel and Jesus by inserting physician material into the Story of the Pearl Merchant. This physician material (as well as the name Lithargoel) was of course absent from the resurrection appearance source. The redactor's seam is once again visible in the resurrection appearance material, since the figure in the second source is first called "the Savior" (9.5) and then "Jesus Christ" (9.11) but not "physician" or Lithargoel.

In summary, the redactor attempted to insert two new concepts which betray his or her theological agenda into the Story of the Pearl Merchant: 1) a reinterpretation of the pearl, and 2) the physician material. The second concept was of considerably more importance to the redactor, to judge from the space that was committed to each: the insertion of the name Lithargoel and its interpretation occupy 10.22–30, whereas the physician material comprises 8.15–9, 34; 9.30–32; 10.31–11.26. This discrepancy in the amount of material committed to each concept may also be connected with the novelty or difficulty of each in the redactor's circle. Hence I shall seek to show that the redactor's interpretation of the pearl was known in various Christian circles, while the physician material and its assertion that Church ministers be physicians both of bodies and souls was decidedly more contentious.[2]

Now that I have briefly reviewed the redactor's work in constructing *ActsPet12Apost.*, I shall turn to an examination of the redactor's material found in 9.30–12.19, lines that are crucial for understanding his or her theology. In this section, the redactor betrays several main theological interests and several adaptions or refinements of concepts presented in the two major sources, principally 1) Jesus' healing ministry and its continuing reality in the Church in general and 2) the identity of the "pearl." Both of these are deeply rooted in the Pearl Merchant = Lithargoel = physician = Jesus identity equation, and are difficult to deal with separately. Other adaptions or refinements of concepts in the Story of the Pearl Merchant source include 1) the roles and relationships of the rich and poor in regard to the disciples and 2) the conception of asceticism and ascetical demands made by the text.

THE CONNECTION OF THE PEARL MERCHANT, LITHARGOEL, THE PHYSICIAN AND JESUS: HEALING AND THE CHURCH

A major indication of the redactor's theological interests is the relationship between the Pearl Merchant and the character of Lithargoel. In Patterson's view the pearl merchant episode was inserted as a whole into what he has called the "I, Peter Source":

> First, in the I, Peter Source the action at Habitation would have
> been dominated by the exchange between Peter and Lithargoel.
> Lithargoel would have been essentially a mystagogue in the I,
> Peter Source, concerned with providing Peter and the Disciples
> with the ascetic regime which would prepare them for the ascent
> to the heavenly city. But with the insertion of the story of the pearl
> merchant, the character of Lithargoel is changed. His main
> concern is no longer with Peter, who slips to the sidelines to

---

[2] A detailed consideration of the physicians of bodies/ souls material appears in the final chapter.

narrate the action as a spectator, but with the poor, to whom he offers the pearls — perhaps a symbol of soteriological significance — free of charge. No longer simply an angelic mystagogue, Lithargoel has become a Christ figure, whose primary concern is the request of the poor.[3]

While Patterson may be right in thinking that the Pearl Merchant and Lithargoel were originally two separate figures, I must disagree with his conclusions regarding the exact relationship of these characters to the text. Patterson views the character of the Pearl Merchant as having been inserted into the text and the character of Lithargoel to be original; however, just the opposite may be the case.

The translation of Lithargoel is significant. It derives from two Greek words (λίθος - stone; ἀργός - shining, bright) and the Semitic appellative of deity 'el. Presumably rendered "the shining stone of God," this would seem to be implying that the Pearl Merchant is the "pearl of God," a possible reference to the parable of the pearl in Matt 15:46.[4] According to Schenke, Lithargoel is an angelic physician.[5] However, in

---

[3] Patterson, "Sources, Redaction and Tendenz," 14.

[4] Krause uses the same etymology to arrive at the name "God of the Pearl" ("Die Petrusakten," 51).

[5] Schenke ("Die Taten des Petrus," 14) quotes two sources from antiquity where a name resembling Lithargoel can be found. The first is literary: the *Book of the Installation of the Archangel Gabriel*. This document, vaguely dated as before the seventh century by Detlef Müller, exists in only one recension, a Sahidic manuscript. Müller locates the place of origin as Egypt (*Die Bücher der Einsetzung der Erzengel Michael und Gabriel* [CSCO 226, Scriptores Coptici 32; Louvain: CSCO, 1962] iv–v). In 86.23–25, Litharkuel, along with four other angelic rulers, appears before Jesus and the apostles. The key section reads as follows: "The fifth angel answered: I am Litharkuel, in whose hand the medical bag is, filled with the medicine of life — I heal every soul." The second reference is a fresco and dedicatory inscription in the cathedral of Faras in Nubia. The inscription accompanying the damaged picture reads, "Lord Jesus Christ [and] Litaxkuel, guard, bless, protect, confirm and stand by thy servant Martere, daughter of Isusinta. So be it. Amen" ("The Acts of Peter and the Twelve Apostles," 419). While the first instance is related to the character presented in

ActsPet12Apost. the question as to who Lithargoel is and how he is related to the Pearl Merchant may be more complicated then has previously been supposed. The problem is related to identity. The Pearl Merchant is first identified in 5.15–18 as Lithargoel in response to a request by Peter for the merchant's name.

With this connection established, the text proceeds to associate Lithargoel with medicine, presenting him as disguised in a physician's dress (8.15–19). However, when the physician reveals himself in the resurrection appearance material, he reveals himself not as Lithargoel but as "Jesus Christ, the son of the living God" (9.11–12). We are led to believe that "the physician" is Jesus.

There are various problems with the connection Lithargoel = physician = Jesus. Certainly there are problems with redactional seams in 8.11–9.1. Krause notes that there are contradictions in the narrative:

> In the first narrative only Peter spoke with Lithargoel. The disciples remained in the harbor (2.7–8) and Peter started out twice to call his companions. In the second narrative it is presupposed that all the apostles took part in the conversation and that they know Lithargoel, since 8.20 says: "...we (the apostles) did not recognize him (Lithargoel as the doctor)."[6]

---

our text (a healer figure with medical bag and the connection with healing souls) and may represent a later use of the Lithargoel tradition, the second offers little more than an angelic guardian figure with a similar name.

[6] Krause, "Die Petrusakten," 49. Parrott also finds problems with the Lithargoel = physician = Jesus connection. Besides reiterating Krause's arguments, he makes two additional points that suggest the physician material is secondary:

1) It (the physician material) compromises the identification of Lithargoel with Jesus, which is most important for the narrative. The physician is the intermediate figure between the two, but within the narrative itself the physician is never recognized as Lithargoel but only as Christ by Peter and the disciples. To be sure, Peter, as narrator, makes the identification of Lithargoel with the physician, but we do not know how, since the text says explicitly, "We did not recognize him" (the physician as Lithargoel) (8.20). Only in 10.12–3 do the words of the Lord himself make clear the connection, and these are not said

In addition to the observations of Krause, Parrott, Patterson and Schenke, there are other difficulties with 8.11b–9.1. There is the enigmatic use of OYⲰⲰ⳰ⲂⲈ which indicates missing material between 8.20 and 8.21. In addition, 8.11 is problematic. In 8.10–11a, the disciples are presented as contemplating the faith and talking about the things of God. Then in 8.11b, they are suddenly discussing the robbers. This may indicate a redactional seam. Certainly, one aspect of the physician material is particularly confusing. I refer to the peculiar presence of a physician in Nine Gates (i.e., Heaven). In 8.33–35, the text portrays this heavenly physician as actually practicing his craft ("Rest yourselves a little so that I may go and heal this man and come back"; M̄TON M̄MⲰTN̄ N̄OYKOYEI N̄TⲀBⲰK N̄TⲀP̄ ⲠⲀ⳰ⲢⲈ ⲈⲠⲈⲓⲢⲰⲘⲈ N̄TⲀⲈⲓ). I find this striking in that it implies that sickness and infirmity (things strongly associated with the physical body) continue to exist — even in Nine Gates! This is the same place that is described in glowing terms in 8.4–11 ("A great joy [came upon] us [and a] peaceful carefreeness [like that of] our Lord. We [rested ourselves] in front of the gate [and] we talked with each other [about that] which is not a distraction of this [world]. Rather we continued in contemplation of the faith"). Usually, Heaven and its mythic counterparts are conceived as places free from physical suffering (e.g., Virgil, *Aeneid* 6; Lazarus's place of comfort from his sores, Luke 16:19–25; Revelation 21:1–5 and the restoration described for Perpetua's brother, Dinocrates; *Mart. Perpetua and Felcitas* 7–8) and physical pain in the afterlife is associated with

---

in such a way as to make the reader think that something new is being revealed to the disciples. If the physician material is removed, the identification problem disappears.

2) There is no reason within the narrative why Lithargoel, who is already a disguised figure, should appear in a second disguise to the disciples (*Nag Hammadi Codices*, 201).

Patterson comes to similar conclusions. He describes the physician material as "the work of the redactor" ("Sources, Redaction and Tendenz," 13–14). See also Schenke, "The Acts of Peter and the Twelve Apostles," 418–19.

suffering (e.g., the vision of Er). Surely this instance of an active physician in Nine Gates (heaven) reflects the hand of the redactor who, in his or her zeal to emphasize Jesus' role as physician, took it one step too far — not considering the narrative surroundings of his or her "physician." For these reasons I am persuaded , like Krause, Parrott, Patterson and Schenke, to consider the physician material as reflecting the hand of the redactor.

Whether or not one views the physician material as secondary, questions remain as to the connections between the Pearl Merchant = Lithargoel = physician = Jesus. I offer the following explanatory theory:

The redactor had the story of Peter and the Pearl Merchant (Jesus incognito) before him and decided to alter the story's object (the identity of the pearl). (Let us remember that in the initial part of the Story of the Pearl Merchant, the merchant is trying to give away the pearl as something separate and exterior to himself. One must go to the merchant's city to collect one's free pearl — not correctly recognize the identity of the merchant!) The redactor chose to make Jesus, or more specifically Jesus' name, the pearl. Thus, the redactor constructed the name "Lithargoel" from his or her imagination (a suggestion that Jesus himself is "the pearl of God"),[7] added it to the Story of the Pearl Merchant and proceeded to interpret the pearl of the Story of the Pearl Merchant as referring to the mystical power of Jesus' name (10.23–30). I am suggesting that in the original Story of the Pearl Merchant there was no request by Peter for the merchant's name. I regard both the words in 5.9 that make this request and the response in 5.15b–20a, "If you seek my name...and also..." as from the hand of the redactor.

However, because of the interest of the redactor in healing (bodies and souls), the redactor also consciously attempted to link Lithargoel with physician material. Not only is Lithargoel presented in the disguise of a

---

[7] Parrott suggests this idea: "it seems more reasonable to think that the identification of Lithargoel with Jesus Christ (9.8–15) was the intention when the word was first coined" (*Nag Hammadi Codices*, 200–201; see also "The Acts of Peter and the Twelve Apostles," *ABD* 5.265).

physician (8.15–19); the redactor may have inserted medical allusions into the initial description of the Pearl Merchant to strengthen this association. I am referring to 2.26–29, which is part of 2.17b–29, the rather peculiar second description of the merchant: "A book cover like those of my own books was in his left hand. A staff of styrax wood was in his right hand." The mention of the "staff of styrax wood" may have medical significance in that storax, the resin from the styrax tree (*styrax officinalis*, found in Asia Minor and Palestine among other locations) was used in perfume, incense and medicine.[8] Furthermore, the staff itself may be significant in its similarity to the staff typically pictured with Ascelpius whose symbols of the staff and entwined serpent remain as a symbols for medicine to this day.[9]

---

[8] Theophratus, ca. 300 B. C., mentions its use as a perfume (*Enquiry into Plants* 9.7.3). More importantly for our purposes, Dioscorides Pedanius, a 1st century A. D. Roman army physician from Anazarbus, describes its medical uses in *De materia medica* 1.68, "It is useful for coughs, for inflammation of the mucous membranes [of the nose and throat], hoarseness, heaviness in the head, for difficulties breathing and for a lost voice. It is proper for the stopping and hardening of the places natural to women and applied or taken in a drink it induces coughing." For further details on the lives of Theophrastus and Dioscorides see N. G. L. Hammond and H. H. Scullard, *The Oxford Classical Dictionary* (2d ed.; Oxford: Clarendon, 1970) 353–54, 1058–59. For more on *Styrax officinalis* see Harold N. and Alma I. Moldenke, *Plants of the Bible* (Plant Science Books 28; Waltham, MA: Chronica Botanica, 1952) 224–25.

[9] "The staff, particularly the long one which reached up to the armpit, was the walking stick which people used when on a journey. Asclepius, the physician, had to do extensive traveling, not only while he was a human being, but also later when he had become a god.... He wandered all over the earth to help everybody everywhere. The staff, therefore, may have at first been the natural attribute of the traveling physician, and with this significance it may have been retained on images of the gods even in late centuries" (Edelstein and Edelstein, *Asclepius*, 229). For example, Eusebius writes, "Of the safeguarding power (of the sun) a symbol is Asclepius to whom they attribute a staff, as a sign of support and relief for invalids; the serpent is twined about it, being the sign of preservation of body and soul" (*Praeparatio evangelica*, 3.11.26).

If the redactor did attempt to connect Lithargoel with the physician, what was his or her purpose?[10] First, as I have already suggested, the character of Lithargoel was an entity created by the redactor to strengthen the connection between Jesus and the "pearl." This was a deliberate reinterpretation of the "identity" of the pearl which was indigenous to the Story of the Pearl Merchant. Second, the redactor is not really interested in linking Lithargoel and the physician material. With the connection between Lithargoel/ Jesus and the pearl established, the redactor then intended to proceed to his or her revelation discourse material, which included important instructions on the disciples's role as "physicians of bodies and souls."

To make the transition from one issue (Jesus as pearl) to the next (Jesus as model physician for a new cadre of physical/ spiritual physicians) the redactor inserted the physician material. However, this process of redaction has left noticeable seams. First, Lithargoel appears (in disguise) as a physician in 8.11–15. To this point there is no hint that the merchant/ Lithargoel has any medical association (with the exception of the second description of the merchant in 2.17b–29, i.e., the mention of the staff of styrax wood). However, the redactor slipped up in that he

---

[10] Parrott suggests a link between the concern for healing and the challenge presented to Christianity by the cult of Asclepius: "The intent of this physician material may be to identify Christ and Asclepius. The identification of Asclepius with other gods of healing was not at all uncommon, and probably symbolized the belief in the ultimate unity of all healing power. An alternative explanation is that this material was added to convince believers that since Christ himself is a physician they do not need Asclepius" (*Nag Hammadi Codices*, 201–2). Another possible solution is that there existed a separate angelic-healer entity called Litharkuel (possibly a Jewish healing figure) that was challenging the healing prowess of Jesus at the time that the redactor put together *ActsPet12Apost.* In an attempt to absorb syncretistically this figure and fuse the figure of Jesus (already known as a healer from the numerous gospel accounts) and Litharkuel, the redactor altered the name of Litharkuel to Lithargoel. The implication would be that any appearance or healing of Litharkuel known from past legend or experience was really the work of Lithargoel ("the Pearl of God"/ Jesus incognito). Thus, Jesus is affirmed to be the source of all healing, both of body and of soul.

or she failed to inform the reader how Peter knew that the physician was Lithargoel, since when the physician reveals himself it is as Jesus, not Lithargoel. Second, the plastic and obviously hastily penned 8.33–35 is nonsensical: "Rest yourselves a little so that I may go and heal this man and come back. He hurried and came back quickly."[11] The specific connection of the name Lithargoel and the physician is not an important connection for the redactor. It happens almost incidentally as the redactor goes about his or her task of addressing pertinent issues. I suggest that for the redactor there are really not three characters: the pearl merchant (Lithargoel), the physician and Jesus. Lithargoel ("pearl of God") is another title for Jesus, no different in the redactor's mind from "the bridegroom" (Matt 9:15) or "the vine" (John 15:1–8). All three characters are one to the redactor, despite their separateness in the sources.

Exactly how the redactor conceptually connected the Pearl Merchant, Lithargoel, the physician and Jesus may never be known, but one thing is certain: the redactor was obviously interested in healing. The disciples are twice presented with the pouch of medicine (9.31; 10.31–32). Then, through the dialogue between the Lord and John, the redactor presents a view of healing that, while not denying the real need for bodily healing ("Heal the bodies first"; ⲀⲢⲒ ⲠⲀϨⲢⲈ ⲞⲨⲚ ⲈⲚⲒⲤⲰⲘⲀ ⲚϢⲞⲢⲠ̄; 11.19–20), sets up a proper priority and understanding of its role in the larger picture ("so that through the real powers of healing for their bodies, without medicine of the world, they may believe in you, that you have power to heal the illness of the heart also;" 11.20–26). The unguent box and pouch of medicine have been transformed from "tools of the physician's trade" into symbols of the disciples's commission to be more

---

[11] As I stated in chapter one, this peculiar section just doesn't make any narrative sense. An important character is described as taking his leave from the main group yet nothing is accomplished in the meantime. Since the author does not have to make Lithargoel depart, in the original source there had to have been some purpose for his departure. However, that purpose has become unclear because of the redactor's elimination of any intervening interaction between the disciples. As they now stand these lines serve no purpose other than to demonstrate Lithargoel at work as a physician.

than worldly physicians ("physicians of this world"; N̄Cⲁⲉ1N N̄Tⲉ
Ⲡ1KOCMOC; 11.16). They are to be physicians who treat both bodies
and souls (11.18).

The text includes a commission for the disciples to become "medics"
of both the body and the soul. This implies a perceived need on the part
of the redactor for medical ministry (albeit subordinated to spiritual
ministry). The redactor also recognizes that the potential ministers's (or
physicians's) lack formal medical training (cf. 11.6–13), yet presses them
into service anyway. This may well suggest extraordinary (and possibly
dire) circumstances.

THE REDACTOR'S REINTERPRETATION OF THE PEARL

> The Lord answered and said, "O Peter, it was necessary that you
> understand the parable that I told you! Do you not understand that
> my name, which you teach, surpasses all riches, and the wisdom of
> God surpasses gold, and silver and precious stones? (10.22–30)

This interpretation of the pearl, while apparently satisfactory to the
redactor, does not easily fit with the pearl as presented in the Story of the
Pearl Merchant. In his introductory article, Krause recognized difficulties
in the interpretation of the pearl in *ActsPet12Apost.* 10.22–30: "The image
of the pearl is found not only in the New Testament, but also in the
apocryphal acts of the apostles, the writings of the gnostics, Manicheans
and Mandeans and this makes an unambiguous interpretation
impossible."[12]

The question of the identity of the pearl is an interesting one. In each
case, the word translated pearl is MⲁⲢⲅⲁⲢ1THC, a direct loanword
from Greek (μαργαρίτης). Despite translations to the contrary in 2.32
and 3.13, the word always appears in the Greek feminine nominative
singular form (e.g., 4.5, 10, 19, 24, 26–27; 5.8). Certainly, it is one,

---

[12] Krause, "Die Petrusakten," 53–54.

singular pearl that is being offered to the people of Habitation, rich and poor alike. It is one thing, capable of being shared by many, but only attained outside of Habitation, in Nine Gates. If the pearl is Lithargoel (as is suggested by 5.15–18) or Jesus' name (ΠⲀⲢⲀⲚ; 10.26) as the redactor would have us believe, it is very peculiar that the merchant stresses the need to make the trip to Nine Gates (specifically, "my city"; ⲦⲀⲠⲞⲖⲓⲤ) in 4.29–34. Obviously, Lithargoel and Jesus' name are things that are attainable in Habitation as is evidenced by Lithargoel's presence and his question to Peter in 6.14–16 ("if, indeed, you know this name 'Jesus' and believe...").[13]

The pearl offered by the merchant can only be seen and obtained by virtue of a journey to Nine Gates (cf. 4.10–15; 30–34). As the reader soon finds out, the trip to Nine Gates is not without effort. The trip makes strict ascetical demands upon the wayfarer (5.19–6.8). Especially in light of the Habitation/ Nine Gates = the Earth/ Heaven (Pleroma) symbolism present in the Story of the Pearl Merchant, it is peculiar to think that the pearl could be something like the name of Jesus/ wisdom of God. In fact, the statement of Lithargoel in 6.14–19 actually conflicts with the redactor's interpretation of the pearl:

> He said to me, "Why do you sigh, if you, indeed, know this name 'Jesus' and believe him? He is a great power for giving strength. For I too believe in the Father who sent him."

From these lines we can see that Lithargoel assumes that Peter already possesses access to the use of Jesus' name. Why should he need to go to

---

[13] However, 10.8–13 seems to nuance the issue further. In 10.26 the pearl is identified as Jesus' name, something to be had while in Habitation. But 10.8–13 assumes that the Poor do not yet have this name (i.e., that the Poor are not, as yet, believers simply by virtue of their social status). For the Poor the pearl is still a reality that is yet to be attained.

Nine Gates to attain it?[14] However, leaving the world is precisely what is required to obtain the pearl.

In attempting to impose his or her interpretation of the role of the pearl the redactor did not merely pen 10.22–30. As suggested above, the redactor also inserted the name Lithargoel ("the pearl of God"; 5.14–18) into the text and then connected this name with the second source (9.8), which, as an appearance text, was ideal for "revealing" the symbolically named Lithargoel as Jesus. It is significant to this thesis that while Peter asks the merchant for his name, it has no significance in the story other than its symbolic meaning. Knowledge of the name Lithargoel is not important later in the text. It does not serve as a password, has no bearing on the journey to Nine Gates or on the story itself. Except for the later redactional connection of Lithargoel (the pearl) with Jesus in the second source (9.8), and the interpretation of Jesus' name as the pearl (10.22–30), the name of Lithargoel could be removed from the Story of the Pearl Merchant without doing any violence to it.

Therefore there are two interpretations of the pearl at work in our text: 1) the pearl in the Story of the Pearl Merchant is something that must be obtained outside of this world (e.g., salvation); and 2) in the Author/ Redactor's Theology, the pearl is the name of Jesus/ wisdom of God. However, as Krause notes, differing interpretations of the identity of the pearl were not uncommon to early Christianity.

Paul-Hubert Poirier, referring to the diversity of understanding present in just Syriac-Christian sources, summarizes the complexity one encounters when considering the varied Christian understandings of the pearl:

> In Syriac Christianity, the symbolism of the pearl is nevertheless greatly exploited: the pearl becomes in turn the symbol of Christ [Aphraate, *Demonstrations* 17.11], the word of God [Aphraate,

---

[14] One would hope that one need not leave this world to attain such a basic component of the Christian faith (e.g., cf. Peter's dramatic usage of the name to work a healing in Acts 3:6).

Demonstrations 22.26], of faith [Ephrem, *Hymns Against the Heresies* 41.2], of virginity [Ephrem, *Hymns on the Epiphany* 6.17; *Hymns on the Nativity* 12.7], and of the Eucharist [Ephrem, *Sermons* 2.4.9–10]. In an Armenian sermon on Matt 13:45–46 attributed to Ephrem, after a development on the origin of the pearl (from a flash of lightning from heaven descending in the water), symbol of virginal birth, one makes of the merchant who researches the pearl, the symbol of Christ in his kenosis: he rids himself of his domain so as to recover the pearl, i.e., to save humanity. The theme of the pearl is also found in Manicheism: the first work of the Living Spirit is in effect to extract from combat the Primordial Man as one extracts a pearl from the sea [*Kephalaia* 32].[15]

Now that some of the difficulties attached to interpreting the meaning of the pearl have been delineated, an examination of other Christian interpretations of the pearl will help shed further light upon this discussion.

The Christian usage of the pearl as a symbol stems primarily from the parable found in Matt 13:45: "Again, the kingdom of Heaven is like a merchant in search of fine pearls, who, on finding one pearl of great value, went and sold all that he had and bought it."[16] While this parable is not accompanied by an interpretation it was interpreted by the Church

---

[15] Poirier, *L'Hymne de la Perle des Actes de Thomas* (Homo Religious 8; Liége: Louvain-la-Neuve, 1981) 418–19. [I have supplied the references Poirier provides for these various points. Poirier also provides ample bibliography on the tradition history of the pearl in mid-eastern and Greco-Roman culture, which further serves to demonstrate the varied usage of the image of the pearl in the ancient world.]

[16] There is another version of this parable in *Gos. Thom.* 76: "Jesus said, 'The kingdom of the father is like a merchant who had a consignment of merchandise and who discovered a pearl. That merchant was shrewd. He sold the merchandise and bought the pearl alone for himself. You too, seek his unfailing and enduring treasure where no moth comes near to devour and no worm destroys.'" Stephen J. Patterson suggests that this parable is earlier than its synoptic counterpart ("Gospel of Thomas," 95).

in at least three ways which may have direct bearing upon its role in *ActsPet12Apost.* The first interpretation is similar to that which I am suggesting was used by the redactor. In this view Jesus is identified as the pearl. For example, Clement of Alexandria, commenting upon Matt 13:45, writes:

> A pearl, and that pellucid and of purest ray, is Jesus, when of the lightning flash of Divinity the Virgin bore. For as the pearl, produced in flesh and the oyster-shell and moisture, appears to be a body moist and transparent, full of light and spirit; so also God the Word, incarnate, is intellectual light, sending His rays, through a body luminous and moist. (*Fragments* 2.5)

Jesus is also called "a pearl" by Peter in a homily delivered to the brethren in the house of Marcellus in *Acts of Peter* 20:

> this Jesus you have, brethren, the door, the light, the way, the bread, the water, the life, the resurrection, the refreshment, the pearl, the treasure, the seed, the abundance, the mustard-seed, the vine, the plough, the grace, the faith, the word: He is all things, and there is no other greater than he.[17]

Likewise, Origen, in his *Commentary on Matthew* 10.7–10, interprets Matt 13:45 by describing Christ as "the one very precious pearl" and "the very costly pearl."[18] These texts seem to be along the same lines as the redactor's interpretation of the pearl as the name of Jesus/ wisdom of God (10.22–30).

---

[17] Jesus is also called "the inexpressible Pearl" in Acts of John 109.

[18] Origen offers yet another interpretation of the pearl, stating that every spiritually mature soul will receive as its "patrimony" the "very costly pearl" which he relates to "the excellency of the knowledge of Christ" (10.9). This is interesting in that it demonstrates that it was possible for a theologian to hold to two separate, even contradictory understandings of the pearl.

The second way that the pearl was interpreted is evidenced in *Gos. Phil.* 62.18–26. This text describes the sons of God as pearls thrown in the mud yet none the less valuable to God:

> When a pearl is cast down into the mud it becomes greatly despised, nor if it is anointed with balsam oil will it become more precious. But it always has value in the eyes of its owner. Compare the sons of God, wherever they may be. They still have value in the eyes of their father.[19]

The third way the pearl was interpreted is demonstrated in The Hymn of the Pearl in *Acts of Thomas* 108–113. Bentley Layton describes this mystical story of a prince sent to retrieve a lost pearl as a "folktale or fairy tale"[20] and interprets this story as follows:

> The first principle of the spiritual realm providentially causes the individual soul to descend past the heavenly bodies into incarnate life in a material body, in order to be educated (get salvation). The soul becomes unconscious and inert because of matter. But it disengages itself in response to the savior or message of philosophy (wisdom). It becomes acquainted with itself and its career and is metaphysically reunited with itself (i.e., becomes integral) and with the first principle, gaining true repose.[21]

---

[19] A similar understanding of people as pearls, held by the Naasseni, is described by Hippolytus, *Ref.* 5.3: "They assert, however, that the living 'are rational faculties and minds, and men — pearls of that unportrayable one cast before the creature below.' This, he says, is what (Jesus) asserts: 'Throw not that which is holy unto the dogs, nor pearls unto the swine.'" In this case the key scriptural text that is referred to is Matt 7:6, rather than Matt 13:45. See also the description of Ptolemy's system in Irenaeus, *Adv. haer.* 1.6.2.

[20] Layton, *Gnostic Scriptures*, 369.

[21] Ibid., 367. Heinz Kruse generally agrees with this evaluation, stating: "In the PH, the acquisition of the Pearl is little more than the human contribution to salvation, the condition for readmission and rehabilitation to the heavenly Kingdom." However, Kruse notes that, "Looking back on the Hymn as a whole, we have to admit that the Parable of the Pearl Merchant (Matt 13:45–46) is only

Thus, the pearl is seen here as salvation. A similarity between both The Hymn of the Pearl and the Story of the Pearl Merchant is that both texts envision a journey as part of the attainment of the pearl. However, the directions in which the journeys are directed seem to be the reverse of each other. The Story of the Pearl Merchant envisions a program of asceticism and renouncing the world as the path to heaven. The direction is toward the other world and away from this one. On the other hand, the Hymn of the Pearl, while envisioning a journey, teaches the reader the necessity of being born or coming into the world as a prerequisite for salvation. The pearl must be found here on earth so the prince may take up his royal position.

Since I have examined three of the many differing interpretations of the pearl available in early Christian literature, it is possible to reconsider the two different interpretations of the pearl present in *ActsPet12Apost.* Krause is correct in his assessment of the redactor's view of the pearl as a "Christian reinterpretation"; some Christian circles viewed Jesus as the pearl. On the other hand, the second and third interpretations of the pearl (probably gnostic in outlook) separated the pearl from Jesus — using it as a symbol for the "sons of God" and salvation respectively. It is an understanding of the pearl similar to that found in the third interpretation that reflects the original intention of the Story of the Pearl Merchant. It is right to speak of a Christian reinterpretation of the pearl.

---

one motif among others taken from Scripture; it is neither the starting point nor the main topic" ("The Return of the Prodigal: Fortunes of a Parable on its Way to the Far East," *Orientalia* 47 [1978] 194, 211). A. F. J. Klijn takes a similar position, comparing the understanding of the pearl in the Hymn with that in Matt 13:45–46: "The meaning of the parable is that 'it is with the kingdom as with a man finding the one pearl.' The same idea is found in the hymn. To fetch the one pearl means partaking in the kingdom. The hymn adds a great deal of mythological and theological matter, but the structure of the parable is clearly seen" ("The So-Called Hymn of the Pearl," *VC* 14 [1960] 158).

NEW INTERPRETATIONS OF CONCEPTS FROM THE STORY OF THE
PEARL MERCHANT

New interpretations of concepts presented in the Story of the Pearl
Merchant source include 1) the roles and relationships of the rich and
poor in regard to the disciples and 2) the conception of ascetical demands
made in the text. The sections which address the question of the rich and
poor in the Author/ Redactor's Theology reveal a subtle shift.

The basic assumption has changed. No longer are the Poor presented
as possible travelers to Nine Gates (cf. 4.10–5; 30–4). In the view of the
redactor the Poor now must be given the pearl (i.e., "what is better";
10.11) by Jesus. They can no longer "go and get it"; it must be "given"
to them. When the Poor are mentioned by Jesus in 10.8–13, they have
become objects of the disciples's ministry (especially corporal works of
mercy) and possible members of the Church. The disciples are told to
give to the Poor "what they need in order to live."

As for the rich, in 11.26–12.13 they are assumed to be part of the
Church, or at least to be associated with it. In the Story of the Pearl
Merchant, the merchant is utterly rejected by the rich (3.25–27). In
response to this rejection, the merchant chooses to reject the rich by not
revealing himself to them. There is no explicit contact between Peter and
the rich (or, for that matter, between the merchant and the rich). On the
other hand, the text implies that he stands by and narrates the dialogue
between the merchant and the Poor. Some degree of relationship between
the Poor and Peter is implied.

There is also a shift, albeit very slight, in the ascetical demands that
are made by the Story of the Pearl Merchant and the redactor. In the
former an extremely severe asceticism is suggested (5.21–6.8). All things
must be forsaken and daily fasting is prescribed. According to the
description of the desires of the hostile creatures which infest the road to
Nine Gates one must truly separate oneself from even the most basic of
bodily desires, even bread and water. While this kind of regime could not
be kept up indefinitely, it might be sustained long enough to achieve
spiritual purification or salvation (i.e., the pearl). Nevertheless, while the
redactor agrees with renunciation of the world (10.15–18), the redactor

has Peter speak not of daily fasting but of being concerned about "the food for a single day." This is reliance upon God's daily provision as is advocated in Matt 6:31–34 and 10:9–10, not a demand for daily fasting.

THE STORY OF THE PEARL MERCHANT:
HYPOTHESIZING A BASIC STRUCTURE

Since I have now discussed the overall work of the redactor, it is possible to examine more closely his or her sources. A key question which must be addressed is: What did the Story of the Pearl Merchant look like before it was altered to become part of our text? While this question cannot be answered completely, the text does seem to provide some indications of its original structure and focus.

The basic structure of the Story of the Pearl Merchant was as follows: 1) the apostles receive a commission from the Lord to a ministry for which they are not fully prepared; 2) they arrive in Habitation and Peter meets a mysterious merchant who is offering a pearl to everyone in Habitation; 3) interested by this offer, Peter takes a step no one has yet taken in Habitation: he requests specific directions to the merchant's city; 4) upon receiving these directions, Peter gathers his friends and they depart (thereby putting into practice these directions) and subsequently arrive at Nine Gates;[22] 5) upon arrival, the group again encounters the Merchant, who turns out to be the Lord in disguise;[23] 6) they are then

---

[22] Note that I have not mentioned Peter's encounter with the mysterious old man (6.27b–7.19a). The reason I do not include this little narrative aside is that its originality to the Story of the Pearl Merchant is questionable (particularly 7.5b–19a) — more on this in the pages that follow.

[23] They receive revelatory material, which includes the revelation that the "pearl" they desire is in fact the salvation of their own souls, now polished and purified by their journey and ready for heaven. It is possible that much of this material was either not acceptable or, most likely, did not reflect the immediate concerns of the redactor, concerns which I have previously suggested were very practical (pastoral). This is evidenced by the fact that very little remains concerning Nine Gates, the ascetical journey and its rigors or the pearl itself — excepting 10.24–30.

ordered to go back, their mission clarified, and teach the Poor about their hidden treasure (the salvation of their souls) and exactly how to make the journey to Nine Gates.

EXAMINING THE STORY OF THE PEARL MERCHANT

Now that I have set out a basic outline of the Story of the Pearl Merchant, it is possible to examine the text for indications of its particular characteristics. There are two important aspects of the Story of the Pearl Merchant that can be identified by even the most cursory of readings: 1) the document's otherworldly trajectory; and 2) its Petrine and Christian-Gnostic flavor. First, it can be said that this text, like the two other *narrationes fabulosae* I have discussed (*Scipio's Dream* and the vision of Er), is "otherworldly" in its emphasis. By "otherworldly" I mean that the focus of the text is upon both the need for and the "how to" of a journey to another realm. In fact, one could even describe the Story of the Pearl Merchant as "anti-world" and possibly even "dualistic." How is this the case?

Initially, it is clear that to obtain the pearl one must leave Habitation and travel to Nine Gates (4.10–5). There is no immediate mention of a return to Habitation in either the Pearl Merchant's invitation or the directions he provides to his city. The only mention of a return to Habitation is made in the material I have designated as part of the Author/ Redactor's Theology (10.1–13).

However, despite its otherworldly tone, it is probable that the Story of the Pearl Merchant did not end in Nine Gates. When we compare this story with the other two *narrationes fabulosae* I have considered (*Scipio's Dream* and the vision of Er), both of these texts also have a strong otherworldly emphasis, yet both stories describe a return to earth by the visionary: Scipio awakens from his dream and Er regains his life while stacked like cordwood upon the funeral pyre. To be practical, a *narratio fabulosa* must be "down to earth." In other words, the visionary must return to witness his or her vision and revealed wisdom to the world, otherwise the story cannot be told (at least with the power of first person report) and there can be no didactic value.

Furthermore, the journey to Nine Gates can be made only by "one who has forsaken everything and fasted from stage to stage" (5.23–25). Thus the emphasis is upon separating oneself from one's possessions, even from those possessions which are basic to the physical preservation of life (e.g., bread, garments and water). Furthermore, both of the key "heroes" in the text, Peter (and his friends) and the Pearl Merchant, describe themselves as "strangers" in relation to Habitation (3.4–11). On the other hand, Nine Gates (or at least the gates of the city) is described as a place where the Petrine group experiences "great joy" (**OYNOϬ NPⲀϢⲈ**), "peaceful carefreeness like that of our Lord" (**OYⲈ1P[HNH N̄ΘⲈ M̄] [Π]Ⲉ[T]N̄ΠⲈNⲨOⲈ1C**) and "rest" (**M̄TON**).[24] Thus there is a consistent and decidedly negative portrayal of Habitation (the world) while Nine Gates (heaven/ the Pleroma) is presented as the ideal place.

The second conclusion that can be reached about the Story of the Pearl Merchant is that it is Petrine and, therefore, Christian. Its preferred term for Jesus is "Lord" (**ⲨOⲈ1C**), which appears four times (1.12, 16, 23; 8.6). This exclusive usage of the term "Lord" to refer to Jesus may reflect the "otherworldly" emphasis of this source. Its Christological emphasis is placed upon a heavenly ruler figure (cf. Phil 2:9–11, without the tempering effect of 2:5–7) and not upon the earthly itinerant preacher of the synoptic tradition.

The terms used to refer to the Petrine group are diverse yet, for the most part, consistent. The term "apostles" is used once (1.5). The terms "brother(s)" (**CON / CNHY**) "stranger(s)" (**ϢMMO**) and "friend(s)" (**ϢBHP**) appear four, three and five times respectively.[25] However, each of these terms is also used in reference to the Pearl Merchant (2.35; 3.10). The term "servants of God" (**ϨⲈNBⲀⲓ̈Ⲁⲓ̈K N̄TⲈ ΠNOYTⲈ;**

---

[24] I recognize that the Coptic verb for "rest" (**M̄TON**) is a theoretical reconstruction of the text. Only the prefix "we" (**ⲀN**) remains.

[25] "Brother(s)" appears in 2.35; 3.2, 6, 9; "stranger(s)" in 3.7, 10; 5.11; "friend(s)" in 2.35; 3.3, 9; 6.28; 7.21.

5.11–12) is also used to refer to the Petrine group in connection with their ministry (mentioned first in 1.10–12).[26] Furthermore, as noted above, this text was also gnostic in its cosmology and soteriology, as well as its anthropology. This has already been sufficiently demonstrated in my analysis of the tradition history of this source.

REDACTIONAL ELEMENTS
There are five sections within the material designated The Story of the Pearl Merchant that are redactional. Three have already been addressed in consideration of the Author/ Redactor's Theology. In order of their appearance in the text, these redactional sections are 1) the second description of the merchant, in 2.17b–29; 2) the reference to the disciples's ability to interpret their "hardships" (sufferings) in 5.5b–6; 3) the symbolic name of Lithargoel, in 5.9 ("name and"), 5.15–18 (and supplementary insertions in 7.22; 8.14, 25); 4) the editorial elaboration that follows the episode with the mysterious old man in 7.5a–19a; and 5) the physician insertions in 8.14–19, 33–35. Having already covered the first, third and fifth of these redactional sections, I now turn my attention to the fourth (and the second which is related).

The section which includes 6.27b–7.19a is intriguing. In this section Peter, having received his "travel" instructions from the merchant, suddenly encounters a mysterious old man. Although this section interrupts the flow of the story by delaying the disciples's attempt to reach Nine Gates (see 7.19b), it need not necessarily be a secondary addition to the text. Schenke views this section as the ending of the first of three originally separate source texts:

> The first text was the legendary narrative of a marvelous voyage by
> Peter and the other apostles, which brings them out of time and
> space to an imaginary small island, which signifies the world and

---

[26] Peter's conception of his ministry ("it is necessary for us to spread the word of God in every city harmoniously," 5.12–14) reflects the same Christian universal mission theology as found in Matt 28:18–19 and Acts 1:8.

is accordingly symbolically named. Its high points are the imparting of this name, the wonderful display of the truth of this name, since the island city still endures although it ought properly to be swallowed up by the sea, the conversation about the significance and power of endurance, and a kind of application in the style of the peroration of a sermon. The original end of this text (with the catch-word "kingdom of heaven") may still be recognizable at 7.18.[27]

I accept Schenke's characterization of 6.27b–7.5 as a "wonderful display of the truth of this name, since the island city still endures although it ought properly to be swallowed up by the sea." This section actually helps advance the Story of the Pearl Merchant by dramatically illustrating the circumstances under which those in the city must live, and by illustrating the appropriateness of the city's name. However, I am far from convinced that the second half of this section (7.5b–19a) is original to the Story of the Pearl Merchant.

There is a noticeable shift in chronological framework between the apostolic period used in the Story of the Pearl Merchant and the Resurrection Appearance, and the present of the author/ redactor's own time. This is especially reflected in the discussion of the circumstances within the churches involving the rich in 11.26b–12.13a. What is especially important about 7.5b–19a is that this same time shift has occurred again. The mention of "apostasies" (7.14) is out of place in the early evangelistic stage reflected in Peter's words, "It is necessary for us to spread the word of God in every city harmoniously" (5.12–14). According to Peter's words, churches do not exist in which such apostasies could take place. These "apostasies" would be more at home within troubled times of the author/ redactor, times where sinful church leaders show partiality toward the rich, thereby leading others into sin (11.26–12.8). Furthermore, 7.5b–19a speaks of "the burden (suffering) of his yoke of faith," which implies persecution. It is premature to speak

---

[27] Schenke, "The Acts of Peter and the Twelve Apostles," 417.

of persecuted believers who do not as yet exist! Therefore, 7.5b–19a is an editorial comment added by the author/ redactor. This is also the case with 5.5b–6 (the second redactional insertion). It too reflects a period of persecution. How else could the disciples, having not yet begun their ministry, be exposed to persecution so as to be in a position to interpret its significance?

However, just because a time shift occurs in 5.5b–6 and 7.5b–19a, it does not prove that these sections are secondary. Certainly such editorial comments could have been inserted into the text by the original writer of the Story of the Pearl Merchant. The Story of the Pearl Merchant was written in a Christian period. Therefore even if the author did attempt to reflect the earliest apostolic period in the story, in the author's own experience there existed the possibility of apostasies and persecutions.[28] This shift in time frame could feasiblely represent either the actual author or the redactor. As will become clear later, this material is redactional. However, regardless of how one chooses to view this section, Schenke's evaluation of 7.5b–19a as "the original end of this text" is illogical, since the journey (discussed in 5.19–6.8) has not yet taken place.

A RESURRECTION APPEARANCE[29]

9. He said to Peter,
   "Peter!" And Peter was frightened,
   for how did he know
   that his name was Peter?

---

[28] An example of the kind of thing to which I am referring is found in John 9 with the story of the man who was blind from birth. While this story has its setting during Jesus' ministry, it actually reflects the current situation of the redactor. The trial and casting out of the follower of Jesus from the synagogue (i.e., the blind man) does not reflect the period of Jesus' ministry but rather the experience of the redactor's community.

[29] This source is most certainly secondary. As Patterson points out, it is unique to our text in that it has a change not only in voice but also in the identity of the narrator. This section alone is narrated from the voice of one of the apostolic group (Patterson, "Sources, Redaction and Tendenz," 6).

5. Peter responded to the Savior
    "How do you know me,
    for you called my name?"
    Lithargoel answered, "I
    want to ask you who gave the
10. name Peter to you?" He
    said to him, "It was Jesus Christ, the
    son of the living God. He
    gave this name to me." He answered
    and said, "It is I! Recognize me.
15. Peter." He loosened the garment,
    which clothed him — the one into which
    he had changed himself because of us —
    revealing to us in truth that
    it was he. We prostrated ourselves
20. on the ground and worshiped him. We
    comprised eleven disciples.
    He stretched forth his hand
    and caused us to stand. We spoke with
    him humbly. Our heads were
25. bowed down in unworthiness
    as we said, "What you
    wish we will do. But
    give us the power to do
    what you wish at all times."

If this section can be described properly as a resurrection appearance, then any analysis of its contents can only be strengthened by a form-critical evaluation of its constituent parts. In 1975, John E. Alsup examined the NT resurrection appearance stories as well as numerous extra-canonical, Jewish and Hellenistic sources. In his attempt to delineate a *Gattung* for the resurrection appearance narratives, Alsup studied two major complexes of appearance stories: 1) the group appearance[30] (Matt 28:16–20; Luke 24:36–49; John 20:19–23, 24–29) and 2) those simply known as appearance stories[31] (Luke 24:13–33, 35; John 20:14–18, 21:1–14). Alsup states that the formal similarities between these two complexes "overlap one another in many aspects almost identically": 1) the crisis situation; 2) Jesus' coming into their presence; 3) a failure to recognize Jesus (or the pre-eminence of the doubt motif); 4) his address and verbal exchange; 5) the moment of recognition; and 6) the commission.[32]

---

[30] Alsup, *The Post-Resurrection Appearance Stories of the Gospel Tradition* (Calwer Theologische Monographien 5; Stuttgart: Calwer, 1975) 147–89. Alsup notes five key structural elements in this complex of stories: 1) the gathering of the disciples after the Crucifixion; 2) the appearance and address of Jesus; 3) the reaction of partial acceptance and partial skepticism; 4) the recognition and 5) the commission and sending forth. He also identifies two additional elements which he describes as "ancillary but possibly with some claim to an early union." They are: 6) the cross and resurrection as fulfillment of OT prophecy and 7) the Holy Spirit's activation of the commission (*Appearance Stories*, 190).

[31] Likewise, Alsup points out five structural points of contact: 1) a crisis situation; 2) Jesus' unexpected arrival; 3) the failure to recognize Jesus; 4) the address and verbal exchange and 5) the eventual recognition of the Lord made concrete by some expression recalling the familiarity of that former experience (*Appearance Stories*, 211).

[32] Alsup, *Appearance Stories*, 212. This may be compared with the formal pattern offered by Charles H. Dodd:
A. The situation: Christ's followers bereft of their Lord.
B. The appearance of the Lord.
C. The Greeting.
D. The Recognition.
E. The Word of Command.
Dodd divides appearance stories into two types: Class I, the "concise" type, characterized by brevity "like a water-worn pebble, until nothing but the essential remains, in its most arresting and meaningful form" (Matt 28:8–10, 16–20; John 20:19–21) and Class II, the "circumstantial" type similar to "tales" (Luke 24:13–35; John 21:1–14) ("The Appearances of the Risen Christ: an Essay in Form-Criticism of the Gospels," in D. E. Nineham, ed., *Studies in the Gospels: Essays in Memory of R. H. Lightfoot* [Oxford: Blackwell, 1957] 10–11). Dodd builds upon the work of Martin Albertz, "Zur Formengeschichte der Auferstehungsberichte," *ZNW* 21 (1922) 259–69 and Lyder Brun, *Die*

With such a statement of the formal qualities of resurrection appearances,[33] it remains to compare these elements with *ActsPet12Apost.* 9.1–29. However, before I make this comparison I must stress that I do not view 9.1–29 as a complete appearance story for two reasons. First, it lacks a proper introduction which describes the setting in which this appearance takes place. Certainly, in its current position it does have a "setting," that of the disciples's journey to Nine Gates and subsequent restful discussion and encounter with the physician. However, I have already outlined the problems with 8.11–35 (the text that provides much of the current setting) and how, taken together with the voice shift in 9.1–29, I view it as part of a separate source. Thus I suggest that the original setting was omitted by the redactor as part of the process that led to the composition of *ActsPet12Apost.* as it now exists. The redactor, intending to reveal or unveil Lithargoel as Jesus, needed a text which narrated an incident in which Jesus, heretofore unrecognized, revealed himself to his disciples. The redactor simply removed the original setting, trusting in the context to provide a new setting, and made only minor attempts to provide a narrative motivation for a revelation of Jesus (e.g., the statement in 8.20 "We did not recognize him," which seems out of chronological order).[34] Second, if my division of *ActsPet12Apost.* stands,

---

Auferstehung Christi in der urchristlichen Überlieferung (Giessen: Töpelmann, 1925).

[33] By opting for Alsup's formal qualities I reject the surprisingly simplistic view of Bultmann that prefers to view these appearances not as stories but rather as the use of the two motifs — whether separately or combined — of "proving the Resurrection by the appearance of the risen Lord" and "the missionary charge of the Risen Lord" (*The History of the Synoptic Tradition* [rev. ed.; London: Blackwell, 1963] 288).

[34] What I mean by "out of chronological order" is that up until this point (after the merchant's queer instructions about the way to Nine Gates and the disciples' mystical journey) there is no reason to expect that a character just encountered might be incognito. This statement smacks of an editorial insertion to ease the transition into new source material — material that includes a revelation of a previously indistinguishable character.

the resurrection appearance in 9.1–29 lacks its original commission, an element viewed by both Alsup and Dodd as being a formal aspect of appearance stories.[35] As with the setting, a commissioning scene is quite obviously present but I have attributed 9.30–12.19 to the hand of the redactor. This presents no problem. As Alsup has aptly demonstrated in the case of the canonical resurrection appearances, the commission remains a part of the traditional matrix of gospel appearance stories despite being "cast entirely in the style, vocabulary and intention of the three evangelists in question."[36] Thus I suggest that the redactor of our text simply replaced the resurrection appearance's original commission, probably a much simpler construction, with his or her own commissioning scene. Now that these points have been made, we can proceed to an examination of the formal characteristics of a resurrection appearance and how they apply to *ActsPet12Apost.* 9.1–29.

Alsup's first formal element, the crisis situation, is directly impacted by this view of the redactor's activity. As the text currently stands there is nothing in the setting to imply a feeling of crisis. The nearest thing to such a situation would be the hostile animals encountered by the disciples on their journey to Nine Gates (7.19–8.13), but as the text clearly states these threats were "evaded" ($\overline{\text{P}}$ **BO\;** 7.26, 29, 32; 8.1, 13). However, these elements were not part of the original resurrection appearance.

---

[35] Alsup concludes: "in view of the...historical fact that the primitive community at the earliest stage of the traditions's development was conscious of having been sent and did not, in fact, become a closed community or sect retreating from the world into itself — acknowledging of course that exceptions did exist —, that the commission in the form of the sending motif was original to the basic form of the appearance Gattung for the first complex and perhaps remotely for the second as well" (*Appearance Stories*, 213). Reginald H. Fuller takes much the same position, albeit from a more theological perspective, describing appearances as "revelatory events... in which the recipient was called to a particular function in salvation history" (*The Formation of the Resurrection Narratives* [rev. ed.; Philadelphia: Fortress, 1980] 48).

[36] Alsup, *Appearance Stories*, 212–13.

Therefore if we limit ourselves to 9.1–29, it must be admitted that there is no explicit reference to a crisis situation.

On the other hand, there is the odd phrase in 9.2–4, "And Peter was frightened, for how did he know that his name was Peter?" The words "And Peter was frightened" (ⲀϤⲚⲞⲨⲰⲠ ⲆⲈ ⲚϬⲒ ⲠⲈⲦⲢⲞⲤ) seem out of place. Fear is an extreme reaction, which is not in keeping with the actual narrative situation. As the text now stands Peter reacts fearfully because a physician whom he has just met knows his name. Since earlier in the story Lithargoel's description of the killer "robbers and wild beasts" on the road to Nine Gates (5.26–27) evoked only sadness from Peter and not fear (6.9–14), it is odd that a stranger's knowledge of his name should elicit such a powerful emotion. However, this element of fear is found in a number of NT resurrection appearance stories, primarily texts associated with the empty tomb.[37] This fear of Peter's may be a vestige of an original setting in which it made better sense such as, Luke 24:36–37 ("As they were talking about all this, there he was, standing among them. Startled and terrified, they thought they were seeing a ghost").

Alsup's second formal characteristic, Jesus' coming into their presence, is of course assumed both from the current context ("He hurried and came back quickly"; 8.35b–9.1a) and the type of dialogue which occurs in 9.1–15, in which there is a sense of an initial encounter.

---

[37] Cf. Matt 28:4 (φόβου), 5 (μὴ φόβεῖσθε), 8 (φόβου), 10 (μὴ φόβεῖσθε); Mark 16:8 (ἐφοβοῦντο); Luke 24:5 (ἐμφόβων). There is one NT instance where the motif of fear is associated with an appearance story not involving the tomb ("But they were startled and frightened [ἔμφοβοι] and supposed they saw a spirit," Luke 24:37). Further, the motif of fear appears also in John 20:19, although it is used to provide a motivation for the disciples's hiding ("for fear [φόβον] of the Jews") and not as a reaction to Jesus' arrival. In *ActsPet12Apost.* there are three different words that express fear or a related emotion: 1) ⲢⲞⲞⲨⲰ (πτόησις) "an anxious care, concern" (1.8); 2) ⲚⲞⲨⲰⲠ (μέριμνα) "fright" (9.2) and 3) Ⲣ ϨⲞⲦⲈ (φόβος) "fear, to be afraid" (11.1, 7) (Crum, *A Coptic Dictionary*, s.v. 236; 306b–308a; 720b–721b). In the Coptic NT texts the typical choice is Ⲣ ϨⲞⲦⲈ in all the passages except Mark 16:8, which uses ⲤⲦⲰⲦ.

The third formal element, a failure to recognize Jesus, and the related fourth characteristic, Jesus' address and verbal exchange, are certainly the most obvious motifs in 9.5–14:

> Peter responded to the Savior, "How do you know me, for you called my name?" Lithargoel answered, "I want to ask you who gave the name Peter to you?" He said to him, "It was Jesus Christ, the son of the living God. He gave this name to me." He answered and said, "It is I! Recognize me. Peter."

It was this recognition scene that attracted the redactor in the first place. Since in the Story of the Pearl Merchant the merchant was an allegorical figure representing Jesus and given the fact that two new identities (Lithargoel/ the physician) were imposed upon the merchant, the redactor needed a scene in which Jesus revealed himself. This scene served a dual role: 1) it allowed for the merchant/ Lithargoel/ physician (the last two identities being redactional) to be revealed as Jesus and 2) its revelation of Jesus could set the stage, as in all revelation dialogues, for new instructions and theology.[38]

The fifth formal characteristic, the moment of recognition, is found in 9.15–20:

> He loosened the garment, which clothed him — the one into which he had changed himself because of us — revealing to us in truth that it was he. We prostrated ourselves on the ground and worshiped him.

---

[38] Judging from Peter's failure to recognize Jesus, I suggest that this appearance of Jesus was originally presented as a "first" appearance of the risen Lord. Lack of recognition is part of several of the "first" appearances of Jesus that are described in the gospels (cf. the road to Emmaus, Luke 24:13–35; Mary Magdalene, John 20:11–18; and also Peter and the disciples, John 21:1–14 — which, based on evidence provided by the *Gospel of Peter*, may have been used as an initial appearance story).

A key question in regard to this formal aspect of the resurrection appearance source is what is happening when Jesus "loosens" his garment (9.15–19). Jesus is presented as loosening his garment so as to reveal definitively his identity. Readers of the canonical gospels might expect some display of the crucified one's wounds to verify his identity (cf. Luke 24:39; John 20:19–20, 24–29). It is peculiar that at the point in our text where a verification of Jesus' identity based on the evidence provided by his wounds would be expected, the text instead portrays Jesus as stripping off his body as if it were a suit of clothes.[39] Certainly, the original purpose for Jesus' loosening his garments was to show his wounds. This understanding is keeping with basic human experience and Greco-Roman literary techniques.

This use of distinguishing marks, scars or wounds to identify a character was a literary convention long before the gospel appearance stories. In *Poetics* 16.1, Aristotle writes:

> Discovery in general has been explained already. As for the species of discovery, the first to be noted is the least artistic form of it, of which the poets make most use through mere lack of

---

[39] The flesh is envisioned as a garment. This is hardly foreign to the Nag Hammadi corpus (e.g., *Gos. Thom.* 21, 36; *Gos. Phil* 57.19–22; *Auth. Teach.* 32.2–8; *Sent. Sextus* 346; *Paraph. Shem* focuses on the spiritual garments that are to replace the fleshly one). This is also the case in *Hermetica* 10.18: "Then, when the mind has got free of the earthly body, it immediately puts on its own tunic, a tunic of fire, in which it could not stay when in the earthly body." Of course, this concept is not foreign to Greek and Roman literature in general (e.g., Lucian, *Dialogues of the Dead* 10.5):
"Hermes: You! The tubby fellow! Who might you be?
Damasias: Damasias the athlete.
Hermes: Yes, I remember your face. I've seen you many a time at the sports grounds.
Damasias: Yes, you have. Let me on; I've stripped.
Hermes: Stripped, my dear fellow? With all that flesh on you? You get it off. You'll sink the ship if you put one foot on. And throw away those wreaths and first prizes.
Damasias: There, I really am stripped — see for yourself. I'm no heavier than the rest of the corpses."

invention, discovery by signs or marks. Of these signs some are congenital, like the "lancehead which the Earth-born have on them," or "stars," such as Carcinus brings in his *Thyestes*; others acquired after birth — these latter being either marks on the body, e.g., scars, or external tokens, like necklaces, or (to take another sort of instance) the ark in the discovery in *Tyro*. Even these, however, admit of two uses, a better and a worse; the scar of Ulysses is an instance; the discovery of him through it is made in one way by the nurse and in another by the swineherds.[40]

Using scars or wounds for identification is not limited to living characters. This is evidenced by both Homer (*Odyssey* 11, The Book of the Dead) and Virgil (*Aeneid* 6, The Underworld). The dead met by Odysseus and Aeneas continue to bear the marks inflicted upon them in their death. In fact, Aeneas recognizes his ex-mistress, the Phoenician queen Dido, by her suicide wound.

Obviously, these examples are not found in ancient Greek and Roman appearance scenes. They demonstrate that this ancient motif was not exclusively an element of the resurrection appearance stories currently under examination. This motif has been borrowed by the canonical and non-canonical authors so as to concretely "prove" Jesus' identity.

In light of this lack of emphasis upon the wounds of Jesus I pose the question: Exactly what was the theological position of this source on the salvific suffering of Jesus? I suggest that at its most primitive stage this resurrection appearance, like Luke 24:39 and John 20:19–20, 24–29, described Jesus showing the disciples his wounds. However, at some point, either by some later editor of this source or by the redactor of *ActsPet12Apost.*, a docetic theology was introduced into the text. A variation on the bodily proof motif was provided. Instead of showing his wounds as proof of his identity, Jesus now strips off the body of Lithargoel and reveals his own body — obviously recognizable to the

---

[40] Ingram Bywater, trans., *Aristotle: Rhetoric and Poetics* (New York: Random House, 1954) 243–44.

disciples — as proof. Thus it is not the wounds but the (spiritual) person of Jesus that is the focus, a person that can assume alternate bodily appearances in much the same way that we can put on different suits of clothes.

I propose that it was the redactor who had docetic leanings. As evidence for this position I point to 2.17b–29, which Patterson describes as a problematic "second description" to be attributed to "the work of the redactor":[41]

> I was staring at the man, because he was beautiful in his form and stature. There were four parts of his body that I saw: the soles of his feet and a part of his chest and the palms of his hands and his visage. These things I was able to see. A book cover like (those of) my books was in his left hand. A staff of styrax wood was in his right hand.[42]

If this "second description" of the Pearl Merchant (2.17b–29) reflects the "hand of the redactor," as Patterson argues, then the content of these lines provides support for a docetic redactor. In this passage the merchant, known by the redactor to be Jesus incognito, is described. Peter says that he can see the hands, feet, face and chest of the merchant. Presumably if

---

[41] Patterson, "Sources, Redaction and Tendenz," 13.

[42] The text is correctly translated "soles of his feet" (N̅ϭⲞⲠ N̅Tⲉ NⲉϥⲞⲨⲈⲠⲎTⲉ) and "palms of his hands" (ⲐⲰⲘⲈ N̅Tⲉ Nⲉϥϭⲓⲭ) but this may reveal haste and a lack of continuity in the redactor's thought. There seems to be a tension even between 2.17b–24 and 25–29. It is physically impossible to see the soles of one's feet when he or she is standing and equally impossible to see one's palms when grasping a staff and book. This peculiar from a literary point of view as the redactor could have easily written NⲉϥⲞⲨⲈⲠⲎTⲉ and Nⲉϥϭⲓⲭ. It seems odd to take the trouble to specifically mention a character's palms and the soles of his or her feet — only to have this mean nothing to the story. This especially true in a Christian context which would have been informed by the famous Thomas story in John 20. My suggestion is that this peculiarity is linked with the revelation of Jesus through the stripping of the flesh in 9.15–19. The point of the redactor would be that Jesus is not to be identified through a physical body but recognized through spiritual means.

there were any scars or wounds to report (to provide a hint at the merchant's identity) this would have been an appropriate place to introduce them. The redactor obviously did not choose to do so.

Parrott, Schenke and Patterson[43] suggest that the presence of σουδάριον in 2.14 indicates that the merchant is wearing "grave clothes." This conclusion could be taken as evidence for a post resurrection-setting and therefore as an allusion to a crucified Lord. But this is simply not the case. While σουδάριον can refer to burial rags (John 11:44; 20:7; of Lazarus, Origen, *Comm. John* 28.7; of Jesus, *Acts of Pilate* [A] 15.6), it can also refer to a napkin or handkerchief used to wrap possessions, particularly valuables (Luke 19:20).[44] It is this latter definition that is undoubtedly referred to in our text. This is made clear when the rich spurn the merchant because, having seen his σουδάριον, they see no bundle inside it — "And they did not see (that they could gain) anything from him, because there was no pouch on his back nor bundle inside his cloth and napkin; 3.23–25. This is an indication to them that he does not actually have precious stones on his person. Thus there is no reference (explicit or otherwise) in *ActsPet12Apost.* to Jesus' crucifixion. At the moment when a Christian reader would most expect a reference to Jesus' wounds, it is absent. This evidence suggests that the redactor of *ActsPet12Apost.* had docetic leanings.

---

[43] See Parrott, *Nag Hammadi Codices V,2–5 and VI*, 207; Schenke, "The Acts of Peter and the Twelve Apostles," 2.418; and Patterson, "Sources, Redaction and Tendenz," 13.

[44] In addition the σουδάριον can refer to the towel "reputed to have been worn at the left side by Jewish priesthood and symbolized by the pallium (as a precursor of the maniple)" (cf. *LPGL*, s.v. σουδάριον [1244b]). It derived from a Latin loanword, *sudarium*, which was typically used to refer to a napkin or sweatcloth (see Catullus, *Poems* 12.14; 25.7; Martial, *Epigrams* 11.39; Quintilian, *Institutio oratoria* 6.3.60; 11.3.148; Seutonius, *Twelve Caesars* [Nero] 25; 48; 51 and Petronius Arbiter, *Satyricon* 67) (E. A. Andrews, *Harper's Latin Dictionary* [New York: American Book Company, 1907] s.v. 1790).

As for Alsup's sixth formal characteristic, the commission, only the original introduction to this traditional motif remains in 9.21–29 (especially 24–29):

> We comprised eleven disciples. He stretched forth his hand and caused us to stand. We spoke with him humbly. Our heads were bowed down in unworthiness as we said, "What you wish we will do. But give us the power to do what you wish at all times."

As already suggested, the redactor simply replaced the resurrection appearance's original commission with his or her own commissioning scene. To accomplish this task the redactor added 9.30–10.1a: "He gave them the unguent box and the pouch that was in the hand of the young disciple. He commanded them like this, saying...." In this seam the redactor picks up again the elements of the unguent box, the pouch and young disciple (cf. 8.16–18) in an attempt to ease the transition to his or her material in the rest of the revelation dialogue. However, this seam, while neatly linking the material before and after the resurrection appearance, actually serves to underline the original separateness of the appearance.[45] From this brief inspection it can be seen that 9.1–29, despite the activity of a redactor, does possess the formal characteristics of a resurrection appearance. Having established this it is profitable to examine more closely some of the lesser motifs that are present and compare them with other resurrection appearances. A reading of the extant text provides the following motifs: 1) Peter's role is magnified;[46]

---

[45] There is no mention of the physician in 9.1–29. When Jesus is revealed, it is because he sheds his identity as Lithargoel, not the physician (9.8). Furthermore, the unguent box, medicine pouch and, most importantly, the young disciple are absent from 9.1–29. Except for 9.32 the young disciple is never mentioned again and disappears from the story. He is nothing more than a prop, serving only to emphasize the redactor's medical imagery.

[46] Jesse Sell notes the central position of Peter within *ActsPet12Apost.*, and suggests that this may be a clue as to why this particular resurrection appearance was chosen ("Simon Peter's "Confession," 352–53). As a resurrection

2) its reference to the "eleven disciples" (implying a missing Judas Iscariot) associates it with a post-crucifixion period and with the tradition recorded in the canonical gospels;[47] and 3) the sense of unworthiness on

---

appearance it is not surprising that 9.1–29 should involve Peter. In the earliest known source which lists those to whom the risen Lord appeared (1 Cor. 15:3–8), Paul clearly states that Peter was the first: "For I delivered to you as of first importance what I also received, that Christ died for our sins in accordance with the scriptures, that he was buried, that he was raised on the third day in accordance with the scriptures, and that he appeared to Cephas, then to the Twelve. Then he appeared to more than five hundred brethren at one time, most of whom are still alive, though some have fallen asleep. Then he appeared to James, then to all the apostles. Last of all, as to one untimely born, he appeared also to me." The tradition which suggests the importance of Peter's experience of the risen Christ is supported by other empty tomb and appearance stories in the NT (cf. Mark 16:7; Luke 24:34; John 21:1–14). Peter's crucial position in regard to appearances of the risen Christ is also attested in non-canonical sources. For example, *Ep. Apost.* 11.2–3 describes an appearance to the disciples as a group in which Peter is addressed first: "And we doubted and did not believe. He came before us like a ghost and we did not believe that it was he. But it was he. And thus he said to us, 'Come, and do not be afraid. I am your teacher whom you, Peter, denied three times, and now do you deny me again?" Again, *Gos. Pet.* 14.58–60 relates what can only be a resurrection appearance, similar to John 21:1–14, in which Peter (in the first person) begins to describe how he, Andrew and Levi encountered Jesus. *Ep. Pet. Phil.* 132.1–134.18 contains a letter in which Peter, apparently having seen the risen Lord, writes to Philip entreating him to come together with the rest of the other apostles and witness the risen Lord. Lastly, *Ap. Jas.* 1.1–2.39 records a resurrection appearance in which Jesus reveals special information to both James and Peter.

[47] Despite the use of the phrase ἔνδεκα μαθηταί or simply ἔνδεκα in the synoptics (Matt 28:16; Mark 16:14; Luke 24:9, 33) and Acts 1:26 to refer to a specific group of Jesus' followers, it is extremely rare in other NT or extra-canonical writings. For example, in the famous passage in 1 Cor. 15:3–8 which records Jesus' appearances the experience of Peter is associated with that of the Twelve (τοῖς δώδεκα). This is strange in that according to both these synoptic reports and Acts 1:12–26, a replacement for the traitor, Judas, was not elected until after the appearances of the risen Lord. It is probable that Paul's use of the phrase τοῖς δώδεκα is an anachronism which reflects the already current (A.D. 55) practice of referring to a specific leadership group by a collective title. The use of the phrase "eleven disciples" in *ActsPet12Apost.* further links it with resurrection appearances as four of the five known occurrences of this phrase are used in such a context. Certainly there may be those who might wonder if this

the part of the disciples (9.24–25) is part of the original resurrection appearance. In its original setting it reflected the disciples's sense of guilt for acts of betrayal and abandonment of Jesus.[48]

There are quite obviously numerous parallels between *ActsPet12Apost.* 9.1–29 and other resurrection appearances along formal lines. However, the appearance story found in *Ep. Apost.* 11–12 is strikingly parallel with that found in our text. The similarities go far beyond the formal characteristics shared by resurrection appearances. They go beyond some of the lesser motifs I have discussed above (e.g., the prominence of Peter). These similarities lie in areas that are distinctive in *ActsPet12Apost.* I suggest that, in light of the above considerations (i.e., formal characteristics, lesser motifs and the

---

reference to "eleven disciples" in our text might refer to the disciples who were accompanying Peter as is the case in Acts 2:14 (But Peter, standing up with the eleven, lifted up his voice and addressed them..."). However, the text itself seems to militate against this possibility in that all the disciples (presumably including Peter) are described as prostrating themselves and invited to stand. It is specifically within this context that the number of the disciples is stated ("We comprised eleven disciples," 9.20b). For more on the curious usage of the number twelve when from a historical point of view the number eleven would seem the more appropriate choice see, Wolfgang A. Bienert, "The Picture of the Apostle in Early Christian Tradition," in W. Schneemelcher, ed., *New Testament Apocrypha* (2 vols; Philadelphia: Westminster/ John Knox, 1992) 2.16–17.

[48] However, it is far from clear that this reflects genuine guilt. A sense of guilt on the part of the disciples is only a minor part of the gospel tradition. The examples of it are few (cf. Mark 14:72 and parallels; John 21:15–17). It may be that the disciples are merely expressing proper respect in the presence of divinity. Certainly, such prostration is not uncommon to resurrection appearances whether they be found in the NT (Matt 28:9; John 20:17) or extra-canonical sources (*Ap. Jas.* 15.5–9; *PS* 5–6). However, in 9.22 the phrase "He stretched out his hand..." (as if offering pardon) is included in the formula. While the formula a) prostration, b) worship and c) being caused to stand is similar in 9.19–23 and 12.16–19 (the terms translated "prostrate" are different in 9.19 [ⲡⲁϩⲧ̄ⲛ̄] and 12.16 [ⲛⲟⲩϫⲉ]) the phrase "He stretched forth his hand..." (ⲁϥⲥⲟⲩⲧⲛ̄ ⲧⲉϥϭⲓϫ) only occurs in 9.22. The different terminology and formulaic construction leads me to consider 9.19–23 and 12.16–19 as representing two different hands, which in turn suggests that 9.24–25 was original to the resurrection appearance source.

following, more obscure, similarities), there is no other resurrection appearance with greater correlation to our text.

> 11. Then the Lord said to Mary and also to her sisters, 'Let us go to them.' And he came and found *us* inside, veiled. He called us out. But *we* thought it was a ghost, and *we* did not believe it was the Lord. Then he said to *us*, 'Come, do not be afraid. I am your master whom you, Peter, denied three times; and now do you deny again? But *we* went to him, doubting in our hearts whether it was possibly he. Then he said to *us*, 'Why do you still doubt and are you not believing? *I am he who spoke to you concerning my flesh, my death, and my resurrection. That you may know that it is I, put your finger, Peter, in the nailprints of my hands*; and you, Thomas, put your finger in the spear-wounds of my side; but you, Andrew, look at my feet and see if they do not touch the ground. For it is written in the prophet, 'The foot of a ghost or a demon does not join to the ground.''
>
> 12. But *we* touched him that *we* might truly know whether he had risen in the flesh, and *we fell on our faces confessing our sin, that we had been unbelieving.* Then the Lord *our* redeemer said, 'Rise up, and I will reveal to you what is above heaven and what is in heaven, and your rest that is in the kingdom of heaven. For my Father has given me the power to take up you and those who believe in me.'

There are at least three significant similarities between *Ep. Apost.* 11–12 and *ActsPet12Apost.* 9.1–29. First, both resurrection appearances are presented in the first person plural, non-Petrine, apostolic voice. The only other text I have found that is similar in this regard is *Apocryphon of James* (NHC 1.2). However, while it is in the first person, it is primarily presented in the first person singular — representing the personal voice of James.

Second, while both *Ep. Apost.* 11–12 and *ActsPet12Apost.* 9.1–29 obviously exhibit Petrine prominence (despite the presence of the other disciples), they also share the rare motif of Peter being the primary recipient of the bodily proof of Jesus' identity in the recognition scene.

While bodily proofs of Jesus' identity occur in the NT, it is unique that
the bodily proof in *ActsPet12Apost.* 9.13b–19a is specifically, although
not exclusively, directed toward Peter. This peculiarity is shared by only
one other early Christian text: Ignatius, *Smyrn.* 3.1–2:

> For I know and believe that he was in the flesh even after the
> resurrection; and when he came to Peter and those with him, he
> said to them: 'Take hold of me; handle me and see that I am not a
> disembodied demon.' And immediately they touched him and
> believed, being closely united with his flesh and blood.[49]

The similarity of this tradition and Luke 24:36–43 has ignited
substantial debate. This is especially the case when one considers: 1)
Origen's claim in *De principiis* 1.preface.8 that this statement was found
in the apocryphal *Teaching of Peter*; 2) the claim of Jerome in *De viris
illustribus* 16 that this saying belonged to a *Gospel of the Hebrews* of
which he had knowledge; and 3) the statement by Eusebius in *Hist. eccl.*
3.36.11 that he did not know the source of this Ignatian saying.[50] Despite
the testimonies of Origen and Jerome, there are those such as Philipp
Vielhauer who view the evidence as having "less weight than the
similarity of the passage with Lk. 24:36ff."[51] However, Vielhauer's

---

[49] Hills notes that "Jerome, paraphrasing Ignatius, removes any doubt
that Peter was invited to touch: 'When he came to Peter and to those with Peter...'
(*De vir. ill.* 16)" (*Tradition and Composition in the Epistula Apostolorum*, 87 n.
62). I am indebted to Hills for both his literary analysis of the texts in question
and his personal advice in this matter.

[50] The intricacies of this argument are too detailed to explore here. For
a full discussion see Philipp Vielhauer, "Introduction: The Testimonies of the
Early Church Regarding Jewish-Christian Gospels," in Wilhem Schneemelcher,
E. Hennecke, eds., *New Testament Apocrypha* (Philadelphia: Westminster, 1963)
1.126–30.

[51] Vielhauer goes on to conclude, "in my opinion the antidocetic
tendency of Ignatius and the actual front-line in which he stood sufficiently
explain the formulation of the saying of the Lord and make the assumption of any
source other than Lk. 24:36ff. unnecessary" (ibid., 130). Cf. also Robert Joly, *Le*

position has not received universal affirmation. William R. Schoedel admits that Ignatius' saying is closely related to Luke 24:39 ("see my hands and my feet that it is I; handle me and see that a spirit does not have flesh and bones as you see me have").[52] Schoedel opines:

> Ignatius is probably not simply presenting a loose version of the Lukan text since further evidence for dependence on Luke is virtually absent in Ignatius and because the terms "bodiless and demonic" in Sm. 2, otherwise foreign to his vocabulary, were presumably prompted by the exact wording of the tradition under discussion... Thus it is perhaps most likely that Luke and Ignatius rely on a common tradition.[53]

This conclusion is significant in that it supports the thesis being suggested here: the existence of a resurrection appearance tradition which included the use of the bodily proof motif in connection with Peter.

Third, as I have noted prostration is not unique in resurrection appearances. However, both *ActsPet12Apost.* and *Ep. Apost.* supply a different motivation for the act of prostration. It is not just an act of worship or reverence; rather it is associated with repentance for past failures (cf. "we fell on our faces confessing our sin, that we had been

---

dossier d'Ignace d'Antioche (Université libre de Bruxelles, Faculté de Philosophie et Lettres 69; Brussels: Éditions de l'Université de Bruxelles, 1979) 53–54. However, neither Vielhauer nor Joly explains the existence of the material we have examined in *Epistula Apostulorum*, nor do they show awareness of the *Acts of Peter and the Twelve Apostles.*

[52] Cf. also John Lawson, *A Theological and Historical Introduction to the Apostolic Fathers* (New York: Macmillan, 1961) 137.

[53] Schoedel, *Ignatius of Antioch: A Commentary on the Letters of Ignatius of Antioch* (Hermeneia; Philadelphia: Fortress, 1985) 226–27. Cf. Christine Trevett, who describes Ignatius' saying as "a reminiscence of a not entirely canonical post-resurrection story" (*A Study of Ignatius of Antioch in Syria and Asia* [Studies in the Bible and Early Christianity 29; Lewiston, NY: Mellen, 1992] 157). See both Schoedel and Trevett for further bibliography on the debate over this saying.

unbelieving"; *Ep. Apost.* 12.2; "We prostrated ourselves on the ground and worshiped him.... He stretched forth his hand and caused us to stand. We spoke with him humbly. *Our heads were bowed down in unworthiness*"; *ActsPet12Apost.* 9.19–25). Here "in unworthiness" ($\overline{\text{2N}}$ OYMN̄T X̄TI1HT) can be probably better translated "shamefacedness." However, this is not certain as the meaning "modesty" is also allowed.[54]

The similarities between these two texts are important. They provide a clue as to the tenor of the original source that lies behind 9.1–29. Both texts were obviously influenced by a source or sources that employed an apostolic diary-like presentation of early Christian resurrection appearance traditions. While it is unlikely that these texts shared an underlying source, *Ep. Apost.* is significant in that its similarities with 9.1–29 demonstrate in no uncertain terms the likelihood of the existence of my proposed Petrine resurrection appearance source.[55]

With these thoughts our consideration of the process of redactional composition is complete. Certainly the separation of the redactor's insertions and emendations is a complicated and problematic undertaking. However, it is essential in understanding the priorities and interests of the redactor, a prerequisite for taking the next step in our analysis of *ActsPet12Apost.* — proposing an underlying community.

---

[54] Crum, *Dictionary*, s. v. X̄TIO, 778b.

[55] After comparing 9.1–29 with numerous other resurrection appearances, I can only see one factor that could militate against a first-century dating for its underlying source — the rather docetic tone of the recognition scene. However, I have already argued that I consider this docetic tone to be a redactional insertion. On the other hand, the presence of the phrase "eleven disciples," virtually non-existent in anything but first-century texts, suggests an early dating for the source behind 9.1–29.

Chapter 5
Painting a Community Portrait:
Clues from the Text

In the first four chapters of this study I have attempted to employ the techniques of source criticism, genre analysis and redactional composition to understand *ActsPet12Apost*. Furthermore, I have tried to explain the mythical structure that lies behind the allegory of the Story of the Pearl Merchant. All this has been done so as to understand the composite parts of the text and the actual process the redactor used to mold these parts into a coherent whole. Truly, all of these analyses rely on my belief that the material from 9.30 to 12.19 most closely represents the distinctive voice of the redactor. Not only does this material represent a different voice (third person) but also a different identity (non-apostolic narrator). Further, it is different in that it is only minimally narrative and primarily instructional. These differences, coupled with a shift in time frame (apostolic period to redactional present), strongly suggest that this section should serve as our primary material when attempting to study the redactor.

In the final two chapters of this study, I shall continue to analyze the redactor but no longer with an eye to trace his or her shaping of previous tradition. Rather, I am interested to know if the activity and interests of the redactor are of any help in determining the historical setting of his or her community and, further, in positing an actual date for the final composition of *ActsPet12Apost*. Of necessity this will involve a movement from the more "scientific" (and I say this with a knowing wink) methods of source, genre and redaction criticism which rely on hard evidence (e.g., aporias, vocabulary shifts, theological and thematic [in]consistencies) to a less scientific reliance on reading between the lines. I recognize that these next two chapters will be highly speculative in nature and that I will be opening myself up to a myriad of criticisms by those less daring. However, I forgive myself in advance, not expecting my every assertion to stand the test of time. Rather, I believe that there is much to be gained in probing out into the unknown — for it is only in taking great risks that great rewards are acquired. With this in mind, let us probe into the darkness...

SOME THOUGHTS ON SITZ IM LEBEN

With our new appreciation of the theology and ethics of the redactor of *ActsPet12Apost.*, I shall consider how the text might have been used by its community. In the first section of this study I noted the general voice shift from the first to the third person that occurs at 8.21. At this juncture, I would like to suggest that there may be a shift in purpose as well. With the beginning of the Resurrection Appearance (9.1–29) and throughout the Author/ Redactor's Theology (9.30–12.19) there is a conscious decision to use the third person. Source questions and textual seams aside, the author/ redactor did not act to smooth out the changes in voice that are present in the text. It is reasonable to assume that the author/ redactor was at least aware of this major shift from first to third person. If one assumes authorial awareness, then the question arises as to the author/ redactor's purpose for maintaining the differing voices of the sources and for choosing the third person as the voice in which to express his or her own theology.

In attempting to answer the question of authorial purpose, the shift in voice from first to third person signals the shift from "story" to the "didactic" aspect of *ActsPet12Apost.* As I have argued above, the text moves from the mythic *narratio fabulosa* to the inspirational resurrection appearance. (This serves to establish the revealer's authority, in this case the fact that it is Jesus himself who is giving the instructions which follow.) The text concludes with a revelation dialogue with similarities to the genre, church order. The emphasis on teaching is connected with the sustained use of the third person. This shift from first to third person affects the impact the text has upon the reader. It marks the transition between an intensely personal and exclusive "story" of one man's experience to a more "objective," impersonal and general experience of the disciples's commissioning.

In addition to these shifts in voice and purpose, there is a shift in the time frame of the tractate, which is present primarily in the Author/ Redactor's Theology. This shift in time frame from the apostolic period to the time of the author and the post-apostolic church is best evidenced in the apostles's self-expression of their ministry. There is a development in the disciples's ministry. In 1.10–12, Peter speaks on behalf of the others in his group in describing the launching of an apostolic mission. He says, "We agreed to fulfill the ministry to which the Lord appointed us." Clearly this reflects an initial evangelistic effort on the part of the apostles. This sense of a new beginning of ministry is heightened by the initiation of a "covenant" (1.12–13). Later, Peter's words to Lithargoel seem to reinforce this impression: "It is necessary for us to spread the word of God in every city harmoniously" (5.12–14), i.e., this type of universal mission is a work that still lies ahead.

While this sense of the apostles being on the verge of beginning their evangelistic efforts is uniform in the Story of the Pearl Merchant, there is no such sense in the Author/ Redactor's Theology. If there is a need for the most preliminary evangelistic work to be done as is the impression from the texts reviewed above, then how could the churches of 12.4–13 exist to favor the rich? Parrott describes this occurrence in the text:

> The narrative intention of the final editor appears to have been to depict the disciples's preparation for apostolic activity. In the course of the account, he shifts the time frame from the earliest apostolic period to that of his own time. The result is that, at the conclusion of the final segment, it is not really the original disciples who are being commissioned, but their latter day representatives.[1]

---

[1] Parrott, *Nag Hammadi Library*, 288.

If it is the "latter day representatives" that are addressed, then the details of the commission (the specifics to which they are directed) can speak to us about the priorities of the author's community. By way of commissioning, the disciples are given articles of healing (the unguent box and pouch; 9.30–31) and commanded to teach and care for the needs of the poor (10.1–13). They are given instruction in the specifics of ministry: reliance on the powerful name of Jesus to provide (10.13–30); healing (11.6–26) and the dangers of association with the rich (11.26–12.4). They are also given the right to judge (12.4–13).

It is these final two points (Jesus' warning about association with the rich and the disciples authority to judge; found in 11.26–12.13) that help shed light upon the question of how this text was used in its community. To fully understand the significance of this section an examination of 12.4–13 is crucial:

> For many (ⲘⲎⲎ₩Ⲉ) in the churches have shown partiality to the
> rich (ⲚⲒⲢ̄Ⲙ̄Ⲙⲁⲟ), because they are also sinful, and they give
> occasion for others to sin. But judge them with uprightness, so
> that your ministry may be glorified, and that my name also, may be
> glorified in the churches.

The primary goal of the interpreter in this section should be to determine the identity of the "many" to which Jesus refers. I suggest that the "many" (ⲘⲎⲎ₩Ⲉ) refers to church leaders. This should be a somewhat questionable suggestion based on the typical definition of ⲘⲎⲎ₩Ⲉ ("a multitude, crowd, many"; usually translating Greek words such as πλῆθος, πολλοί).[2] However, to my mind there are two elements within 12.4–13 that suggest this conclusion. First, throughout *ActsPet12Apost.* there are only three groups of people: 1) the rich, who reject the pearl merchant and whose partiality brings sinfulness to the churches; 2) the poor, who rejoice at the pearl merchant's invitation and become (in the

---

[2] Crum, *Dictionary*, s. v. 202a.

redactor's view) the target of the apostolic group's ministry; and 3) the apostolic ministers themselves (and their counterparts in the author's own time). It is simply a matter of deduction to determine the group which is showing or has shown partiality toward the rich. Since the rich are not showing partiality to themselves and the poor lack the power, position and resources to do so, only the third group (contemporary leaders) is left.

Second, the verbal phrase "to give judgment" (ⲧ ϩⲁⲡ) is used to describe the action the ministers are to perform with the result that both the ministry and Jesus' name might be glorified. When this phrase is used in the Coptic translation of the OT it is used in parallel connection with the nation's highest offices (e.g., Deut 1:16 [Israel's legal authorities]; Isa 33:22, the term, equated with king and lawgiver is applied to God; Hosea 7:7 the term is associated with the nation's king).[3] This sentence, found in 12.8–13, has been placed by the redactor in opposition to or contrast with the previous sentence. In these sentences the partiality of the "many" (which has *already* led to sin) is being contrasted with the ministry of righteous judging that the disciples are being called to perform. It is logical that if these two statements are being juxtaposed and the subject of the latter is a group of ministers from the author's own time, then the subject being contrasted negatively should be another group of ministers (i.e., the current church leadership or that of the recent past). It is not the churches themselves or even the concept of church that is being attacked. Rather, it is the leadership of the "many," those who are (or were) partial, who give occasion for sin and, by implication, who judge in unrighteousness.

These considerations suggest a possible use for *ActsPet12Apost.* I see the text used as a sophisticated teaching tool (as compared to *Hyp. Arch.* or *Tri. Trac.*). By "sophisticated" I mean that instead of presenting the reader with thoroughgoing myth or theology, the reader or, more appropriately, the listener is presented with a vicariously experiential lesson in discipleship. The reader/ listener hears first hand from Peter,

---

[3] Crum, *Dictionary*, s. v. 694b.

their father in the faith, about the origins of his ministry, and can "experience" these events along with him by virtue of first person testimony. I would describe the ideal setting for such a work as a school or seminary where the "spiritual" are trained to guide the churches. This text may have been used as subject matter for a sermon reminding the new disciples of their true calling and mission.[4] This is quite plausible in light of the strong emphasis in the text on Jesus' direct commission to his disciples in regard to their future actions in the church.

THE COMMUNITY ITSELF

I am assuming a functioning faith community lies behind *ActsPet12Apost.* In the following pages I shall attempt to reconstruct this community on the basis of indicators present in the text. My goal is similar to that of a forensic artist, to replace flesh upon bones so as to be able once again to behold the face of my subject. An attempt can be made at answering the question: "What did the community that produced *ActsPet12Apost.* look like?"

While modern commentators often assume an underlying community, this carries with it a distinct set of problems. There is the danger of "mirror-reading" the text. This type of interpretation assumes that the text accurately and faithfully reflects the exact situation of the community out of which it proceeds. For example, if a text warns against witches and witchcraft, then the community must be facing a situation in which these issues are pressing in upon it. This kind of naive reading of the text fails to take into consideration questions of genre (what type of text is it?) and

---

[4] I am aware that Parrott's view is different from mine. He views the text as being geared toward those who were already trained for church leadership as opposed to those who were being trained or commissioned for it. He writes: "In view of the shift, it appears that the editor wished to remind contemporary church leaders about their true mission" (ibid., 288). However, in my view the current church leaders are being criticized for their lackluster and even negligent ministerial practices. They are being held up for another group of potential leaders as an example of what not to be as ministers. In short, the "many" are being contrasted with the implied "few."

literary convention. It may well be that, upon further investigation, warnings against witches and witchcraft are typical of other texts of the same genre. Likewise, a commentator would be wrong immediately to assume an active mystical spirituality for the writer of a newly discovered apocalypse just because the apocalysticist describes detailed conversations with heavenly beings. Obviously, heavenly revealers are a well documented element of the apocalyptic genre.[5]

Furthermore, there is the danger of taking for granted that the views expressed in a text are reflective of those adhered to by an actual community. In reality, they may merely reflect the ideal of one disenfranchised radical. Any text, like those discovered at Nag Hammadi, which has been translated from one language (Greek) to another (Coptic) obviously appealed to some audience (regardless how small and marginalized by comparison with the rest of society). Otherwise it would not have been preserved.

There is also the danger of the interpreter's own biases, which he or she brings to the text. Is the interpreter approaching the text with an "agenda," assuming the answers to his or her questions before allowing the text to speak? Or is the interpreter willing to allow the text to speak, regardless of how he or she feels about its message? There is some risk to be assumed when postulating a community behind any text. The commentator can be mindful of issues of genre and literary convention, as well as the possible "ideal" nature of the text and the blinding effect of his or her own biases. However, the truth is that these dangers are inextricably linked with the text and impossible to overcome fully. Ultimately, the text itself is our primary (if not only) evidence for the moment of Christian activity (singular or communal) and struggle (real or

---

[5] "Apocalypse is a genre of revelatory literature with a narrative framework, in which a revelation is mediated by an otherworldly being to a human recipient, disclosing a transcendent reality which is both temporal, insofar as it envisages eschatological salvation, and spatial insofar as it involves another, supernatural world" (John J. Collins, "Apocalypse: The Morphology of a Genre," *Semeia* 14 [1979] 9).

imagined) that is captured in its pages. Despite these dangers, the temptation to postulate an underlying community is great. The desire to know more about the way the early Christians lived is mesmerizing, like the undulating flames of a campfire.

Therefore, mindful of these dangers, it is necessary to be forthright with my method of analyzing the text for clues to its possible community setting. There are three important elements within the Author/ Redactor's Theology which set it apart: 1) a shift in voice from the personal first person to the more inclusive third person; 2) a shift in time frame from the apostolic period to the time of the author/ redactor; and 3) a pastoral focus which culminates in a commissioning scene. Having concluded that this material represents the voice of the redactor (and by association his or her community), I suggest that this material (and other material inserted by the redactor) should be the primary material used to understand the hypothesized community. The specific details of the commission contained in this material are crucial in determining both the community's priorities and its immediate situation in regard to the surrounding world. In examining these hypothesized priorities, I shall be especially attentive to elements within the redactor's material that reflect different, uncommon or unique positions when compared with other early Christian texts. Taken together with theological ideas that are more common, I contend that much can be learned about *ActsPet12Apost.* and its life setting. Therefore, I shall begin by discussing four aspects of this hypothesized community: 1) its tendency toward self-centeredness; 2) its spirituality (which was both mystical and ascetical); 3) its experience of persecution; and 4) its desire for utter rejection and exclusion of the rich from the churches.

A TENDENCY TOWARD SELF-CENTEREDNESS
In *ActsPet12Apost.*, the text which contains the commissioning of the disciples is 10.1–11.26:

> "Go into [the] city from which you came, which is called Habitation. Continue in endurance as you teach all those who

have believed in my name, because I have endured in hardships of
the faith, I will give you your reward. To the poor of that city give
what they need in order to live until I give them what is better,
which I told you that I will give you for nothing."

Peter answered and said to him, "Lord, you have taught us to
forsake the world and everything in it. We have renounced them
for your sake. What we are concerned about (now) is the food for
a single day. Where will we be able to find the needs that you ask
us to provide for the poor?"

The Lord answered and said, "O Peter, it was necessary that you
understand the parable that I told you! Do you not understand that
my name, which you teach, surpasses all riches, and the wisdom of
God surpasses gold, and silver and precious stones?"

He gave them the pouch of medicine and said, "Heal all the sick of
the city who believe in my name." Peter was afraid [to] reply to
him for a second time. He signaled to the one who was beside
him, who was John: "You talk this time." John answered and said,
"Lord, before you we are afraid to say many words. But it is you
who asks us to practice this skill. We have not been taught to be
physicians. How then will we know how to heal bodies as you
have told us?"

He answered them, "Rightly have you spoken, John, for I know
that the physicians of this world heal what belongs to the world.
The physicians of souls, however, heal the heart. Heal the bodies
first, therefore, so that through the real powers of healing for their
bodies, without medicine of the world, they may believe in you,
that you have power to heal the illnesses of the heart also."

In these lines the disciples are told by Jesus to teach (10.5), to provide for
the basic necessities of the poor (10.8–10) and to heal both bodies and
souls (10.31–11.26). While none of these ministries is unusual when
compared with the kind of ministerial activities which were typical of the
early Church (with the possible exception of that of physicians of souls;
11.18), the recipients of the ministry have changed from those designated
by the Story of the Pearl Merchant. In the Story of the Pearl Merchant
Peter tells the merchant, "It is necessary for us to spread the word of God

in every city harmoniously" (5.12). It would appear from this statement that Peter is expressing a type of ministry that is both evangelistic and universal. However, this is not the case with the Author/ Redactor's Theology (10.1–11.26). The commission in 10.1–11.26 reveals a different vision of ministry. When the disciples are commissioned to teach, their audience is described as those "who have believed in my name" (ΕΤΑΥΝΑ2ΤΕ ΕΠΑΡΑΝ; 10.5–6).[6] Again, when they are told to heal, the designated recipients are described in a similar fashion: "Heal all the sick of the city *who believe* (ΕΤΝΑ2ΤΕ) in my name" (10.33–11.1). Even when the disciples are told to care for the poor the implication is that these poor are also related to Jesus. Thus, the Poor, while not specifically designated as those who believe, are certainly well within the sphere of influence of the redactor's disciples and are envisioned as inevitably receiving the pearl as have the disciples. They too will be given by Jesus "what is better" (10.11).

The sphere of the disciples's ministry is missing the evangelistic and universal tone described by Peter in 5.12. Rather, the focus has been collapsed in upon the community. The community is to care for its own. Gone is any hint of outreach into the world. The author/ redactor has literally reshaped and redefined the commission that was initially part of the Story of the Pearl Merchant (the commission, 1.10–12; its guiding principle, 5.12). There are quite literally two different types of commissions at work within our text. As a first community trait I conclude that this theoretical community tended toward self-centeredness, all religious activities were to be in service of the community — or, better put, this is the policy that is advocated by the redactor.

---

[6] Note the use of the Coptic first perfect (which corresponds to the English simple past tense) "have believed" (ΑΥΝΑ2ΤΕ), which indicates an established church. This is further evidence of the chronological shift which I mentioned above.

SPIRITUALITY

The second aspect of the community to consider is how it conceives the activities that are part of its spiritual life. Patterson makes some interesting observations in regard to this subject. He notes that there are two conceptions of spirituality in our text. As evidence for this Patterson points to the peculiarity that while the disciples make the ascetic journey to Nine Gates and arrive at its gates they never enter the city. Instead, "Jesus turns them around, sending them back to the city from which they have come — Habitation, the earthly abode — to pursue the very down-to-earth task of serving the poor and the sick."[7] Patterson distinguishes between two understandings of the mystical experience. First, he claims that his "I, Peter" Source is a myth of apostolic origins stemming from "circles which valued asceticism and mysticism, and, so one might guess, still required such discipline from its leaders." Second, he claims that the author "creates a text which stands over against the earlier myth in a position of critical dissent." He views the author of our text as arguing that "it is not other-worldly, mystical visionary experience which establishes one in the apostolic office. The true apostolic commission is to serve the poor and the sick, and to avoid the injustice wrought in the world by the rich."[8]

I hesitate to accept Patterson's analysis completely. Patterson is correct in finding it peculiar that the disciples never actually enter Nine Gates. However, we do not know that the disciples were not given a tour of Nine Gates in the original Story of the Pearl Merchant. I have suggested above that they probably did receive just such a tour. If the Story of the Pearl Merchant was a *narratio fabulosa*, then, like the vision of Er and *Scipio's Dream* (as well as Lucian's satirical *A True Story*), it had some kind of heavenly tour.

Furthermore, it should not be regarded as strange that the disciples are sent back to Habitation. As noted in my reconstruction of the Story

---

[7] Patterson, "Redaction, Sources and Tendenz," 15.

[8] Ibid., 15.

of the Pearl Merchant in the section on the activity of the redactor, the disciples would have had to return to Habitation. In short, I argued that for a *narratio fabulosa* to function the visionary must return to reveal his or her vision and imparted wisdom to the world. Otherwise, there could be no story and no didactic content.

Another aspect of Patterson's understanding of these two spiritual viewpoints that I disagree with is his claim that the author "creates a text which stands over against the earlier myth in a position of critical dissent." If the author/ redactor were really so critical in his or her dissent, why keep the ascetical journey at all? However, the author/ redactor did keep the ascetical ascent section and made no attempt to deny its possibility or discredit it in any way. Rather, the author/ redactor has merely refocused the Story of the Pearl Merchant. In short, the original message of the Story of the Pearl Merchant was that "Other-worldly, mystical visionary experience leads to salvific knowledge." On the other hand, the message the author/ redactor is advancing is: "Other-worldly, mystical visionary experience leads to a proper understanding of one's own ministry." The author/ redactor's position on "other-worldly, mystical visionary experience" is accepting and respectful.

I suggested in my consideration of the Author/ Redactor's Theology that the author/ redactor has a different view of fasting than that which is presented in the Story of the Pearl Merchant. However, the author/ redactor's inclusion of the extreme ascetical demands prescribed by the merchant signals an appreciation for such discipline, if not an adherence. The demand that the world be renounced put forth in the Story of the Pearl Merchant is echoed by the author/ redactor (cf. 5.23–24 and 10.13–19). Therefore, I conclude that the community behind our text accepted "other-worldly, mystical visionary experience" and was ascetical in nature. It accepted extreme versions of this asceticism (e.g., the stringent requirements outlined by the merchant in 5.21–6.8) but was not unbendingly rigid, in that it did not demand such extreme asceticism from all of its members. Renunciation of the world was fundamental for everyone in the community, but it was recognized that those related to the community had basic needs. Evidence for this can be seen in the concern for the poor, who, according to the text, are not only the object of ministry but have a relationship with Jesus: "To the poor of that city give what they need in order to live until I give them what is better" (10.8–11). Further evidence is provided by Peter's statement, in relation to the community's leaders, that the disciples, apparently following the guidelines set forth in the Lord's Prayer, are now only concerned about the "food for a single day" (10.19). The community's asceticism, while open to sterner expressions, was pastorally balanced in its application of ascetic practices and realistic in its appreciation of its members's basic needs. It is possible that the redactor and his or her community viewed the different groups within the churches as capable of only certain levels of asceticism due to their inherent differences in nature. This leads us back to the three classes of people assumed by the Story of the Pearl Merchant.

AN EXPERIENCE OF PERSECUTION

A third question to examine is "How does the community perceive the world around it?" and the corresponding question, "What is the situation of the community in relation to the world?" The material found in 7.5b–19a is helpful in attempting to answer these questions:

> I responded, saying, "Justly [...] have men named it [...], because (by) everyone [who] endures his trials, cities are inhabited, and a precious kingdom comes from them, because they endure in the midst of the apostasies and the difficulties of the storms. So that in this way, the city of everyone who endures the burden of his yoke of faith will be inhabited, and he will be included in the kingdom of heaven.[9]

---

[9] In my previous treatment of the redaction question I discussed this section and suggested that these lines were secondary. This was primarily because they seem to reflect the same time frame as the material found in the Author/ Redactor's Theology.

According to these lines the world is a place where one must endure
"trials," "apostasies," and "storms." Furthermore, one's belief is
described as "the burden of his yoke of faith." There is a thoroughly
negative tone to these statements. The phrase translated "endures his
trials" uses two Greek loanwords, ὑπομένειν (to endure, submit) and
πειρασμός (temptation, testing) which may be referring to a situation of
persecution. This same combination of words is also used in Jas 1:2, 12,
in which sufferings for the sake of the faith are implied: "Count it all joy,
my brothers, when you meet various trials.... Blessed is the man who
endures trial, for when he has stood the test he will receive the crown of
life which God has promised to those who love him."[10]   There is a
violence in the imagery the redactor has chosen to employ. The phrase in
7.14, "difficulties of the storms," uses two descriptive Coptic words,
ⲔⲀϨ and ⲦⲎⲞⲨ, which are literally translated "buffeting of the wind."
Furthermore, the phrase in 7.16–17 "the burden of his yoke of faith"
(ⲠϨⲒⲤⲈ ⲚⲦⲈ ⲠⲈϤⲚⲀϨⲂ ⲚⲦⲈ ⲠⲒⲚⲀϨⲦⲈ) employs the word
ϨⲒⲤⲈ translated "burden" but which also means "suffering." This word
is used four times in *ActsPet12Apost.* The first occurrences, in 5.2 and
6.11, are part of the merchant's question to Peter about the "hardships"
on the road to "Nine Gates" and Peter's despairing response. When these
"hardships" are described they involve shadowy robbers and curious
animals that seek not only to dispossess the traveler of his or her

---

[10] Martin Dibelius notes, "Rejoice over trials (πειρασμοί) — that is the
first thought presented in the document. The reader, especially if he is not
thinking of 1:13, will not be able to interpret 'trials's here in any other way than
the persecutions which befall the entire group of "brethren" who are here
addressed." In regard to 1:12, he states, "The saying obviously belongs to the
theme touched upon in 1:2–4; therefore, 'to endure trial' (ὑπομένειν
πειρασμόν) is to be understood in the same sense as 'trials's (πειρασμοί)
'endurance' (ὑπομονή) in 1:2 and 1:3" (Dibelius, *James: A Commentary on the
Epistle of James* [Hermeneia; Philadelphia: Fortress, 1976] 71, 88). Heinrich
Seesemann agrees with this evaluation and points to 1 Pet 1:6, 4:12 as other
instances where πειρασμός refers to persecution, Seesemann, "πεῖρα κτλ,"
TDNT 6 (1968) 29–30.

belongings but also to kill and/ or eat the traveler. Of course, this material is found in the Story of the Pearl Merchant, so it should not receive the same weight as that deemed to be redactional. However, it is still valuable in that it demonstrates that ϩ|ⲤⲈ can be used to refer to violent circumstances.[11]

Again, in 10.7, Jesus recalls his own "hardships of the faith" (ϩⲈⲚϩⲒⲤⲈ ⲚⲦⲈ ⲦⲠ|ⲚⲀϩⲦⲈ). This is probably making reference to his persecution by the religious and political powers of his own day and the result, his crucifixion. When the word ϩ|ⲤⲈ is coupled with the metaphor, "yoke of faith," it can be taken as a reference to persecution and suffering. The phrase "yoke of faith" (ⲚⲀϩⲂ ⲚⲦⲈ ⲦⲠ|ⲚⲀϩⲦⲈ was probably originally ζυγὸς πίστεως) is unusual in extant early Christian literature. In Christian literature when similar constructions do appear, they have more positive connotations than that found in *ActsPet12Apost.* However, in general, ζυγός itself, when used metaphorically, conjures up much more negative images.[12]

---

[11] Indeed, in the Coptic NT ϩ|ⲤⲈ is regularly used to refer to Jesus' suffering on the cross or to the sufferings inflicted upon Christians in the world. It translates a variety of Greek words including: πάσχειν (Matt 16:21; 17:12; Mark 5:26; 8:31; 9:12; Luke 9:22; Phil 1:29; 2 Tim 1:12), συμπάσχειν (Rom 8:17), συγκακουχεῖν (Heb 11:25) and πάθημα (Rom 8:18; Heb 2:10).

[12] But cf. *Did.* 6.2; "if you are able to bear the whole yoke of the Lord, you will be perfect"; *1 Clem.* 16.17, "we have come under the yoke of his grace"; Clement *Strom.* 2.20, "we shall have put on us the mild yoke of the Lord from faith to faith"; see also *Pss. Sol.* 7.9; "and we shall be under your yoke forever, and under the lash of your chastening"; 17.32; "and he shall have the peoples of the Gentiles to serve him under his yoke." Such positive use of the metaphor of the yoke may have been influenced by the saying attributed to Jesus in Matt 11:28–30, "Come to me, all who labor and are heavy laden, and I will give you rest. Take my yoke upon you, and learn from me; for I am gentle and lowly in heart, and you will find rest for your souls. For my yoke is easy and my burden is light." However, it should be observed here that Jesus, using a "conscious paradox" is juxtaposing the approach to life he is advocating with that lived by his listeners. Jesus is reversing a negative image which symbolized the day-to-day existence of the peasant-class laborers who followed Jesus and using it in exactly the opposite way his listeners expected. This is demonstrated by the movement

Further light may be shed upon this possible situation of persecution if one examines the phrase "yoke of faith," and more specifically, the word ΝᏘϨΤЄ (faith, belief, trust). This word appears in five other places (6.16, 18; 10.5, 34; 11.24). Since in 7.17 belief is described negatively as a "yoke," these other passages may shed light upon the content of what is it believed that causes such "suffering." In three of these five passages, the "name" of Jesus is the object of belief (cf. 6.16; 10.5, 34).[13] It may be deduced that adherence to the name of Jesus has been the cause of the suffering. This is precisely the situation, also in reference to persecution, that is described in 1 Pet 4:14, "If you are reproached for the name of Christ, you are blessed, because the spirit of glory and of God rests upon you." The issue of belief in the name Jesus was part of the conflict between the Roman state and the early Church. Pliny the younger (ca. 110), the governor of Bithynia, in a letter to the Emperor Trajan describes how he ordered the Christians brought before him to revile the name of Christ as part of fulfilling the mandatory sacrifices to the Roman emperor and state gods. As to the Christians "reviling the name of Christ," Pliny states: "there is no forcing...those who are really Christians into any of these compliances" (*Ep.* 97).[14]

---

in the above quotation from the typical negative images associated with the yoke ("labor," "heavy laden") to Jesus' positive alternative (a yoke that is "easy" and "light"). However, it was the former of these two images (that of the negative) that was most commonly used when ζυγός is used metaphorically by Greek writers. In the NT, ζυγός is combined with δουλεία as in Gal 5:1, "Paul warns the Galatians who have been released by the Gospel from slavery not to rob themselves of this divinely effected and established freedom" (Karl Heinrich Rengstorf, "ζυγός in the NT," *TDNT* 2 [1964] 898–901). See also Acts 15:10 and 1 Tim 6:1. For classical examples see *LSJ*, s.v. 757a–b.

[13] The other two uses are related to belief in the Father (6.18) and the sick people's belief in the disciples's ability to heal (11.24).

[14] The ancient martyrologies are replete with precisely this kind of clash between the Church and the Roman state, e.g., *Mart. Polycarp* 9; *Mart. Carpus, Papylus and Agathonice* 2; *Acts of the Scillitan Martyrs* in Herbert Musurillo, *The Acts of the Christian Martyrs* (Oxford Early Christian Texts; Oxford: Clarendon, 1972). See also Justin, *1 Apol.* 1.4; Athenagoras, *A Plea for the Christians* 2 and

While the exact nature or cause of these persecutions facing the community, analogously described as "trials," "storms," and "hardships," is for now unclear, the reader is given a far more definite clue as to the community's situation with the mention of "apostasies."[15] Apostasy, or the abandonment of one's faith, results in a situation where the community "body" experiences the psychic shock of an "amputation" of one of its members. In this case the situation is described in the plural (ⲚⲓϬⲞⲬ), implying multiple amputations. This interior community problem suggests an exterior force at work upon the community. As to the identity of this exterior force one can only speculate. However, the usual list of suspects is a short one: 1) political (Roman) or 2) religious authority (intolerance by the Great Church).

My judgement is to rule out intolerance by the Great Church due to the fairly positive view the text holds of the churches. In 7.11, a

---

Tertullian, *Apol.* 2.

[15] It should be noted here that Schenke challenges the translation of Wilson and Parrott: "The Coptic word used here does indeed look like the normal (Sahidic) term for 'a lie' (so Krause: 'in the midst of the lies;' Wilson/ Parrott: 'in the midst of the apostasies'). Since however this is completely out of keeping with the context, we have to interpret our word as a homonym resulting from the influence of a lower Egyptian dialect (B,F), with the meaning 'wave'" ("The Acts of Peter and the Twelve Apostles," 425 n. 12). Schenke's translation is indeed possible (especially given the proximity of the metaphor "difficulties of the storms" — literally, "the buffeting of the wind"). Walter E. Crum allows for a translation of ϬⲞⲬ which means "curling back," which could be a reference to rolling waves (*Dictionary*, s.v. 807a). However, there are two reasons Wilson/ Parrott's translation makes sense: 1) the typical Coptic word for waves, ϨⲞⲈⲓⲘ is already used in 6.29 (granted, this could reflect differences in terminology between the Story of the Pearl Merchant and the Author/ Redactor), and 2) in this section, the Redactor is obviously mixing obvious (albeit vague) references to persecution ("trials" and "burden/ suffering") and metaphor ("difficulties of the storms" and "yoke"). Therefore, there is no reason to assume that ϬⲞⲬ must be interpreted metaphorically. Ultimately, both the obvious references and the metaphors must refer to real-world realities. Thus, Schenke is wrong to assume that the context forbids the translation "apostasies." In fact, I have demonstrated that the context (referring to persecution) would support Wilson/ Parrott's translation.

"precious kingdom" is described as emerging from the trials. This "kingdom" (MNT PPO), expressed in the traditional Christian phrase "kingdom of heaven" (TMNT PPO NNTΠHYE; 7.19), will be made up of those who endure "the burden (suffering) of this yoke of faith" (7.16–17) — a reference to martyrdom (whether that be in the form of confession or in blood). In 11.26–12.13, which I have argued came from the same hand as 7.5b–19a, even while "many" of the current church leaders are described as sinful and leading others to sin the validity of the churches as organizations is never questioned.

Thus I suggest that Roman authority (either on an Empire-wide level or only its local representatives) was the exterior force. To cause a significant portion of the community to resort to apostasy the exterior force would have to be able to pose a real threat. Roman authority would certainly fulfill this requirement. The section 11.26b–12.8a sheds further light upon the specific details of these apostasies:

> The rich men of the city, however, *those who did not see fit to acknowledge me* (NTOOY ETE MΠOYMΠϢAPϢ EϢNT EϨPAï), but who reveled in their wealth and pride — with such as these, therefore, do not dine in their houses nor be friends with them lest their partiality influence you. For many in the churches have shown partiality to the rich, because they also are sinful, and they give occasion for others to sin.

I have noted above in my redactional analysis that one of the differences in this section as opposed to the Story of the Pearl Merchant is that in 11.26b–12.8a, it is assumed that the rich have had a past (and presumably ongoing) relationship with the churches. However, in the Story of the Pearl Merchant the rich completely reject the merchant and subsequently drop out of the picture. If the same hand did write both this section and 7.5b–19a, then the failure of the rich to "acknowledge" Jesus may be referring to more than rejection of the merchant by the rich. It is probably a veiled reference to apostasy on the part of wealthy members of the community or, more precisely, the churches in general.

I make this distinction because the specific community that produced our text, with its strict policy of "renunciation" of the world, probably did not have wealthy members. This would explain the rather vague reference to apostasies. The community is commenting upon the apostasies they have witnessed (probably from some distance) in the less ascetical, more worldly churches. This is not to say that this community was unaffected by the Roman pressure. The tone of 7.5b–19a is too genuinely negative. In my judgement the redactor has witnessed the persecution from afar, as those in today's suburbs hear of the violence and crime of the inner city through the medium of television and the news media but are only occasionally personally touched by it. The redactor may well have been a member of a more rigorist sect of Christianity, loyal yet desirous of a greater expression of their faith, that had withdrawn to a location outside a major city. They were close enough to remain well informed of the current state of affairs in the churches yet far enough removed from the daily politics of the churches to be a prophetic voice of correction.

Due to the simple fact that wealthy members of the churches would stand to lose the most in a persecution[16] (at least in terms of possessions)

---

[16] Banishment and the confiscation of lands and goods was a punishment of the Roman authorities which would be specifically injurious to those wealthy Christians who might consider confessing their faith. *Shepherd of Hermas*, Par. 1.1.1–6 provides a metaphor of dual citizenship (the world and heaven). In this parable the effects of riches, the threat of banishment, confiscation of goods and the peril of apostasy are discussed: "He said to me: 'You know,' he said, 'that you who are servants of God are living in a foreign country, for your city is far from this city. If, therefore, you know,' he said, 'your city in which you are destined to live, why do you prepare fields and expensive possessions and buildings and useless rooms here? The one who prepares these things for this city, therefore, does not plan to return to his own city. Foolish and double-minded and miserable man, don't you realize that all these things are foreign to you, and under someone else's authority? For the lord of this city will say, 'I don't want you to live in my city; instead, leave this city, because you do not conform to my laws.' So, you who have fields and dwellings and many other possessions, what will you do with your field and your house and all the other things you have prepared for yourself when you are expelled by him? For the lord of this country has every right to say to you, 'Either conform to my laws, or get out of my country.' So what are you going to do, since you are subject to the law of your own city? For the sake of

it is possible that they would be the first to waver in their commitment.[17]
Even if they desired to retain their belief in Jesus they would be the first
to look for some kind of safe compromise that would allow them to avoid
confrontation with the Romans (and subsequent punishment) and yet
retain their faith.   Hence, they might physically apostasize (e.g., by
offering sacrifice) yet justify it to themselves and others by mentally
withholding consent. This tendency to compromise might be the sin to
which this section refers.   Furthermore, if the wealthy Christians
compromised they might have attempted to persuade the leaders of the
churches to follow suit with the noble intention of preserving the
churches. The relationship between the church leaders and the wealthy
members of their communities might have given "occasion for others to
sin" (12.7–8) by those leaders (who were influenced by the wealthy)

---

your fields and the rest of your possessions, will you totally renounce your own
law and live according to the law of this city? Take care; it may not be in your
best interest to renounce your own law, for if you should want to return to your
city, you will certainly not be accepted, because you have renounced the law of
your city, and will be shut out of it." The Roman historian, Dio Cassius (*Roman
History* 67.14) describes a period of persecution under Domitian, "And the same
year Domitian slew, along with many others, Flavius Clemens the consul,
although he was a cousin and had to wife Flavia Domitilla, who was also a relative
of the emperor's. The charge brought against them both was that of atheism, a
charge on which many others who drifted into Jewish ways were condemned.
Some of these were put to death, and the rest were at least deprived of their
property."   This passage, traditionally suspected to refer to persecution of
Christians, is significant regardless if it refers to the persecution of Christians or
not because it too mentions the confiscation of property.

[17] Once again, *Hermas* provides evidence for linking wealth and
apostasy. In Vis. 3.6.5, part of the vision of the building (the Church) and the
many stones (types of people) is explained in relation to the wealthy: "'And who
are the white and round stones that do not fit into the building, madam?' She
answered and said to me, 'How long will you be foolish and stupid, asking about
everything and understanding nothing? These are the ones who have faith, but
also have the riches of the world. Whenever persecution comes, they deny their
Lord because of their riches and their business affairs.'" Similar sentiments can
also be found in Par. 8.8.2; 8.9.1–3.

encouraging their congregations to follow the example of the rich and apostasize. Further witness to the community's experience of outside pressure is the relationship between Jesus and the community that is described in 10.6–8: "because I have endured in the hardships of the faith, I will give you your reward." Jesus' example is presented to the community so as encourage them "in the midst of difficulties of the storms." The message is simple: "Jesus went through hardships (sufferings), therefore, it is fitting that you (the community) go through hardships (sufferings). But don't despair, there will be a reward for your troubles." It is the same sentiment as that found in John 15:18–20:

> If the world hates you, know that it has hated me before it hated you. If you were of the world, the world would love its own; but because you are not of the world, but I chose you out of the world, therefore the world hates you. Remember the word that I said to you, "A servant is not greater than his master." If they persecuted me, they will persecute you; if they kept my word, they will keep yours also.[18]

---

[18] As I have stated the effect of this passage is really twofold: 1) the disciples (and by implication those who follow them) are told to "continue in endurance" and 2) that which is to be endured is indicated in that Jesus refers to his own sufferings as a model for the community. Thus the community is subtly warned of future sufferings and an example of proper conduct is provided. This is similar to two formal elements typically associated with farewell discourses: the speaker as model and prediction of future persecutions. William S. Kurz explains, "Farewells often portray the speaker as a model for disciples's behavior, as Jesus is in washing their feet (Jn 13) or Paul is in faithfully teaching the whole gospel and working for his own support (Acts 20). Living models of behavior are important for the exhortatory and educational intent of ancient and biblical farewell speeches. Ethical and religious teachers were expected to illustrate their teaching by their behavior, just as a contemporary coach or director teaches fundamentals to the team or cast not only by words but by demonstrating them in action.... Prophecies by an illustrious ancestor, founder or past leader, which play such a central role in farewell addresses, interpret the time of the readers as foretold by God and therefore part of his plan. Distressing incidents in the lives of the readers become more understandable when seen as part of God's plan from of old. They are not meaningless afflictions but foreseen by God who remains in control of history, even when he seems to be absent in such tribulations"

REJECTION OF THE RICH

The fourth point, which is related to our discussion above, is the severity of the community's rejection of the rich: "The rich men of the city, however, those who did not see fit even to acknowledge me, but who reveled in their wealth and pride — with such as these, therefore, do not dine in their houses nor be friends with them, lest their partiality influence you. For many in the churches have shown partiality to the rich, because they also are sinful, and they give occasion for others to sin" (11.32–12.8a). The author/ redactor portrays Jesus as forbidding any further contact with the rich. The rich who are being rejected were at one time associated with the churches, probably as members. Otherwise the outrage that is expressed by Jesus (as a mouthpiece for the redactor) over the rich people's failure "to acknowledge me" loses its power. What surprise is it if those who do not claim to be followers of Jesus fail to acknowledge him? Further, the disciples are forbidden to dine with the rich and are ordered not to extend the title "friend" to them.[19] This title was often used as a self-designation by the early Christians, especially

(*Farewell Addresses in the New Testament* [Zacchaeus Studies: New Testament; Collegeville, MN: Michael Glazier/ Liturgical Press, 1990] 21–23). Cf. also Raymond E. Brown, *The Gospel According to John (xiii–xxi)* (AB 29a; Garden City, NY: Doubleday, 1970) 597–601. Perhaps some further, more contemporary (to *ActsPet12Apost.*), insight can be gained from Pseudo-Clementine *Homilies* 2.3: "It is proper to ply men with words which strengthen the soul in anticipation of evil; so that, if at any time any evil comes upon them, the mind, being forearmed with the right argument, may be able to bear up under that which befalls it: for then the mind knows in the crisis of the struggle to have recourse to him who succored it by good counsel" (cf. also Heliodorus, *An Ethiopian Story* 2.24).

[19] In *ActsPet12Apost.* this title is used six times. Of these six instances, three describe the relationships between either the merchant and Peter and, by extension, the rest of the disciples (3.3, 9) or Peter and the disciples (7.21), two describe the relations between the various poor people (4.9, 25) and one, the text currently being examined, uses it as a term which is exclusive to the community. This, of course, is in agreement with that usage in 3.3, 9 and 7.21. This term is never used in reference to the wealthy — except in 12.2, where it is denied them.

those groups with ties to gnosticism.[20] Apparently, in the recent past other church leaders have both dined with the rich and extended the title "friend" to the rich. If this were not the case, what would be the sense of such a prohibition?

The position which is advocated by the author/ redactor for the community is, quite obviously, an extreme one. It is also obvious that this was not the policy of the churches referred to in the text. As evidence of this I would point to the contact of the "many" (leaders) with the rich mentioned in 12.4b–8a. It is a "new" instruction of the Lord, a reaction to a situation deemed critical enough to warrant a radical break from previous norms. This rejection leaves no room for any exceptions. This severe rejection and exclusion of the rich is not typical of the NT and early Christian literature.

The Jesus of the gospels is presented as associating with a variety of people, spanning the social strata from outcasts (e.g., a leper; Mark 1:40–45; the possessed man; Mark 5:1–20) to the wealthy tax collectors, Levi and Zacchaeus (Luke 5:29–32; 19:1–10). Likewise, Luke's gospel, which has an obvious empathy for the poor, strongly encourages the reader: "Sell your possessions, and give alms; provide yourselves with purses that do not grow old, with a treasure in the heavens that does not fail, where no thief approaches and no moth destroys" (12:33). However,

---

[20] "Evidently the natural term οἱ φίλοι did not gain currency in the catholic church, owing to the fact that οἱ ἀδελφοί was preferred as being still more inward and warm. In gnostic circles, on the other hand, which arose subsequently under the influence of Greek philosophy, οἱ φίλοι seems to have been used during the second century. Thus Valentinus wrote a homily περὶ φίλων (Clem., *Strom* 6.6.52); Epiphanius, the son of Carpocrates, founded a Christian communistic guild after the model of the Pythagoreans, and perhaps also after the model of the Epicurean school and its organization (Clem., *Strom* 3.5–9); while the Abercius-inscription, which is probably gnostic, tells how faith furnished the fish as food for (τοῖς) φίλοις. Clement of Alexandria would have had no objection to describe the true gnostic circle as "friends." It is he who preserves the fine saying (*Quis Dives* 32): "The Lord did not say [in Luke 16:9] give, or provide, or benefit, or aid, but make a friend. And friendship springs, not from a single act of giving, but from invariable relief vouchsafed and from long intercourse" (Harnack, *The Mission and Expansion of Christianity*, 421).

in this gospel's version of the Story of the Rich Young Man (18:18–27), despite the rich ruler's inability to renounce his possessions he is not rejected by Jesus. Salvation for the rich is still presented as being "possible with God."

In regard to the attitudes expressed toward wealth/ poverty in the NT as a whole, Boniface Ramsey has discovered what he calls "five data that are pertinent to any discussion of poverty and wealth in the early Church": 1) allusions to the existence of both rich and poor in the early communities (e.g., 1 Cor 1:26); 2) a concern for helping the poor (e.g., Paul's "offering for the saints" in 2 Corinthians 9); 3) an occasional yet marked predisposition for the poor and against the rich (Luke 1:46–55); 4) the ideal of voluntary poverty for the Gospel (Matt 19:16–30); and 5) the descriptions found in Acts of the early Church and its holding all things in common (2:44–47; 4:32–36).[21]

One possible exception to Ramsey's summary is the fierce invective of James against the rich. Dibelius isolates three instances where James attacks the rich: 1:9–11; 2:5–12 and 5:1–6:

> Let the lowly brother boast in his exaltation, and the rich in his humiliation, because like the flower of the grass he will pass away. For the sun rises with its scorching heat and withers the grass; its flower falls, and its beauty perishes. So will the rich man fade in the midst of his pursuits.

> Listen, my beloved brethren. Has not God chosen those who are poor in the world to be rich in faith and heirs of the kingdom which he has promised to those who love him? But you have dishonored the poor man. Is it not the rich who oppress you, is it not they who drag you into court? Is it not they who blaspheme the honorable name which was invoked over you? If you really fulfill the royal law, according to the scripture, "You shall love

---

[21] Ramsey, "Christian Attitudes to Poverty and Wealth," in Ian Hazlett, ed., *Early Christianity: Origins and Evolution to A.D. 600* (Nashville: Abingdon, 1991) 256.

your neighbor as yourself," you do well. But if you show
partiality, you commit sin, and are convicted by the law as
transgressors. For whoever keeps the whole law but fails in one
point has become guilty of all of it. For he who said, "Do not
commit adultery," also said, "Do not kill." If you do not commit
adultery but do kill, you have become a transgressor of the law. So
speak and so act as those who are to be judged under the law of
liberty.

Come now, you rich, weep and howl for the miseries that are
coming upon you. Your riches have rotted and your garments are
motheaten. Your gold and silver have rusted, and their rust will be
evidence against you and will eat your flesh like fire. You have
laid up treasure for the last days. Behold, the wages of the laborers
who mowed your fields, which you kept back by fraud, cry out;
and the cries of the harvesters have reached the ears of the Lord of
Hosts. You have lived on the earth in luxury and pleasure; you
have fattened your hearts in a day of slaughter. You have
condemned, you have killed the righteous man; he does not resist
you.

In these statements, Dibelius sees as background the ancient Jewish
tradition of defending the pious poor against the onslaught of the
oppressive power of their rich enemies, which was subsequently
employed by the Jesus movement.[22] He argues that James's own
community did not contain rich Christians: "James shouted his threats out
the window for all the world to hear; no doubt he still did not have in his

---

[22] "The preaching of Jesus and the movement it stirred up supplied new
strength to this pauperism by revitalizing the eschatological hope. Whereas the
eschatology of salvation in the time of the exile proclaimed the overthrow of the
national order — 'poor' Israel would be exalted and her enemies destroyed —, the
gospel of Jesus proclaimed the overthrow of the social order, in the manner of the
Jewish apocalyptic literature of the Poor (*1 Enoch* 94ff): salvation to the poor and
destruction for the rich (Luke 6:20ff)" (Dibelius, *James*, 42).

own house very many of these rich who are attacked."[23] Dibelius states this position most clearly in his comments on 1:9–11:

> Whom does he have in mind? In any event, it must be people who are spiritually alien to the pious community, for otherwise the conclusion of the saying could not read as it does. Therefore, he may have had in mind primarily non-Christians; but if he was thinking here of Christians as well, then these are people whom he considers no longer to be included in a proper sense within Christendom.

The rich rejected by James were, most likely, never part of the community but, may have been its oppressors.[24]

In other early Christian teachings the rich are consistently assumed to be part of the Church community. Consequently, the emphasis is upon the rich sharing their wealth with the Church so that the needs of the poor may be supplied.[25] In *Hermas*, Par. 2.5–7, the interdependence of the rich and poor in the Christian community is stressed. The rich provide for the poor and the poor intercede for the rich. The rich are urged to give "unhesitatingly" to the poor. This is described as "a great and acceptable deed in the sight of God" because the rich person has learned to "administer his riches correctly" and "rightly accomplishes the Lord's

---

[23] Ibid., 45.

[24] Ibid., 87–88.

[25] Examples of this are numerous. See *Didache* 4.5–8, *1 Clem.* 38.1; *Diognetus* 10.6 and Irenaeus, *Adv. haer.* 4.30.3. For a collection of quotations from the early Fathers on these questions see Peter C. Phan, *Social Thought* (Message of the Fathers of the Church 20; Wilmington: Glazier, 1984); also see Charles Avila, *Ownership: Early Christian Teaching* (Maryknoll, NY: Orbis, 1983) and William J. Walsh and John P. Langan, "Patristic Social Consciousness — The Church and the Poor," in John C. Haughey, ed., *The Faith that Does Justice: Examining the Christian Sources for Social Change* (Woodstock Studies 2; New York: Paulist, 1977) 113–51.

ministry." After examining Hermas's treatment of the rich and poor, Carolyn Osiek concludes:

> Wealth and the wealthy are discussed frequently throughout
> Hermas. The rich are at times severely criticized, but they are
> never condemned without hope. Their traditional obligation to
> give to the needy is reinforced, but outside of Sim. 2 the poor have
> no role of their own...the poor and the needy are never addressed
> and are mentioned only as recipients of charity, while the rich are
> addressed several times and it is their perspective to which appeal
> is consistently made. Consequently, there can be no doubt that the
> paraenesis of Hermas about wealth and poverty is intended for the
> rich, who are presented as insiders called to repentance.[26]

In many early Christian works which address this subject, even when the dangers of wealth or the greed of the rich man are expounded upon, the goals of these teachings are 1) that those who are rich may attain salvation by learning how to use properly their wealth,[27] and/ or 2) that the rich might understand what is the nature of true wealth.[28]

---

[26] Osiek, *Rich and Poor in the Shepherd of Hermas: An Exegetical-Social Investigation* (CBQMS 15; Washington, DC: Catholic Biblical Association, 1983) 57.

[27] For example, Lactantius *Divine Institutes* 6.12: "this is the greatest and most authentic fruit of riches: not to use wealth for one's own personal enjoyment but for the benefit of many; not for one's own present profit, but for justice, which alone endures forever."

[28] This is a major issue for Clement of Alexandria. In *The Tutor* 2.3.38 he writes: "True wealth is poverty of desires, and the true nobility is not that founded upon riches, but that which comes from a contempt for them." This theme of true wealth and poverty is taken up in *Who is the Rich Man that Shall be Saved?* 14–20: "He then is truly and rightly rich who is rich in virtue, and is capable of making a holy and faithful use of any fortune. While he is spuriously rich who is rich, according to the flesh, and turns life into outward possession, which is transitory and perishing, and now belongs to one, now to another, and in the end to nobody at all. Again, in the same way there is a genuine poor man, and another counterfeit and falsely so called. He that is poor in spirit, and that is the

Thus utter rejection of the rich as members of the Christian community as is found in *ActsPet12Apost.* is not typical of early Christian teaching. This is not to say that there were not others who also rejected the rich. However, these elements seem to be associated with heretical theologies and even these extremists still concern themselves with the salvation of the rich. Ramsey writes:

> Yet sentiments hostile to wealth survived and exerted their influence elsewhere. Cyril of Jerusalem, among others, reports that the Manicheans said that gold and silver belonged to the devil, to which he replied, citing Haggai 2:8: "God says plainly by the prophet: The silver is mine and the gold is mine, and I will give it to whomever I desire" (*Catechetical Lectures* 8.6–7). The Synod of Gangra, held in Asia Minor toward the middle of the fourth century, had to condemn a sect of heretics called Eustathians who insisted that the rich who did not forsake their property had no hope of being saved. The Pelagians held the same opinion, and Augustine counters it by pointing out that the patriarchs of the Old Testament were all wealthy and were not on that account denied salvation. (*Epistle* 157.23)[29]

If we take this prohibition of Jesus against the rich in *ActsPet12Apost.* seriously, then we must conclude that something very significant has occurred so as to cause the redactor to advocate such a radical and new position. These thoughts have led me to consider a possible dating for the final redaction of *ActsPet12Apost.*

---

right thing, and he that is poor in the worldly sense, which is a different thing" (19).

[29] Ramsey, *Beginning to Read the Fathers* (New York: Paulist, 1985) 185.

Chapter 6
Healers of Bodies and Souls:
A Post-Decian Dating

ActsPet12Apost. functioned in the redactor's community setting as an "origins text." By "origins text" I mean that this text attempts to provide an apostolic authority and Christological mandate for the currently advocated practice of a particular community. As an origins text, it narrates an initial apostolic commission which provides a reasonably detailed picture of what Jesus wants from his ministers. Consideration of *ActsPet12Apost.* as an origins text leads to an interesting question which is related to the issue of dating.

At this point in the history of scholarly analysis of *ActsPet12Apost.*, the commentators who have mentioned the issue of dating have generally assigned this text to the 2nd or 3rd century A.D.[1] This begs the question: Why would an origins text be needed in the 2nd or 3rd century? This is especially interesting in light of the existence and use of the major

---

[1] Patterson suggests that "the issues of its date and provenance have yet to be settled, but a second or third century date in Syria seems likely" ("Redaction, Sources and Tendenz," 1). In addressing the issue of date Schenke writes, "There is also scarcely any serviceable indication in the text for answering the question of the date of composition, i.e., how long before the first half of the 4th century, the terminus post quem non, the ActPt was composed. We are practically reduced to estimates. Thus scholars speak in quite general terms of the 2nd and/ or 3rd century. To my mind we ought by all means to reckon with the possibility that ActPt could already have come into being in the 2nd century" ("The Acts of Peter and the Twelve Apostles," 414). Parrott was more specific as to the dating of the text's component parts: "As to the date, the allegory and Peter's vision are probably no later than the middle of the second century A.D., in view of their affinities with the Shepherd of Hermas (dated mid-second century or before). The final form of the tractate then would be dated late in the second century or early in the third" ("The Acts of Peter and the Twelve Apostles," in Aziz S. Atiya, ed., *The Coptic Encyclopedia* [10 vols; New York: Macmillan, 1991] 1.63).

"origins texts" (i.e., the canonical gospels). I propose this answer: This origins text was needed because the community in question was rebuilding and recovering from persecution, and they wished (or felt the need) for a Christological mandate and apostolic sanction for the new rules they were proposing as normative for their community.

What are these new rules? The commands to teach, care for the poor and heal can hardly be described as novel. If this is so, what is the new element in these instructions that necessitates their being written down? At first glance there are two new aspects in Jesus' instructions. First, there is the self-centered tendency of these instructions to place an exclusive focus on the community as the recipient of all ministry. This tendency would seem to fly in the face of the universal mission theology which was common in the early church and is evidenced to us by such NT texts as Matt 28:19–20; Luke 24:46–48 and Acts 1:8, as well as the obvious spread of Christianity that characterizes the first three centuries of the Christian era. Second, there is the intriguing rejection of the rich. This rejection is not a simple chastisement or censure but rather a disassociation, a disassociation which clearly excludes without mention or hope of reprieve.

Why? The answer is to be found in the redactional material in 7.5–19, with the references to persecution and apostasies. It is a direct result of this situation of recent persecution/ apostasies that the two aforementioned new elements in Jesus' commission have been advocated. (I refer to that material found in the second commission in the Author/ Redactor's Theology.) These elements were an extreme response to an extreme situation. The rich are the logical candidates for apostasy. The promise of a bountiful hereafter carries far less weight for one who already possesses everything than it does for those who are destitute. I am not trying to imply that no wealthy Christians remained faithful. This would be patently untrue as is evidenced by the devotion of Perpetua (*Mart. Perpetua and Felicitas* 2) and Cyprian (Pontius, *Life and Passion of Cyprian* 2). Rather I am merely stating the obvious, that he rich have more to lose, and therefore in times of persecution it is reasonable to think that in a situation of persecution that they would be first to seek a compromise. Hence, the rich are rejected as a reaction to their rejection (apostasy) of the community.[2] Furthermore, a post-persecution setting would explain the self-centered tendencies of the community.

In this model the community would naturally be recoiling from an obviously hostile world to "lick its wounds." After emerging from a period of severe persecution a community would need to focus all its energy upon itself so as to regain some semblance of normalcy. If one accepts this hypothesis of a community that has been shocked by persecution and apostasies, then the question remains whether these clues in the text suggest a particular post-persecution period for the final redaction of this text. This is no easy task.[3] Persecution is very slippery

---

[2] This is really an attempt at rationalizing the situation. It is similar in spirit to 1 John 2:19: "They went out from us, but they were not of us; for if they had been of us, they would have continued with us; but they went out, that it might be plain that they all are not of us."

[3] The subject of persecution is a very complicated one. Persecution during the first three centuries of our era can be described as sporadic, local and usually in response to civic disturbances. Despite all the evidence from the key primary sources (Athenagoras, *A Plea for the Christians*; Clement of Alexandria, *Strom.* 4.4–12; Eusebius, *Hist. eccl.* (select passages); Lactantius, *The Divine Institutes*; Lucian, *The Death of Peregrinus*; Origen, *Exhortation to Martyrdom*; Tertullian, *Apology*; *On Flight in Persecution*; *On the Spectacles*; *To the Martyrs*; *To Scapula* as well as numerous martyrdoms of varying reliability) there were only three periods where persecution was directed from an Imperial level (under Decius, ca. 249–51; Valerian, ca. 257–60 and Diocletian, ca. 302–312). As Adela Yarbro Collins has so effectively demonstrated (*Crisis and Catharsis: The Power of the Apocalypse* [Philadelphia: Westminster, 1984]) persecution has a very subjective element. To make matters worse, the legal reasons for the Roman state's persecution of the Church are far from clear as is evidenced by the large volume of often contradictory secondary literature that is available. The most famous dialogue on these questions is that of G. E. M. de Sainte Croix ("Why Were the Early Christians Persecuted?" *Past and Present* 26 [1963] 6–38; "Why Were the Early Christians Persecuted? — A Rejoinder," *Past and Present* 27 [1964] 28–33) and A. N. Sherwin-White ("Early Persecutions and the Roman Law Again," *JTS* 3 [1952] 199–213; "Why Were the Early Christians Persecuted? — An Amendment," *Past and Present* 27 [1964] 23–27). See also Timothy D. Barnes, "Legislation Against the Christians," *JRS* 58 (1968) 32–50; Christopher

and subjective. Every ancient source must be weighed as to its reliability and proximity to the events in question. If the writer is a historian, how reliable are his sources and is there an attempt to gloss over less favorable events? If the writer is an apologist, what about the tendency to exaggerate? If the writer is non-Christian, how much do they really know from first hand experience and what reflects rumor and cultural prejudice?[4] These questions must never be far from our minds as we approach this topic.

I suggest that *ActsPet12Apost.* received its final redaction in the years immediately following the Decian Persecution of late 249 to 251 A.D.[5] This assertion is based on three aspects of striking similarity between *ActsPet12Apost.* and the available details in the historical sources which describe the Decian persecution: 1) the infamous reputation for apostasy (especially among the rich) for which this period is known; 2) the negative impact this persecution had upon the relationship between the Church and its wealthy members;[6] and 3) the unique usage of physicians

---

J. Haas, "Imperial Religious Policy and Valerian's Persecution of the Church," *CH* 52 (1983) 133–44; and L. F. Janssen, "'Superstitio' and the Persecution of the Christians," *VC* 33 (1979) 131–59.

[4] For an excellent collection of non-Christian writers's opinions on Christianity see Stephen Benko, "Pagan Criticism of Christianity During the First Two Centuries A. D.," *ANRW* 2.23.2 (1980) 1055–1114.

[5] I specifically note that I am referring to the final redaction, since there were at least three distinct stages which led to the text as we now have it: 1) the composition of the underlying sources, the Story of the Pearl Merchant, ca. mid-2nd century (as argued by Parrott, *The Coptic Encyclopedia*, 1.63) and the Resurrection Appearance, probably contemporary with the canonical stories, i.e., mid 1st century); 2) the final redaction in which these two sources were combined, edited and expanded upon by the Author/ Redactor (ca. A.D. 251–256); and 3) the translation of this text from Greek to Coptic (before the mid 5th century [James M. Robinson, "Introduction," *The Nag Hammadi Library in English*, 22).

[6] For the details of this persecution I have relied heavily on the reconstruction provided in W. H. C. Frend, *Martyrdom and Persecution in the Early Church* (Garden City, NY: Doubleday, 1967) 285–323. Frend's classic study is invaluable for its citation of the key sources.

of bodies/ souls imagery.[7]   In the pages that follow I shall treat each of these issues in turn.

PERSECUTION AND APOSTASY

Decius, forcibly declared emperor by his legions in Pannonia and Moesia in the summer of 249, was officially recognized as such by the Senate after his defeat of the Emperor Philip in September of 249, at the Battle of Verona. Immediately after ascending the throne in late September, Decius, an efficient and competent administrator, set about an empire-wide campaign of rebuilding infrastructure which included construction and repair of roads along the Danube, in Syria, Galatia, Africa, Spain and Britian as is evidenced by dedicatory inscriptions of the period.[8] His brief reign (September 249 to ca. July 251), which was marked by external pressures on the Empire, produced the first empire-wide persecution of Christians. Decius and his son, Herennius Etruscus, would eventually meet their deaths in the Balkans at the hands of the Goths at Plevna and

---

[7] In making this assertion I recognize that apostasy was not unique to any single persecution. For example, apostasy is mentioned by Pliny in *Ep.* 97 to Trajan regarding the Christians: "An anonymous information was laid before me containing a charge against several persons, who upon examination denied they were Christian, or had ever been so. They repeated after me an invocation to the gods, and offered religious rites with wine and incense before your statue (which for that purpose I had ordered to be brought, together with those of the gods), and even reviled the name of Christ: whereas there is no forcing, it is said, those who are really Christians into any of these compliances: I thought it proper, therefore, to discharge them. Some among those who were accused by a witness in person at first confessed themselves Christians, but immediately after denied it; the rest owned indeed that they had been of that number formerly, but had now (some above three, others more, a few above twenty years ago) renounced that error" (William Melmoth, trans., *Letters of Gaius Plinius Caecilius Secundus* [Harvard Classics; New York: Collier, 1909]). Furthermore, during the initial stages of the Diocletian persecution (ca. 302) Eusebius states that, despite the bravery of various leaders of the church, "countless others, whose souls cowardice had numbed beforehand, readily proved weak at the first assault" (*Hist. eccl.* 8.3).

[8] For a reconstruction of the events of Decius's reign based on inscriptions, coins and other historical sources see F. S. Salisbury and H. Mattingly, "The Reign of Trajan Decius," *JRS* 14 (1924) 1–23.

in the marshes of Dobrudja respectively.[9] However, Decius may not have intended to single out Christians for abuse. Michael M. Sage suggests that Decius's edict of December 249 ordering mandatory sacrifices to the traditional gods was really about encouraging political and religious unity in the empire. The available *libelli*, or certificates proving a person's compliance with the edict, from this period do not indicate any special attention to Christianity:

> The certificates preserved indicate that the edict was not directed specifically against the Christians, but was a general measure of sacrifice to be carried out by all inhabitants of the Empire. Even a priestess of Petesouchos was forced to comply. There was no provision for the specific renunciation of Christianity. A century and a half earlier, when dealing with Christians, Pliny had added to the ceremony of libation and sacrifice the requirement that those who had renounced Christianity had to curse the name of Christ. The Decian certificates, on the other hand, point to a sacrifice to the gods as a universal requirement, without singling out a particular group. They stress that the recipient has always been a worshiper of the gods.[10]

Regardless of why the edict was issued, its result was devastating to the Christian communities in the Empire's leading cities. Sage simply states, "The persecution of Decius had resulted in apostasy on a previously unknown scale." Despite the martyrdoms of Bishop Fabian in Rome, Bishop Alexander of Jerusalem and Bishop Babylas of Antioch,[11]

---

[9] Ibid., 18.

[10] Sage, *Cyprian* (Patristic Monograph Series 1; Cambridge: Philadelphia Patristic Foundation, 1975) 174–75. Sage provides an description of the Decian Persecution in pages 165–266. For Greek texts of these *libelli* with English translations, see John R. Knipfing, "The Libelli of the Decian Persecution," *HTR* 16 (1923) 345–90.

[11] See Eusebius, *Hist. eccl.* 6.39.2–5.

many Christians readily preformed the demanded *supplicatio* (incense or sacrifice) or obtained a *libellus* through bribery or some other means.[12]

THE NEGATIVE IMPACT OF PERSECUTION UPON THE CHURCH AND ITS WEALTHY MEMBERS

An especially infamous aspect of the Decian Persecution is the strong connection between apostasy and wealth. In *ActsPet12Apost.* 10:1–13, the focus of ministry is upon the poor. The rich are utterly excluded, presumably because they were the ones who apostasized ("who did not see fit even to acknowledge me," 11.28–29). In his treatise, *On the Lapsed*, written ca. 251 in the wake of the Decian persecution, Cyprian, bishop of Carthage during and after this persecution, writes quite specifically about the negative impact wealth had upon the community before the persecution:

> Each one was desirous of increasing his estate; and forgetful of what believers had either done before in the times of the apostles, or always ought to do, they with the insatiable ardor of covetousness, devoted themselves to the increase of their property. Among the priests there was no devotedness of religion; among the ministers there was no sound faith: in their works there was no mercy; in their manners there was no discipline. In men, their beards were defaced; in women, their complexion was dyed: the eyes were falsified from what God's hand had made them; their hair was stained with falsehood. Crafty frauds were used to deceive the hearts of the simple, subtle meanings for circumventing the brethren. They united in marriage with unbelievers; they prostituted the members of Christ to the Gentiles. They would swear not only rashly, but even more, would swear

---

[12] For more on the Decian Persecution see George C. Brauer, *The Age of the Soldier Emperors* (Park Ridge, NJ: Noyes, 1975) 19–57; G. W. Clarke, "Double-Trials in the Persecution of Decius," *Historia* 22 (1973) 651–63; Paul Keresztes, "The Decian libelli and Contemporary Literature," *Latomus* 34 (1975) 761–81; and G. W. Clarke, "Some Observations on the Persecution of Decius," *Antichthon* 3 (1969) 63–76.

falsely; would despise those set over them with haughty swelling, would speak evil of one another with envenomed tongue, would quarrel with one another with obstinate hatred. (chapter 6)[13]

In addition, in *On the Lapsed* 2 and 10 Cyprian states that among the punishments endured by the Christian community, "one's country was to be left, and the loss of one's estate was to be suffered." Obviously, it was the rich who were most profoundly affected by such punishments. The poor could be poor in any town or province, while for the rich this would mean a total change in economic condition, i.e., loss of traditional estates, land, businesses, etc. Cyprian proceeds to speak more specifically about wealth, describing it as "the matter and cause of our wound":

A blind love of one's own property has deceived many; nor could they be prepared for, or at ease in, departing when their wealth fettered them like a chain. Those were the chains to them that remained — those were the bonds by which both virtue was retarded, and faith burdened, and the spirit bound, and the soul hindered; so that they who were involved in earthly things might become a booty and food for the serpent, which, according to God's sentence, feeds upon the earth. (chapter 11)

Therefore Cyprian urges the wealthy person to follow the words of Jesus, "If you will be perfect, go, sell all that you have, and give to the poor, and you will have treasure in heaven: and come follow me" (Matt 19:21). While Cyprian himself does not reject the wealthy, he does urge them to divest themselves of their wealth and possessions so that they would not "perish by their riches." According to Cyprian, the wealthy are victims of their own abundance:

---

[13] There is good patristic evidence that documents the gradual increase in wealthy and high born adherents to Christianity from approximately the time of the Emperor Commodus (ca. 180–190). See Eusebius, *Hist. eccl.* 5.21.1; in Alexandria, Origen, *C. Cels.* 3.9; also in North Africa, Tertullian, *Ad. nat.* 1.1; *Apol.* 1.7 and *Ad. Scap.* 2.

But how can they follow Christ, who are held back by the chain of their wealth? Or how can they seek heaven, and climb to sublime and lofty heights, who are weighed down by earthly desires?[14] They think that they possess, when they are rather possessed; as slaves of their profit, and not lords with respect to their own money, but rather the bond-slaves of their money. (chapter 12)

and again:

Wealth must be avoided as an enemy; must be fled from as a robber; must be dreaded by its possessors as a sword and as poison. To this end only so much as remains should be of service, that by it the crime and the fault may be redeemed. Let good works be done without delay and largely; let all your estate be laid out for the healing of your wound; let us lend of our wealth and our means to the Lord, who shall judge concerning us. (chapter 35)

While Cyprian's position of rejection of the chains of wealth as a path of salvation for the rich themselves is not the same as the utter rejection of the rich in *ActsPet12Apost.*, it is not difficult to imagine how extremists in a community might speak these same words and come to a much harsher conclusion than Cyprian.

Further evidence for widespread apostasy on the part of the rich during this persecution is provided by Dionysius, bishop of Alexandria. In a letter to Fabius, bishop of Antioch, preserved in Eusebius, *Hist. eccl.* 6.41.10–12, Dionysius describes the initial reaction of his community to Decius's general edict of 250:

The decree had arrived, very much like that which was foretold by our Lord, exhibiting the most dreadful aspect; so that, if it were

---

[14] How much different is this concept from that advocated by the merchant in his instructions as to the way to Nine Gates (see 5.19–6.8)? In these instructions the travelers are told to divest themselves of all worldly possessions for exactly the purpose of seeking heaven and climbing "to sublime and lofty heights," or, as *ActsPet12Apost.* puts it, "from stage to stage."

possible, the very elect would stumble. All, indeed, were greatly alarmed, and *many of the more eminent immediately gave way to them*; others, who were brought by their acquaintance, and when called by name, they approached the impure and unholy sacrifices. But, pale and trembling, as if they were not to sacrifice, but themselves to be the victims and the sacrifices to the idols, they were jeered by many of the surrounding multitude, and were obviously equally afraid to die and to offer the sacrifice. But some advanced with greater readiness to the altars, and boldly asserted that they had never before been Christians. *Concerning whom the declaration of our Lord is most true, that they will scarcely be saved.*

With this last remark it is clear that Dionysius is referring to Jesus' statement after encountering the rich young man: "Truly, I say to you, it will be hard for a rich man to enter the kingdom of heaven" (Matt 19:23 and parallels). This interpretation is reinforced by Dionysius's reference to the apostasy of "many of the more eminent" (πολλοὶ... τῶν περιφανεστέρων). This problem of apostasy among the rich was apparently also a problem at Rome during this period. In Cyprian, *Ep.* 8.2, the Roman clergy (questioning Cyprian's retirement in the face of persecution) also mention the apostasy of the wealthy in their area of jurisdiction:

The Church stands in faith, notwithstanding that some have been driven to fall by very terror, whether that they were *persons of eminence* (*insignes personae*), or that they were afraid, when seized, with the fear of man: these however, we did not abandon, although they were separated from us, but exhorted them, and do exhort them, to repent, if in any way they may receive pardon from Him who is able to grant it; lest, haply, if they should be deserted by us, they should become worse.

Yet another example is provided by the *Martyrdom of Pionius*. In this tale, set during the Decian persecution, the hero, a Christian presbyter, stands his ground against Polemon, the temple keeper (νεωκόρος). Polemon uses the fact that Euctemon, one of the leading men (ὁ προεστώς) in the Christian community, has already sacrificed to attempt to break Pionius's spirit, but to no avail.[15] These examples serve to demonstrate the widespread problem of apostasy on the part of the wealthy during this period. While these examples cannot prove a link between *ActsPet12Apost.* and the Decian Persecution, this period's many defections on the part of the wealthy would explain the extraordinary rejection of the rich and the mention of apostasies in *ActsPet12Apost.* if the text did indeed receive its final redaction in this period.

A second area of comparison between *ActsPet12Apost.* and the Decian Persecution is the connection between some leaders of the Church and the wealthy. *ActsPet12Apost.* 12.4–8 reviews how in its community's past "the many" (to be identified with church leaders) have shown partiality to the rich, "because they also are sinful, and they give occasion for others to sin" (ЄΒΟΛ ХЄ СЄР̄ ΝΟΒЄ... ΔΥШ СЄϯ ΜΟЄΙΤ Ν̄ϨЄΝΚΟΟΥЄ ЄЄΙΡЄ). It is possible that within the community which produced our text the wealthy have had undue influence with the leaders. Once again Cyprian provides us with evidence. In *On the Lapsed* 6, Cyprian describes the situation regarding the Church's leadership immediately prior to the Decian Persecution as one in which

> not a few bishops who ought to furnish both exhortation and example to others, despising their divine charge, became agents in secular business, forsook their throne, deserted their people, wandered about over foreign provinces, hunted the markets for gainful merchandise, while brethren were starving in the Church. They sought to possess money in hoards, they seized estates by crafty deceits, they increased their gains by multiplying usuries.

Given this involvement of the Church's hierarchy in business and their concern for acquiring worldly wealth (for whatever seemingly noble

---

[15] See *Martyrdom of Pionius* 15 and 18.

purpose), it is not surprising to learn that a number of these bishops apostasized,[16] as did many of the wealthy in their congregations. Cyprian speaks of a certain Fortunatianus, bishop of Assurae, who had apostasized and yet, when the persecution had subsided, desired to regain his episcopal powers. While in this instance Cyprian does not specifically state that the rich influenced the bishop to apostasize, he does note this bishop's connection with wealth:

> Nor is it wonderful if now those reject our counsels, or the Lord's precepts, who have denied the Lord. They desire gifts, and offerings, and gain, for which formerly they watched insatiably. They still long also for suppers and banquets, whose debauch they belched forth in the indigestion lately left to the day, most manifestly proving now that they did not before serve religion, but rather their belly and gain, with profane cupidity. (*Ep.* 65.3)

Furthermore, in Pontius, *Life and Passion of Cyprian*, the reporting deacon records how, at the approach of the executioner the wealthy and affluent in Cyprian's community attempted to persuade him to flee martyrdom. In chapter 14, Pontius writes:

> The coming executioner was instantly looked for who should strike through that devoted neck of the most sacred victim; and thus, in the daily expectation of dying, every day was to him as if the crown might be attributed to each. *In the meantime, there*

---

[16] The Decian persecution is not the only persecution which had a number of its leaders give a poor showing. For example, during the difficulties under Septimius Severus (ca. 202) Tertullian discusses the failure of members of the clergy in *On Flight in Persecution* 11. Also, in the early stages of the Diocletian persecution, "the bishops of Furni, Zama and Abitina are among those who openly co-operated with the authorities and surrendered their scriptures, thus earning for themselves the ill-omened name of '*traditor*.' Even at Carthage, Bishop Mensurius salved his conscience by handing over scriptures of 'the new heretics's (Manichaeans?) to satisfy the authorities. Few ecclesiastics followed Felix, bishop of Thibiuca and accepted martyrdom rather than surrender (15 July 303)" (Frend, *Martyrdom and Persecution*, 372). Cf. Eusebius, *Hist. eccl.* 8.2.1.

assembled to him many eminent people, and people of the most
illustrious rank and family, and noble in this world's distinctions
(*Conveniebant interim plures egregii et clarissimi ordinis et*
sanguinis, sed et saeculari nobilitate), who, on account of their
ancient friendship with him, repeatedly urged his withdrawal; and,
that their urgency might not be in some sort hollow, they also
offered places to which he might retire.

I recognize that this "event" would have taken place in late 258, as a
result of the second edict of Valerian's persecution,[17] and that the rich are
not attempting to persuade Cyprian to apostasize, only to flee martyrdom.
However, I still argue that this is a useful example of how the wealthy in
a community might exert their influence so as to pressure a bishop to
conform to their standards.

The final phrase of *ActsPet12Apost.* 12.4–8, "and they give occasion
for others to sin" (ⲁⲩⲱ ⲥⲉϯ ⲙⲟⲉⲓⲧ ⲛ̅ϩⲉⲛⲕⲟⲟⲩⲉ ⲉⲉⲓⲣⲉ),
may refer to two sins of which the leaders were guilty: 1) the apostasizing
bishop's encouragement of his flock to follow his example of apostasy;[18]
and 2) the encouragement by these lapsed bishops of their flocks to
continue to communicate with them as if their lapse was of no
consequence.[19] Obviously, these sins (apostasy and failure to repent of

---

[17] See Cyprian, *Ep.* 80 for the most comprehensive extant statement of
this edict available. Also see the discussion of both these edicts in Paul Keresztes,
"Two Edicts of the Emperor Valerian," *VC* 29 (1975) 81–95.

[18] We have an example of precisely this behavior in Bishop Repostus of
Suturnica who, in Cyprian's words, "not only fell himself in the persecution, but
cast down by sacrilegious persuasion the greatest part of his people" (*Ep.* 59.10).

[19] See *Ep.* 65.1, in which Cyprian, describing the damage done by
Bishop Fortunatianus, states: "Or as if he would not provoke a greater wrath and
indignation of the Lord against himself in the day of judgement, who, not being
able to be a guide to the brethren in faith and virtue, stands forth as a teacher of
perfidity, in boldness, and in temerity; and he who has not taught the brethren to
stand bravely in the battle, teaches those who are conquered and prostrate not even
to ask for pardon." See also *Ep.* 67.9, where Cyprian argues that those who allow
the lapsed bishops Basilides and Martialis to communicate "become sharers and

apostasy) are related. However, due to the use of the present tense in this phrase (not in the past tense as in 12.4–5, "For many in the churches have shown partiality to the rich"), I suggest that it is primarily to the second of these two sins that reference is being made in the final phrase of 12.4–8. From this vantage point the "partiality" (following the advice and example of the rich to apostasize) is in the past, while the "occasion to sin" (literally: "they give a way to sin"; i.e., the encouragement to continue to communicate as full-fledged Christians) is in the present as an continuing problem. Therefore, the mandate of Jesus to his disciples in 12.1–2, "do not dine in [their] houses nor be friends with them," may be a veiled reference to the community's refusal to celebrate Eucharist with the apostate rich.

AN INTRIGUING USE OF PHYSICIANS
OF BODIES/ SOULS IMAGERY

A third historical aspect of this period which is significant to our text is connected with the special instructions given by Jesus to the disciples in *ActsPet12Apost.* 11.14–26 to be physicians (**NIC&ЄIN**) of bodies and souls.[20] I suggest that the particular way in which these concepts are used in *ActsPet12Apost.* is very significant in helping to narrow down the date of the final redaction.

To fully grasp its impact, one must understand that the connection of "physician of bodies"[21] and "physician of souls" has a long history in the

---

partakers in other men's sins."

[20] See Gervaise Dumeige, "Le Christ médecin dans la litterature chrétienne des premiers siécles," *Revista di archeologia cristiana* 48 (1972) 115–41; Jörg Hübner, "Christus medicus: Ein Symbol des Erlösungsgeschehens und ein Modell ärztlichen Handelns," *KD* 31 (1985) 324–35.

[21] For a concise, yet thorough introduction to medical thought and practice in the Greco-Roman world and its impact upon early Christianity, see Howard C. Kee, *Medicine, Miracle and Magic in New Testament Times* (SNTSMS 55; London: Cambridge University Press, 1986).

Greco-Roman world.[22] It begins with Plato or, probably more accurately, was popularized by Plato. In *Republic* 3.17.409e–410a, Plato compares the work of the ideal physician with that of the ideal state judge. The former is to heal the bodies of the citizens of the state, the latter is to heal their souls:

> This is the sort of medicine, and this is the sort of law, which you will sanction in your state. They will minister to better natures, *giving health both of soul and of body* (τὰ σώματα καὶ τὰς ψυχὰς θεραπεύσουσι); but those who are diseased in their bodies they will leave to die, and the corrupt and incurable souls they will put an end to themselves.[23]

In *Protagoras* 313c–e, Plato shifts this image as Socrates cautions Hippocrates about rushing off and becoming a student of a philosopher about whose character he knows nothing. Socrates compares the unknown philosopher (Protagoras) with those dealers in the marketplace who praise their own wares. Socrates states that just as only a physician or athletic trainer knows enough about the types of food to know if the dealers are speaking the truth, so also the only people who can know the

---

[22] I do not pretend to be presenting an exhaustive analysis of the "philosopher as physician of souls" imagery as it appeared in antiquity. To do so would be to re-invent the wheel as at least two major recent studies have attempted to accomplish precisely this task. See Martha C. Nussbaum, *The Therapy of Desire: Theory and Practice in Hellenistic Ethics* (Martin Classical Lectures 2; Princeton, NJ: Princeton University Press, 1994); and Owsei Temkin, *Hippocrates in a World of Pagans and Christians* (Baltimore: Johns Hopkins University Press, 1991).

[23] Cf. *Gorgias* 480b: "But if he or anyone of those for whom he cares has done wrong, he ought to go of his own accord where he will most speedily be punished, to the judge as though to a doctor, in his eagerness to prevent the distemper of evil from becoming ingrained and producing a festering and incurable ulcer in his soul" (W. R. M. Lamb, trans., *Plato: Lysis, Symposium, Gorgias* [LCL; Cambridge: Harvard University Press, 1967]).

essential differences between genuine and false philosophers are physicians of souls:

> Then can it be, Hippocrates, that the sophist is really a sort of merchant or dealer in provisions on which a soul is nourished? For such is the view I take of him. With what, Socrates, is a soul nourished? With doctrines, presumably, I replied. And we must take care, my good friend, that the sophist, in commending his wares, does not deceive us, as both merchant and dealer do in the case of our bodily food. For among the provisions, you know, in which these men deal, not only are they themselves ignorant what is good or bad for the body, since in selling they commend them all, but the people who buy from them are so too, unless one happens to be a trainer or a doctor. And in the same way, those who take their doctrines the round of our cities, hawking them about to any odd purchaser who desires them, commend everything that they sell, and there may well be some of these too, my good sir, who are ignorant which of their wares is good or bad for the soul; and in just the same case are the people who buy from them, *unless one happens to have a doctor's knowledge here also, but of the soul* (ἐὰν μή τις τύχῃ περὶ τὴν ψυχὴν αὖ ἰατρικὸς ὤν).[24]

The shift which takes place here is significant in that it is now the philosopher who is being compared to the physician. This same analogy is taken up by the philosopher, Lucretius (ca. 92–55 B.C.) in *De rerum natura* 4.1–24. Lucretius compares the tactic of the physician in using honey to help a child take bitter medicine to his own use of poetic verse to present his philosophy:

> For even as healers, when they would essay to give to ailing children bitter draughts of loathsome wormwood, first will overlay the cup's round rim with the sweet golden dew of honey, that

---

[24] W. R. M. Lamb, trans., *Plato: Laches, Protagoras, Meno, Euthydemus* (LCL; Cambridge: Harvard University Press, 1967).

thereby the trustful age of childish innocence may be beguiled to open the portal of the lips, and all unwitting swallow down the nauseous draught of wormwood, thus deceived though not betrayed, but rather by such means may be restored and once again made strong; so now do I, since these my teachings often too bitter seem to those who have not known their taste, and since the common herd doth shrink therefrom in dread. For I have chosen in sweet-tongued melody to Muses now to frame my reasoning for your delight, and as it were to touch my theme with honey'd sweets of poesy, if so perchance I might avail to hold your mind upon my verses, till you come to grasp the nature of the world entire and make the lesson of its use your own.[25]

This same route is followed by the Stoic philosopher, Epictetus of Hierapolis (c. 50 B.C.–A.D. 30) in *Discourses* 3.23.28. Epictetus also compares the philosopher to a physician, dramatically expanding this analogy:

The school of a philosopher is a surgery. You are not to go out of it with pleasure, but with pain; for you do not come there in health; but one of you has a dislocated shoulder; another, an abscess; a third, a fistula; a fourth, a headache. And am I, then, to sit uttering pretty, trifling thoughts and little exclamations, that, when you have praised me, you may each of you go away with the same dislocated shoulder, the same aching head, the same fistula, and the same abscess that you brought?[26]

---

[25] Martin F. Smith and W. H. D. Rouse, trans., *Lucretius: De rerum natura* (LCL; Cambridge: Harvard University Press, 1975).

[26] William A. Oldfather, trans., *Epictetus: The Discourses as reported by Arrian, the Manual and Fragments* (2 vols.; LCL; Cambridge: Harvard University Press, 1925–28). The Cynic philosophers also used this same imagery; see Dio Chrysostom (ca. 40–115) *Discourses* 8.5–10. See also, Pseudo-Diogenes, *Ep.* 49: "if there is any disease afflicting your soul, senselessness for example, get a doctor for it. And pray the gods that you not do more harm than good by choosing one that only seems to be a good physician" (Abraham J. Malherbe, *The Cynic Epistles* [SBLSBS 12; Missoula, MT: Scholars Press, 1977] 181).

As one might expect, Philo of Alexandria, heavily influenced by both Greek philosophical thought and the Jewish scriptures, also employed this imagery. However, Philo adapts this concept to his religious beliefs. For Philo, it is God, not the philosopher, who is the perfect physician of souls. In *De sacrificiis Abelis et Cain* 70, Philo complains that people first try all the medical solutions before looking to God "the only physician (τὸν μόνον ἰατρόν) of the soul's infirmities." This adapted image would eventually be taken up by the Church. With the reputation of Jesus as a healer, it was simply a matter of time before the term physician would be applied to him.[27] With the Christian understanding of Jesus as the Son of God, it is apparent that a designation such as that used by Philo for God might be applied to him.

In *Ephesians* 7, Ignatius of Antioch (martyred ca. A.D. 115), in discussing the damage done to the community by traveling preachers whose doctrines are likened to the bite of a mad dog, states that only Jesus can heal this disease:

> For there are some who maliciously and deceitfully are accustomed to carrying about the Name while doing other things unworthy of God. You must avoid them as wild beasts. For they are mad dogs that bite by stealth; you must be on your guard against them, for their bite is hard to heal. *There is only one physician* (εἷς ἰατρός ἐστιν), who is both flesh and spirit, born and unborn, God in man, true life in death, both from Mary and from God, first subject to suffering and then beyond it, Jesus Christ our Lord.

While this passage does not explicitly state that Jesus is a physician of souls, the implication is most certainly there. This understanding is supported later in 20.2 by the medical terminology Ignatius applies to the Eucharist as the "medicine of immortality, the antidote" (φάρμακον ἀθανασίας) which is provided by Jesus Christ (presumably the physician).

---

[27] Cf. Mark 2:17; Luke 4:23.

This imagery also appears in Clement of Alexandria, Tertullian and Cyprian. In *Paedagogus* 1.1 (ca. 202), Clement, formed by the Greek philosophical tradition, recaptures much of the old "philosopher as physician" imagery while still making Christ the focus. However, this image is slightly altered as the term paedagogue replaces philosopher:

> Hence accordingly ensues the healing of our passions, in consequence of the assuagements of those examples; the Paedagogue strengthening our souls, and by his benign commands, as by gentle medicines, guiding the sick to the perfect knowledge of truth.... As, then, for those of us who are diseased in a body a physician is required, so also those who are diseased in soul require a paedagogue to cure our maladies.[28]

This imagery was not limited to Alexandria. Tertullian writing in Carthage, North Africa, argues that martyrdom has been provided by the Physician (God) as one of God's cures for the illness of the soul:

> Man always first provides employment for the physician; in short, he has brought upon himself the danger of death. He had received from his own Lord, as from a physician, the salutary enough rule to live according to the law, that he should eat of all indeed (that the garden produced) and should refrain from only one little tree which in the meantime the Physician himself knew as a perilous one.... He ate what was forbidden, and, surfeited by the trespass, suffered indigestion tending to death; he certainly richly deserving to lose his life altogether who wished to do so. But the inflamed tumour due to the trespass having been endured until in due time the medicine might be mixed, the Lord gradually prepared the means of healing — all the rules of faith. (*Scorpiace* 5.5, ca. 211 A.D.)

---

[28] See also *Paed.* 12. Not surprisingly, this imagery is also used by Origen, Clement's gifted student; see *C. Cels.* 5.56; 7.60 and 7.72 (ca. 248 A.D.).

Cyprian, in several places, also uses medical imagery to describe the work of "the Lord's priest," comparing the minister to a physician and calling atonement "true medicine" (*On the Lapsed* 14–15):

> And thus also it behooves the Lord's priest not to mislead by deceiving concessions, but to provide with salutary remedies. He is an unskillful physician who handles the swelling edges of wounds with a tender hand, and, by retaining the poison shut up in the deep recesses of the body, increases it. The wound must be opened, and cut, and healed by the stronger remedy of cutting out the corrupting parts. The sick man may cry out, may vociferate, and may complain, in impatience of the pain; but he will afterwards give thanks when he has felt that he is cured.[29]

This imagery was not confined to the works of the great theological pillars of the Church. It is also found in the church order, *Apostolic Constitutions* 2.3 (ca. mid-3rd century). In this ordination text, the image is further stretched so as to apply to the role of the bishop, as representative of Christ:

> As a skillful and compassionate physician, heal all such as have wandered in the ways of sin; for "they that are whole have no need of a physician, but they that are sick. For the Son of man came to save and to seek that which was lost." Since you are therefore a physician of the Lord's Church, provide remedies suitable to every patient's case. Cure them, heal them by all means possible; restore them sound to the Church. Feed the flock, "not with insolence and contempt, as lording it over them," but as a gentle shepherd, "gathering the lambs into your bosom, and gently leading those which are with young."[30]

---

[29] See also chapters 15, 28, 32 and 35 and Pontius, *Life and Passion of Cyprian* 8.

[30] Cf. also 2.5.41.

When this trajectory of thought is compared with Jesus' commission in *ActsPet12Apost.* to be both physicians of bodies and physicians of souls, there is a very important distinction that can be made. In each of the early Christian works cited the emphasis is upon Jesus' ability to cure, heal and treat ailing souls, not bodies as in the canonical gospels. Even in a text such as *AC*, where this role is passed on as it were, to the successors of Jesus, the emphasis is upon what can be done for the soul. In short, when Jesus is pictured as a physician the actual physical healing element of the image is lost. This is probably due to the influence of the underlying Greek philosophical tradition, for which interest in the healing element, apart from its worth as an analogy to healing of the soul, was secondary.[31] The one exception to this tendency to focus primarily on the soul is Philo, who connects the image of God as a physician of souls with God's supernatural ability to heal physically. Likewise, in Christian tradition one would assume that this actual physical healing element would be an added component to the analogy because of Jesus' reputation as an actual healer of bodies. This is not the case in the texts we have examined to this point.[32]

---

[31] I am hardly suggesting that Greco-Roman philosophy was unconcerned with medicine or medical issues. In antiquity there was not the strict dichotomy between the sciences and the humanities that exists today. On the contrary, philosophy played a large role in the development of ancient medical schools. Nowhere was this more obvious than in Alexandria where the formation of such strict philosophical approaches as the Domatic, Empiric and Methodist did more to stymie the growth of scientific knowledge than it did to advance the cause of medicine. See Wesley D. Smith, *The Hippocratic Tradition* (Ithaca, NY: Cornell University Press, 1979) 177–215.

[32] This is not to imply that physical healing was no longer a concern or reality in the patristic churches. On the contrary, Irenaeus asserts in *Adv. haer.* 2.32.4, after denying that the miracles claimed by the heretics are legitimate, the reality of orthodox miracles in his own day: "Wherefore, also, those who are in truth his disciples, receiving grace from him, do in his name perform [miracles], so as to promote the welfare of other men, according to the gift which each one has received from him. For some do certainly and truly drive out devils, so that those who have thus been cleansed from evil spirits frequently both believe and join themselves to the Church. Others have foreknowledge of things to come: they

It is significant that *ActsPet12Apost.* also includes a legitimate and functional healing (medical) component when using the "physician of souls" imagery. However, this dual emphasis on healing bodies and souls is not unique. In the first century, Philo describes (*On the Contemplative Life* 1.2) an ascetical group called the Therapeutae who claim to treat bodies and souls: "they profess an art of healing better than that practiced in the cities — *for the latter cures only the body, while theirs treats also souls mastered by grievous and virtually incurable diseases* (ἡ μὲν γὰρ σώματα θεραπεύει μόνον, ἐκείνη δὲ καὶ ψυχὰς νόσοις κεκρατημένας χαλεπαῖς τε καὶ δυσιάτοις), inflicted by pleasures and lusts, mental pains and fears, by acts of greed, folly, and injustice, and the endless multitude of the other mental disturbances and vices."

This dual emphasis (applied to Jesus) is also present in several apocryphal acts. In *Acts of John* 56, John says to Antipatros, "My physician takes no reward in money, but when he heals for nothing he reaps the souls of those who are healed, in exchange for the diseases." (This is echoed in *Acts of John* 108 and 113). This same emphasis is also found in *Acts of Thomas* 37, in which Thomas says in a sermon: "But believe rather in our Lord Jesus Christ...and he shall be for you a spring gushing forth in this thirsty land, and a house full of food in the place of the hungry, and a rest for your souls, and also a physician of your bodies." Within the apocryphal acts genre this imagery probably reaches its zenith in the *Acts of Philip* 13.4.[33] In this passage, after entering the town of

---

see visions, and utter prophetic expressions. Others still, heal the sick by laying their hands upon them, and they are made whole. Yes, moreover, as I have said, the dead even have been raised up, and remained among us for many years. And what more shall I say? It is not possible to name the number of the gifts which the Church, throughout the whole world, has received from God, in the name of Jesus Christ." For more on miracles se: Justin, *1 Apol.* 2.6; Tertullian, *Apol.* 37; Hippolytus, *AT* 1.15; Origen, *C. Cels.* 1.46; 3.24; Athanasius, *Life of Antony* 56–58; 61 and *AC* 8.1.1.

[33] Regarding the date of *Acts of Philip*, Frédéric Amsler states: "The date and the geographical area out of which the *Acts of Philip* has issued remains unknown. The first mention of the apocrypha figures in a list of books not

Hierapolis, Philip is described as setting up his base of operations in an abandoned medical dispensary:

> Entering into the village, the apostles found a dispensary in the vicinity, which was vacant and none of whose physicians were there. Philip said to Mariamme: "Here our Savior has preceded us and has prepared for us this *spiritual dispensary*. Let us occupy it and find rest, because we are exhausted from the exertion of the road." To Bartholomew, he said: "Where is the unguent box that the Savior gave to us on that occasion when we were in Galilee?[34]

---

received by the ecclesiastical tradition, constructed, it seems, in Gaul around 500 and inserted in the *Decree of Gelasian*. On the contrary, since they know and even cite them, the *Acts of Philip* does not seem to be before the *Acts of Peter*, the *Acts of John* and the *Acts of Andrew*, indeed even those of Paul or Thomas, which the critic dates back to the second- or third centuries. But... an appreciable number of indications contained in the text itself invite us to place the composition of this apocryphal book around the turn of the fourth- and fifth centuries in Phrygia, in Asia Minor, and to attach it to an ascetical movement, one that is a little marginal by the account of the official Church, but one which has established itself in the most fruitful ground of oriental monastic spirituality" (Amsler, François Bovon and Bertrand Bouvier, trans., *Actes de l'apôtre Philippe* [Apocryphes Collection de Poche de l'Aelac 8; Turnhout: Brepols, 1996] 14).

[34] Hypothetically, the Greek word for "unguent box" (translated "coffret" in the French) is νάρθηξ. According to Parrott's judgment, this is the same word that lies behind *ActsPet12Apost.* 9.30 (Parrott, *Nag Hammadi Codices V,2–5 and VI*, 225). This statement by Philip reflects two parallels with *ActsPet12Apost.*: 1) Philip refers back to a time in Galilee (presumably before the apostles part company to go to their designated, geographically separate, missions; cf. *Acts of Philip* 3) when the Savior (note the solitary use of "Savior" in *ActsPet12Apost.* 9.5) presents some apostles (at *least* two: Bartholomew and Philip) with an unguent box; and 2) this unguent box is directly connected with a mission to heal both bodies and souls (as is evidenced by Philip's comments in 13.4). The question arises: Did the author of *Acts of Philip* know a tradition of an apostolic commission to heal bodies and souls? If so, did this tradition look anything like *ActsPet12Apost.*? If Amsler is right and *Acts of Philip* is to be dated at the end of the fourth- or beginning of the fifth century, then it is possible that the author may have been familiar with *ActsPet12Apost.* I base this judgment on cartonnage found in other codices of the Nag Hammadi Library, which indicates that *ActsPet12Apost.* had to have been written before the last half of the fourth century (the period when the codices were created) (Robinson, *The Nag Hammadi*

Let us set up practice in this dispensary and attend to the sick until
we see what purpose the Savior sets for us."

This concern for bodies as well as souls is concretized in the stories that
immediately follow: Stachys (14) and Nicanora (15).[35]

There are also a number of other examples from the third- and fourth
centuries. Eusebius, quoting Bishop Dionysius (ca. 251), describes the
actions of the Christian community in Alexandria as "visiting the sick
without a thought as to the danger, assiduously ministering
(θεραπεύοντες) to them" (*Hist. eccl.* 7.22.6–9). I will discuss this
plague in more detail shortly. My point is that here we have a situation
where Christians are actively fulfilling the role of physicians. Eusebius
also mentions a Bishop Theodotus of Laodicea (ca. A.D. 300) whom he
describes as, "a man who by his very deeds proved true to his own name
and that of bishop. He held first rank in the science of healing bodies, but
in that of caring for souls he was such as was no other man in kindness,
sincerity, sympathy, and zeal for aiding those who need his help" (*Hist.
eccl.* 7.32.23). There is also the "father of monasticism," Anthony (ca.
250–356), whom Athansius refers to as "a physician... given by God to
Egypt" (ca. 356, *Life of Saint Anthony* 87). Basil of Caesarea (mid-fourth
century) mirrors Jesus' mission as the "Great physician" by founding a
"hospital" run by monks trained as physicians.[36]

The concrete emphasis upon physical healing in *ActsPet12Apost.* is
made even more dramatic by the Lord's commission of the disciples to be
actual physicians. It may well provide the final point which, when taken

---

Library in English, 16).

[35] In *Acts of Philip* the image of the physician is applied to both Jesus
(3.4; 4.4.5; 5.27; 6.11–12; 8.6; 12.7) and Philip (2.7; 5.27; 6.11–1213.4–5; 14.4.8;
15.7).

[36] Temkin provides a thorough analysis of the development of this
concretization of the "physicians of bodies/ souls" imagery. See specifically the
practice of both physical and spiritual medicine by Church ministers (*Hippocrates
in a World of Pagans and Christians,* 149–77, 213–16).

together with: 1) a situation of apostasy/ persecution, and 2) an utter rejection of the rich as members of the churches, will help further tie *ActsPet12Apost.* to the period immediately after the Decian Persecution.

In the summer of 250, as the worst of the initial brunt of the persecution had passed, a serious plague swept across North Africa and Egypt. Karl Baus describes the reaction of the bishops of the two major African communities:

> Christian brotherly love had really to prove itself in the times of extraordinary catastrophes which were not lacking in the third century. Dionysius of Alexandria sang a paean to the Christian readiness for sacrifice which distinguished the laity as well as the clergy in Alexandria during the epidemic about the year 250. Without fear of infection, they had cared for their sick brethren and given their lives thereby, while the pagans had avoided their sick relatives and abandoned their dead without burial. When plague was raging in Carthage, Cyprian summoned his flock by word and example to organized relief action which did not deny care and attention to the pagans.[37]

---

[37] Baus, *From the Apostolic Community to Constantine* = Hubert Jedin, ed., *Handbook of Church History*, vol. 1 (New York: Herder, 1965) 311. Eusebius quotes Dionysius's description of the situation: "But when the briefest of breathing-space had been granted us and them, there descended upon us this disease, a thing that is to them more fearful then any other object of fear, more cruel than any calamity whatsoever, and, as one of their own writers declared, 'the only thing of all that proved worse than what was expected.' Yet to us it was not so, but, no less than the other misfortunes, a source of discipline and testing. For indeed it did not leave us untouched, although it attacked the heathen with great strength.... The most, at all events, of our brethren in their exceeding love and affection for the brotherhood were unsparing of themselves and clave to one another, visiting the sick without a thought as to the danger, assiduously ministering to them, tending them in Christ, and so most gladly departed this life along with them; being infected with the disease from others, drawing upon themselves the sickness from their neighbors, and willingly taking over their pains. And many, when they had cared for and restored to health others, died themselves, thus transferring their death to themselves,.... In this manner the best at any rate of our brethren departed this life, certain presbyters and deacons and some of the laity, receiving great commendation, so that this form of death seems in no respect

This situation presented a problem for Cyprian and, by association, Dionysius as well. The onset of the plague brought the threat that large numbers of the lapsed, still considered by the Church to be strayed members of the flock, would die without reconciliation with Christ and his Church.[38] If *ActsPet12Apost.* did receive its final redaction during this period, this background of a plague which threatened strayed Christians may shed some light upon the commands of Jesus in 11.14–26 to be physicians both of bodies and of souls.

It may be postulated that the two types of healing advocated by our text (body and soul) may refer to the community's tasks in the wake of the Decian Persecution: 1) caring for the sick (those caught in the plagues mentioned above); and 2) healing the hearts of those who apostasized (presumably not the church leaders or the rich members of the community but the poor who were led astray by their example).[39] Furthermore this connection of the plague and the Decian persecution may help us in our interpretation of 10.31–11.13:

---

to come behind martyrdom, being the outcome of much piety and strong faith" (*Hist. eccl.* 7.22.6–8). See also Cyprian, *On the Mortality*; *Ep.* 18.1; Pontius, *Life and Martyrdom of Cyprian* 9.

[38] For example see Cyprian, *Ep.* 18 and 19.

[39] There are some other interesting similarities between *ActsPet12Apost.* and material in Cyprian's writings during this period. They can serve to demonstrate the existence of an actual Christian circumstance in which both the social situation (apostasy of the rich, involvement of the church leaders in pursuit of wealth and subsequent apostasy by these leaders) and similar religious motifs existed. First, there is Cyprian's usage of storm imagery to refer to the period of persecution undergone by the Church (*On the Lapsed* 1, "the season of affliction and cloud being dispersed" and, more directly, in chapter 15 "the storm of persecution"). This is similar to the material added by the redactor in *ActsPet12Apost.* 7.11–14: "and a precious kingdom comes from them, because they endure in the midst of apostasies and the difficulties of the storms." A second point of comparison is Cyprian's encouragement of his flock to "renounce the world" (*On the Lapsed* 2, 11–12). While this admonishment could hardly be described as exclusively tied to the Decian context, it is, nonetheless, another point of similarity with our text (see 10.15–19).

He gave them the pouch of medicine and said, "heal all the sick of the city who believe in my name." Peter was afraid to reply to him for the second time. He signaled to the one who was beside him, who was John: "You talk this time." John answered and said, "Lord, before you we are afraid to say many words. *But it is you who asks us to practice this skill. We have not been taught to be physicians* (ⲀⲖⲖⲀ ⲚⲦⲞⲔ ⲈⲦⲰⲒⲚⲈ ⲘⲘⲞⲚ ⲈⲦⲈⲒⲦⲈⲬⲚⲎ ⲈⲀⲀⲤ ⲘⲠⲞⲨⲦⲤⲈⲂⲞⲚ ⲈⲢⲞⲤ ⲈⲢ ⲤⲀⲈⲒⲚ). How then will we know how to heal bodies as you have told us?

If we are to take this commission at face value then we must recognize that there is a legitimate command on the part of Jesus to become physicians of bodies as well as physicians of souls. The reality of this is emphasized by the awarding of the medicine pouch and the apprehension on the part of Peter and John. They recognize that they are being required to perform a profession for which they have no formal training (ⲦⲈⲬⲚⲎ).[40] The protests of Peter and John represent the reservations of the redactor's addressees. They too are being asked to take on the role of physicians, a role for which they too are unprepared.

Such a command with the reply, "We have not been taught to be physicians" (11.10–11) suggests that the community has started practicing medicine of some sort, but its credentials (ability) to do so are being called into question — perhaps by Christians and not simply by pagan physicians. The community feels the need to assert its right and ability to practice medicine in the face of criticism from those who have a recognized authority and "legitimate" claim to practice medicine, that is, those trained at a school of medicine (and those representing that school as its present administrators). If this document is, as I will soon propose,

---

[40] For the use of τέχνη to refer to a definite professional skill see *LSJ*, s. v. τεχνάξω, 1785.

Alexandrian in provenance,[41] one can only imagine the enormous pressure
Christians not trained in medicine would have experienced as they tried
to heal — as if a homeopath were to set up shop across the street from the
Mayo Clinic! This dominical command of Jesus to heal would serve as
a "credential" within the community — it would be meaningless to those
outside the community. It would give those involved the "right," at least
in their own minds, to treat the sick.

The essential point of this text is that a group of ignorant (medically
speaking) Christian ministers are being pressed into service despite their
lack of sufficient medical knowledge. Such an unorthodox and almost
desperate action suggests a crisis situation in which any physician, even
a poorly trained one, is acceptable. In catastrophic situations such as
wars, earthquakes, tornadoes or even epidemics where the casualties are
high, it is quite common for anyone to be recruited to care for the
wounded.

Unfortunately, it is impossible to exclusively associate persecution
and plague to the post-Decian period. Both persecutions and plagues
were all too common occurrences in the first three centuries of our era.
For example, during the reign of Marcus Aurelius (ca. 165), which saw
numerous scattered persecutions (e.g., the martyrs of Lyon, ca. 177), a
plague ravaged the eastern and central provinces (Aristides, *Oratio* 33.6;
48.38–39; 50.9). The very same plague which is spoken of by Dionysius
as attacking Alexandria in 250 dragged on in other regions of the empire
throughout Valerian's persecution in 257–60, as well as for years
afterward (Cyprian, *Ep.* 57; 59; 60; *Ad Demet.* 5.7). Neither was the
Great Persecution of Diocletian (ca. 302–12) immune to such occurrences

---

[41] The medical school in Alexandria was the foremost center of medical
study and anatomical research from the 3rd century B.C. to A.D. 642. It
traditionally enjoyed both royal, then Imperial support and the Alexandrian school
often taught medicine for and to the wealthy and educated. See E. D. Philips,
Greek Medicine (Aspects of Greek and Roman Life; London: Thames and
Hudson, 1973) 139–71; and Heinrich von Staden, trans., *Herophilus: The Art of
Medicine in Early Alexandria* (Cambridge: Cambridge University Press, 1989)
1–34.

(Eusebius, *Hist. eccl.* 8.15; 9.8).[42]

Certainly suffering and apostasy, even that of the rich, can be associated with any number of historical persecutions (whether local or empire-wide). However, the Decian persecution was infamous for its apostasies, especially those of the wealthy and these apostasies can truly be said to have rocked the very foundations of the Church. While such persecutions as those under Marcus Aurelius, Valerian and Diocletian surely had their apostates the general feeling upon the Church's emergence from these periods was one of victory. They must be differentiated from the post-Decian period which left the bitter taste of defeat in the Church's collective mouth. Its aftermath was a time of extreme and polarized problem-solving as is evidenced by Cyprian's epic battle with his Carthaginian opponents over the fate of the lapsed.[43] With *ActsPet12Apost.*'s references to persecution, its extreme position on the wealthy, its distinct medical commission may just provide the key point of contact with this period (i.e., a reference to the Christian community's response to the plague).

A RE-INTERPRETATION OF THE ALLEGORY

In light of the redactor's experience of persecution a further question can be raised in regard to the significance of Lithargoel's description of the hazards on the way to Nine Gates for the redactor. I have argued that the original referents of symbols such as the wild beasts and robbers on the road to Nine Gates in the Story of the Pearl Merchant reflect certain Valentinian gnostic mythological structures. If we accept this position

---

[42] See Frend, *Martyrdom and Persecution,* 198, 286, 298, 309, 332, 506 n. 69.

[43] The classic work on Cyprian is by Edward White Benson, *Cyprian: His Life, His Times, His Work* (London: MacMillan, 1897). See particularly chapter 2, "The Decian Persecution" for a description of Cyprian's policies in regard to the lapsed. Cf. also Karl Rahner, *Penance in the Early Church* (Theological Investigations 15; New York: Crossroad, 1982)152–222 and Cahal B. Daly, *Tertullian the Puritan and His Influence: An Essay in Historical Theology* (Dublin: Four Courts, 1993) 58–74.

can we claim that these symbols maintained this gnostic meaning in their new context? In other words, what meaning did they have for the redactor?

I suggest that there are really two meanings for the enigmatic creatures that threaten the pilgrim on his or her way to Nine Gates. First, there is the gnostic meaning: the creatures are archons seeking to destroy the soul that is still attached to the material elements of this realm. We may consider this to be the latent referent of these symbols. Second, and this is the active referent for the redactor, these creatures are symbolic of the Roman authorities, whether they be local or empire-wide, and their ultimate weapon against the Christians — the dreaded arena. For the redactor the actions of these creatures resonated with his or her experience of persecution. It is a truly horrifying image. For the redactor the Romans were thinking animals, seeking to strip their victims of all worldly goods ("bread," "a costly garment of the world," "water," and "meat and green vegetables") and kill them — this was especially true of the Roman military which was the key mechanism by which the Christians were pressured.[44] For the redactor the statement that "No man is able to

---

[44] The portrayal of one's enemies in bestial form is not unique to *ActsPet12Apost*. The Animal Apocalypse (also an allegory — on the history of Israel) in *1 Enoch* 85–90 uses many wild and predatory animals to symbolize Israel's enemies down through the ages. See Patrick A. Tiller, *A Commentary on the Animal Apocalypse of 1 Enoch* (Early Judaism and its Literature 4; Atlanta: Scholars Press, 1993) 21–60. In the NT, the world into which the disciples are sent is compared to wolves (Matt 10:16; Luke 10:3) and, in probably the most famous example, the Roman Empire is described as a "ten-horned beast" in Revelation 13. Often this imagery is associated with persecution (e.g., *Mart. Lyon* 57–58; *Mart. Pionius* 12; *Mart. Conon* 6; *Sib. Or.* 2.260) the most famous is found in Ignatius, *Eph.* 7.2, where the bishop of Antioch compares his Roman guards to "leopards." Furthermore, the standard bearers of Roman army units were distinguished for actually wearing animal skins as part of their official uniform. "These [the *signiferi*] did not wear a helmet, but a special head-dress of bear-skin (lion-skin for the *signiferi* of the praetorian guard), the skull of the beast (without his jaw) being used as a hood, while the furry skin fell on to the shoulders and down the back, and was fastened at the neck by tying the forelegs together" (Michael Grant, *The Army of the Caesars* [New York: Charles Scribner's Sons, 1974] 296). The Roman standards themselves are also

go on that road, except one who has forsaken everything that he has and has fasted daily from stage to stage" takes on a new meaning. By divesting oneself of all worldly goods the Christians would make themselves a less profitable target for the Roman authorities who, no doubt, were motivated by greed in aggressively targeting the wealthy and affluent members of the Church as much could be gained by confiscating their worldly possessions.[45]

In attempting to fulfill an imperial command such as that ordered by Decius's edict of sacrifice to the traditional gods, a local political

---

significant to our discussion as it was typical for a legion to have an animal associated with it as a type of legionary mascot/ symbol. Often, this animal would be associated with the Zodiac such as the bull (Taurus), the lion (Leo) or the goat (Capricorn), which were related to the month in which the legion was "born." However, legionary symbols were not limited to the Zodiac and, at one time or another, included wolves, dragons, eagles, Pegasus, boars, minotaurs and horses (Daniel Peterson, *The Roman Legions Recreated in Colour Photographs* [Europa Militaria 2; London: Windrow & Greene, 1992] 46–58).

[45] Clarke explains how poverty could provide a measure of protection for many Christians, "In order to escape detection by authorities — or delation by neighbors — there appears to have been a concomitant and widespread refugee movement.... There is little evidence to suggest that any systematic search had been made for them. The authorities appear to have relied on delation as the main weapon for subsequent detection; and if inhabitants were poor, insignificant and unobtrusive they were most unlikely to be victims of delation. And very many Christians were poor and insignificant, and they escaped. This may explain why Cyprian says that he fled because he was an *insignis persona*, an eminent figure, and why Cyprian says his clergy can carry on their work in Carthage because they are not *insignis persona*" ("Observations on the Persecution of Decius," 71–72). On the confiscation of goods, Sage notes that "confiscation of goods appears generally linked to the other penalties, such as *relegatio*. The addition was necessitated by the fact that *relegatio* did not necessarily involve the loss of the exile's property.... Cyprian himself was awarded the penalty of confiscation, and in his letter of remonstrance to Florentius he records part of the edict: '*Si quis tenet possidet de bonis Caecili Cypriani Episcopi Christianorum.*' For a rich man, confiscation in itself could be a serious punishment; the poor have nothing to lose" (*Cyprian*, 186). For a thorough treatment of the economic considerations involved in this persecution see George T. Oborn, "Why Did Decius and Valerian Proscribe Christianity?" *CH* 2 (1933) 67–77; see also Keresztes ("Two Edicts," 88–95).

bureaucracy would be taxed to the breaking point. Such all-out efforts were, of necessity, limited in their duration before such mundane provincial tasks such as taxation and prevention of brigandage once again took center stage.[46] Therefore it would be reasonable on the part of the governor to target wealthy and affluent offenders. Such a course of action would: 1) make the local magistrate appear to his superiors to be actively complying with the imperial decree; 2) set an example for the local population (scare tactics); and 3) serve the never-to-be-underestimated function of lining the local magistrate's pockets with newly-acquired wealth.[47] Lastly, by divesting oneself of worldly goods the Christian prepared himself or herself for the very real possibility of martyrdom. Ultimately, the analogy of the Roman authorities as beasts was made easier by the existence of the arena, where the faithful Christian would often meet his or her end at the claws, teeth or horns of such creatures.[48]

---

[46] Sage describes the strain the attempt to enforce Decius's edict put on the Roman bureaucratic establishment: "The task of enforcing the edict was one of unprecedented magnitude, straining the Empire's administrative resources to the fullest extent. The imperial bureaucracy had always been spread thinly over its area of jurisdiction, and constant attention to the edict's provisions further weakened its effectiveness in performing its customary tasks, even with the aid of local officials. Cyprian's correspondence alone is sufficient indication of the general failure to enforce the provisions of the edict. Even at the height of governmental activity, the clergy functioned" (*Cyprian*, 206). See also Clarke, "Observations on the Persecution of Decius," 71–73.

[47] E.g., the claims of Athenagoras, *A Plea for the Christians* 1 (ca. 177 under Marcus Aurelius and L. Aurelius Commodus) and Eusebius, *Hist. eccl.* 6.2.13–14 (ca. 203 under Septimius Severus) and Cyprian, *Ep.* 80 (ca. 258 under Valerian).

[48] E.g., Eusebius describes the attacks of "leopards, and different kinds of bears, of wild boars and bulls" endured by the martyrs in the arena (*Hist. eccl.* 8.7). *1 Clement* also relates how various Christian women were "persecuted as Dircae" (6.2). Dircae, a figure in Greek mythology, was killed by being tied to the horns of a mad bull. See also Martial, *On the Spectacles*; *Mart. Perpetua and Felicitas* 19–21 and *Mart. Lyons* 37–42. The "robbers" of 5.26 could easily be thought of in terms of gladiators as it is a commonly known fact that criminals were used for this purpose. The four main crimes which led to the arena were murder, treason, robbery and arson (Michael Grant, *Gladiators* [Pageant of

Such asceticism could only heighten their focus upon the mission of the Church — to prepare itself spiritually to make the final journey to heaven.

A CASE FOR AN ALEXANDRIAN PROVENANCE

With these considerations as to the date of the final redaction of *ActsPet12Apost.*, the question naturally arises as to its geographical location. Of necessity my answer will be intimately tied to my proposal regarding a post-Decian persecution dating. It seems to be a given that whenever the question of locating a text geographically arises the usual list of possibilities is a short one. The main cities of the Roman Empire were Rome itself, Antioch of Syria and Alexandria, Egypt. In spite of the fact that a Syrian provenance has already been suggested,[49] I propose an Egyptian milieu for our text. This judgement is based on the following:

1) According to J. E. L. Oulton,[50] the North African epidemic which occurred in the summer of 250 probably began in Alexandria. Be that as it may, we have definite evidence (Dionysius via Eusebius) for its presence in Alexandria.

2) The command in 10.33–11.1 to "heal all the sick of the city who believe in my name," with its rather community-centered focus is interesting in light of the information provided by Dionysius of Alexandria:

> So, too, the bodies of the saints they would take up in their open
> hands to their bosom, closing their eyes and shutting their mouths,
> carrying them on their shoulders and laying them out; they would
> cling to them, embrace them, bathe and adorn them with their
> burial clothes, and after a little receive the same services

---

History; London: Baylis and Son, 1967] 29).

[49] See Patterson, "Sources, Redaction and Tendenz," 1; Guillamont, "De nouveaux Actes," 145; Schenke, "The Acts of Peter and the Twelve Apostles," 414.

[50] Oulton, trans., *Eusebius: The Ecclesiastical History* (2 vols.; LCL; Cambridge: Harvard University Press, 1926) 2.182.

themselves, for those that were left behind were ever following those that went before. But the conduct of the heathen was the exact opposite. Even those who were in the first stages of the disease they thrust away, and fled from their dearest. They would even cast them in the roads half-dead, and treat the unburied corpses as vile refuse, in their attempts to avoid the spreading and the contagion of the death-plague; a thing which, for all their devices, it was not easy for them to escape.[51]

In Dionysius's statement there is no indication that the Christian community cared for any of the affected other than their brothers and sisters in Christ. This can be compared with Pontius's claim that during the epidemic Cyprian "subjoined, that there was nothing wonderful in our cherishing our own people only with the needed attentions of love, but that he might become perfect who would do something more than the publican or the heathen, who, overcoming evil with good, and practicing a clemency which was like the divine clemency, loved his enemies...."[52] This Alexandrian exclusivity would correlate with the command of Jesus recorded in *ActsPet12Apost.* 10.33–11.1, "Heal all the sick of the city who believe in my name."

3) With the medical imagery in *ActsPet12Apost.* (the physician's attendant 8.17; 9.32; the unguent box and pouch 8.18–19; 9.30–31; 10.31–31) a case could be made for Alexandria because of its medical significance in the ancient world.[53] However, this connection is by no

---

[51] Eusebius, *Hist. eccl.* 7.22.9–10.

[52] *Life and Martyrdom of Cyprian*, 9.

[53] As the statement of the famous physician, Galen (ca. A. D. 130–201), regarding the Alexandrian medical school attests. Galen emphasizes Alexandria's significance as a place of medical instruction because of its early legalization of human autopsies: "At Alexandria this (first hand observation) is very easy, since the physicians in that country accompany the instruction they give to their students with opportunities for personal inspection (at autopsy). Hence you must try to get to Alexandria for this reason alone, if for no other" (*On Anatomical Procedure*, 1.2 in Logan Clendening, *Source Book of Medical History* [New York: Dover,

means conclusive in that there were other centers for medical study such as the Asclepicons at Cos, Pergamos, Athens, Epidaurus and Corinth. In any case, this medical imagery is particularly interesting in light of the fact that the two best analogies to the commission in *ActsPet12Apost.* to become "physicians of bodies and souls" are both provided by Philo, i.e., they originate from the Alexandrian milieu.[54]

It must be admitted that these arguments cannot definitively associate *ActsPet12Apost.* with Alexandria. The question of provenance for any text is always complicated by the cosmopolitan character of the Greco-Roman world.[55] However, taken together with my proposal for dating *ActsPet12Apost.*, these points do provide reason to question Patterson, Guillamont and Schenke's unsupported assertion of a Syrian milieu.

In conclusion, I suggest that, taken together, the historical circumstances suggested by *ActsPet12Apost.* are substantially similar to those of the period of the Decian persecution. I have suggested that *ActsPet12Apost.* received its final redaction in the years immediately following the Decian Persecution of late 249 to 251. The three aspects of similarity I have discussed — 1) the connection between persecution and apostasy; 2) the impact of this persecution upon the relationship between the Church and its wealthy members; and 3) the uncommon use of

---

1942] 48).

[54] I refer to Philo's understanding of God as "the only physician (τὸν μόνον ἰατρόν) of the soul's infirmities," in which he accepts God's medical and spiritual competency, and to the similar position of the Therapeutae, an ascetical community allegedly located outside of Alexandria.

[55] As a further complication, it was not uncommon in antiquity for particular cities or regions to have strong connections. For example, the relationship between Alexandria and Rome (Valentius, Galen, Plutarch) was based on the Roman need for grain as is evidenced by Vespasian's desire to secure the loyalty of the Egyptian legions before making his bid for Empire (Tacitus, *History* 2.74). As regards persecution, both Frend (*Martyrdom and Persecution*, 2–3) and Glen W. Bowersock (*Martyrdom and Rome* [Cambridge: Cambridge University Press, 1995] 17–18) discuss the theological and cultural connections between the martyrs of Lyon and the province of Asia.

physicians of bodies/ souls imagery — provide grounds to assign the final redaction of *ActsPet12Apost.* to this period. Taken together with this proposal, the clues provided by Dionysius and Cyprian suggest an Alexandrian provenance for this text.

Conclusion

ActsPet12Apost. is at once fable and dogmatic statement, teaching and whimsical fancy. It is both carelessly spliced and, at times, deftly woven together. It is full of contradiction and correspondence. But despite all this it has a power and grace that no amount of dissection and analysis can tarnish. It is the product of the faith-filled imagination and it is part of the legacy of the Church. In the following paragraphs I shall attempt to summarize the major conclusions which I have advocated in this book:

In Chapter One I suggested that in *ActsPet12Apost.* two originally separate bodies of source material have been brought together, edited and then expanded upon by an author/redactor. I judged that these two previously separate source units have not remained untouched by the redactor's hand. On the contrary, I argued that the redactor added material and thereby altered these sources. I delineated the primary units as *The Story of the Pearl Merchant* (1.1–9.1), *A Resurrection Appearance* (9.1–29) and *The Author/Redactor's Theology* (9.30–12.19).

In Chapter Two I refuted the long-accepted conclusion of Martin Krause that *ActsPet12Apost.* is an apocryphal act in some technical sense. I also closely examined Pheme Perkins's claim that our text is a gnostic revelation dialogue, and concluded that, while our text does contain a revelation dialogue (the Author/Redactor's Theology), its content is not gnostic speculation but rather closer to that of a church order. I noted that most commentators had observed an allegorical element in our text (the Story of the Pearl Merchant) but failed to define it in terms of genre. Finally, I introduced both the ancient rhetorical device of the *homoeosis* and the rhetorician Macrobius's concept of the *narratio fabulosa* (related to the heavenly ascent literature) and concluded that *ActPet12Apost.* is the combination of two major forms: a *narratio fabulosa* (built upon a foundational *homoeosis*) and a revelation dialogue.

In Chapter Three I argued that underlying the allegory of the Story of the Pearl Merchant there are gnostic "perceived real-world realities or constructions of mythic reality" that are the referents of the text. I concluded that the underlying mythical structure presents a pre-existent Savior and disciples who come down to earth on a salvific mission. It envisions an intermediate realm, populated by hostile forces, that separates this world from the Pleroma. It also assumes the existence of three separate classes of people: material, psychic and spiritual. These aspects of the *homoeosis*, with their one-to-one relationships between story and (alleged) "reality," illustrate how story components can be used to refer beyond themselves to perceived real-world realities or constructions of mythic reality. This aspect of *homoeosis* forms the foundation of the Story of the Pearl Merchant. Further, I suggested that the second formal aspect of the Story of the Pearl Merchant, the *narratio fabulosa*, is related to the *homoeosis* aspect as a building is related to its foundation. The proposed journey (Lithargoel's invitation to Nine Gates) and, most importantly, its execution (renunciation of the world and daily fasting) could not make sense without the "reality" created by the *homoeosis*.

In Chapter Four I tried to show how the redactor took over the Story of the Pearl Merchant. As a *narratio fabulosa*, this story included a journey to the heavenly sphere and explanations of both the journey process and other important details about how earthly conduct affects heavenly existence. The redactor, I argued, eliminated the heavenly explanation and replaced it with revelation dialogue material which reflected his or her own concerns. However, there was still a "loose end," i.e., the matter of identifying or explaining the pearl. Therefore the redactor, seeking to alter the meaning of the pearl from what was found in the Story of the Pearl Merchant to something that was more appropriate to his or her needs (i.e., from salvation in the Story of the Pearl Merchant to the "name of Jesus"), inserted the name Lithargoel so as to associate the pearl with Jesus. Finally, the redactor, familiar with the form and function of the revelation dialogue, used an originally separate resurrection appearance source to introduce his or her new revelation. In summation I illustrated how the redactor attempted to insert two new concepts which betray his or her theological agenda into the Story of the Pearl Merchant: 1) a reinterpretation of the pearl, and 2) the physician material.

In Chapter Five I explored both the communal uses of the text and the community which is reflected therein. I determined that *ActsPet12Apost.* was used as a sophisticated teaching tool in a school setting where the "spiritual" are trained to guide the churches. I also argued that the community itself could be distinguished by four characteristics: 1) a tendency toward self-centeredness; 2) a mystical-ascetical spirituality; 3) an experience of persecution; and 4) a rejection of the rich.

In Chapter Six I argued that *ActsPet12Apost.* received its final redaction in the years immediately following the Decian Persecution of late 249 to 251. The main factors suggesting this date were: 1) the connection between persecution and apostasy; 2) the impact of this persecution upon the relationship between the Church and its wealthy members; and 3) the uncommon use of physicians of bodies/ souls imagery. I also theorized that, taken together with this proposal, the clues provided by Dionysius and Cyprian suggest an Alexandrian provenance for this text.

With these arguments I have attempted to demonstrate the need to appreciate this Nag Hammadi text as an independent witness to traditions about Jesus (the resurrection appearance) and not merely as collections of varyingly concrete NT "echoes" and "allusions." Further, I have shown that they can also contain unique expressions of traditional imagery within developing Christianity (e.g., the Story of the Pearl Merchant). Of these results, perhaps the most important is the prospect of a precise dating for a Nag Hammadi text. To my knowledge this is the first document to be pinpointed with such specificity. If the argument can withstand scholarly scrutiny, what can it contribute to our understanding of other tractates? I am not sure. I have taken my text's references to persecution very seriously. What can the study of major historical persecutions teach us about other texts which mention persecution (e.g., *Ap. Jas*, *Treat. Seth* and *Apoc. Peter*)? This calls for exploration in the near future.

Over the last six years of inquiry I have developed a special affection for this little text. It owns a piece of my heart which it has not relinquished since the very first day I laid eyes upon it. This is ultimately my legacy — that I have loved it deeply, even if imperfectly. It is my sincere hope that these conclusions will stimulate further research on *ActsPet12Apost*. My desire is that future scholars will test, challenge and revise my findings, thereby advancing our understanding of its composition and message.

Bibliography

REFERENCE WORKS AND PRIMARY TEXTS

Allenbach, J., et. al., *Biblia Patristica: Index des citations et allusions bibliques dans la littérature patristique* (5 vols.; Paris: Editions du Centre national de la recherche scientifique, 1975–).

Amsler, Frédéric, François Bovon and Bertrand Bouvier, trans., *Actes de l'apôtre Philippe* (Apocryphes Collection de Poche de l'Aelac 8; Turnhout: Brepols, 1996).

Andrews, E. A., *Harper's Latin Dictionary* (New York: American Book Company, 1907).

Athanassakis, Apostolos N., trans., *Hesiod: Theogony, Works and Days, Shield* (Baltimore: Johns Hopkins University Press, 1983).

Bauer, Walter, *A Greek-English Lexicon of the New Testament and other Early Christian Literature* (rev. ed.; Chicago: University of Chicago Press, 1958).

Budge, E. A. Wallis, trans., *Book of the Dead* (London: Routledge and Kegan, 1956).

Butler, H. E., trans., *The Institutio oratoria of Quintilian* (4 vols.; LCL; London: Heinemann, 1921–22).

Bywater, Ingram, trans., *Aristotle: Rhetoric and Poetics* (New York: Random House, 1954).

Caplan, Harry, trans., *(Cicero) Ad C. Herrennium de ratione dicendi* (LCL; Cambridge: Harvard University Press, 1968).

Casey, R. P., trans., *Clement of Alexandria: The Excerpta ex Theodoto* (London: Christophers, 1934).

Chambry, Emile, trans., *Platon: Oeuvres complétes*, vols. 6–7/ 1, 2 *La république* (Collection des universités de France; Paris: Les Belles Lettres, 1947–49).

Charles, R. H., *The Ascension of Isaiah Translated from the Ethiopic Version* (London: Black, 1900).

Clendening, Logan, *Source Book of Medical History* (New York: Dover, 1942).

Conybeare, Fred C., ed., *Philo: About the Contemplative Life* (Oxford: Clarendon, 1895).

Crum, Walter E., *A Coptic Dictionary* (Oxford: Clarendon, 1939).

De Lacy, Phillip H., and Benedict Einarson, trans., *Plutarch's Moralia VII 523c–612b* (Cambridge: Harvard University Press, 1959).

Donaldson, J., and A. Roberts, trans., *Irenaeus. Adversus haereses* in *The Ante-Nicene Fathers*, vol. 1 (1867; repr. Grand Rapids, MI: Eerdmans, 1989) 309–567.

Edelstein, Emma J. and Ludwig Edelstein, *Asclepius: A Collection and Interpretation of the Testimonies* (2 vols; Baltimore: Johns Hopkins Press, 1945).

Fredouille, Jean Claude, trans., *Tertullien: Contre Les Valentiniens*, vol. 1 (SC 280; Paris: Cerf, 1980).

Geoltrain, Pierre, trans., *Le traité de la Vie Contemplative de Philon d'Alexandrie* (Semitica 10; Paris: Librairie d'Amérique et d'Orient Adrien-Maisonneuve, 1960).

Grant, Robert M., ed., *Gnosticism: A Source Book of Heretical Writings from the Early Christian Period* (New York: Harper, 1961).

Haardt, Robert, *Gnosis, Character and Testimony* (Leiden: Brill, 1971).

Hammond, N. G. L., and H. H. Scullard, *The Oxford Classical Dictionary* (2d ed.; Oxford: Clarendon, 1970).

Harris, J. Rendel, ed. and trans., and J. Armitage Robinson, *The Apology of Aristides* (2d ed.; TS 1/1; Cambridge: Cambridge University Press, 1893).

Horner, George, ed. and trans., *The Coptic Version of the New Testament in the Southern Dialect: Otherwise Called Sahidic or Thebaic* (7 vols.; Oxford: Clarendon, 1911–24).

Jowett, Benjamin, trans., *The Works of Plato* (4 vols. in 1; New York: Tudor, n.d.).

Kittel, Gerhard, ed., *Theological Dictionary of the New Testament* (10 vols.; Grand Rapids, MI: Eerdmans, 1949–76).

Koester, Helmut, *Introduction to the New Testament* (2 vols.; Philadelphia: Fortress, 1982).

Lake, Kirsopp, trans., *Eusebius of Caesarea: Ecclesiastical History* (2 vols.; LCL; London: William Heineman, 1924).

Lamb, W. R. M., trans., *Plato: Laches, Protagoras, Meno, Euthydemus* (LCL; Cambridge: Harvard University Press, 1967).

————. trans., *Plato: Lysis, Symposium, Gorgias* (LCL; Cambridge: Harvard University Press, 1967).

Lambdin, Thomas O., *Introduction to Sahidic Coptic* (Macon, GA: Macon University Press, 1983).

Lampe, G. W. H., *A Patristic Greek Lexicon* (Oxford: Clarendon, 1961).

Layton, Bentley, *The Gnostic Scriptures* (Garden City, NY: Doubleday, 1987).

Liddell, Henry G., Robert Scott, and Henry S. Jones, *A Greek-English Lexicon* (rev. ed.; Oxford: Clarendon, 1996).

MacMahon, J. H., *Hippolytus: The Refutation of All Heresies* (Edinburgh: T. & T. Clark, 1868).

Mead, G. R. S., trans., *Pistis Sophia* (London: Watkins, 1947).

Melmoth, William, trans., *Letters of Gaius Plinius Caecilius Secundus* (Harvard Classics; New York: Collier, 1909).

Meyer, Marvin W., ed., *The Ancient Mysteries: A Sourcebook* (San Francisco: Harper, 1987).

————. ed., *Ancient Christian Magic: Coptic Texts of Ritual Power* (San Francisco: Harper, 1994).

Meyer, Robert T., trans., *St. Athanasius: The Life of Saint Anthony* (ACW 10; Westminster, MD: Newman, 1950).

Müller, Caspar Detlef G., *Die Bücher der Einsetzung der Erzengel Michael und Gabriel* (CSCO 226, Scriptores Coptici 32; Louvain: CSCO, 1962).

Musurillo, Herbert, ed. and trans., *The Acts of the Christian Martyrs* (Oxford Early Christian Texts; Oxford: Clarendon, 1972).

Oldfather, William A., trans., *Epictetus: The Discourses as reported by Arrian, the Manual and fragments* (2 vols.; LCL; Cambridge: Harvard University Press, 1925–28).

Oulton, J. E. L., trans., *Eusebius: The Ecclesiastical History* (2 vols.; LCL; Cambridge: Harvard University Press, 1926).

Passage, Charles E., trans., *The Complete Works of Horace* (New York: Ungar, 1983).

Quasten, Johannes, *Patrology*, vol. 1: *The Beginnings of Patristic Literature* (Westminster, MD: Christian Classics, 1990).

Reardon, Bryan P., trans., *Lucian: Selected Works* (Library of Liberal Arts; Indianapolis: Bobbs-Merrill, 1965).

Robinson, James M., ed., *The Nag Hammadi Library in English* (Leiden: Brill, 1977).

———. *The Nag Hammadi Library in English* (rev. 2d ed.; San Francisco: Harper, 1988).

Rousseau, Adelin, and Louis Doutreleau, *Irénée de Lyon; Contre les Hérésies* (SC 264; Paris: Les Éditions du Cerf, 1979).

———. *Irénée de Lyon; Contre les Hérésies* (SC 294; Paris: Les Éditions du Cerf, 1982).

Rudolph, Kurt, *Gnosis: The Nature and History of Gnosticism* (San Francisco: Harper and Row, 1987).

Sabine, George H., and Stanley B. Smith, trans., *Cicero: On the Commonwealth* (Indianapolis: Bobbs-Merrill, 1976).

Sagnard, François L., *Extraits de Théodote / Clément d'Alexandrie* (SC 23; Paris: Éditions du Cerf, 1948).

Schmidt, Carl, ed. and trans., *Koptisch-gnostische Schriften*; vol. 1: *Die Pistis Sophia, Die beiden Bücher des Jeû, Unbekanntes altgnostisches Werk* (GCS 13; Leipzig: Hinrichs, 1905).

———. *Pistis Sophia; Ein gnostisches Originalwerk des 3 Jahrhunderts aus dem Koptischen übersetzt* (Leipzig: Hinrichs, 1925).

———. *Koptisch-gnostische Schriften*; vol. 1: *Die Pistis Sophia, Die beiden Bücher des Jeû, Unbekanntes altgnostisches Werk* (GCS 45: Berlin: Akademie-Verlag, 1954).

Schmidt, Carl, ed. and trans., and Violet MacDermot trans., *The Books of Jeu and the Untitled Text in the Bruce Codex* (NHS 12; Leiden: Brill, 1978).

———. *Pistis Sophia* (NHS 9; Leiden: Brill, 1978).

Schneemelcher, Wilhelm, ed., *New Testament Apocrypha: Gospels and Related*

Writings (rev. ed.; vol 1: Louisville: Westminster/ Knox, 1991).

————. *New Testament Apocrypha: Writings Related to the Apostles; Apocalypses and Related Subjects* (rev. ed.; vol 2: Louisville: Westminster/ Knox, 1992).

Smith, Martin F., and W. H. D. Rouse, trans., *Lucretius: De rerum natura* (LCL; Cambridge: Harvard University Press, 1975).

Stahl, William H., trans., *Macrobius: Commentary on the Dream of Scipio* (Records of Civilization, Sources and Studies 48; New York: Columbia University Press, 1952).

Webb, Robert L., Craig A. Evans and Richard A. Wiebe, *Nag Hammadi Texts and the Bible: A Synopsis and Index* (New Testament Tools and Studies 18; Lieden: Brill, 1993).

Williams, Frank, trans., *Epiphanius: The Panarion, Book 1 (1–46)* (NHS 35; Leiden: Brill, 1987).

Winston, David, trans., *Philo of Alexandria: The Contemplative Life, The Giants, and Selections* (New York: Paulist, 1981).

SECONDARY WORKS

Albertz, Martin, "Zur Formengeschichte der Auferstehungsberichte," *ZNW* 21 (1922) 259–69

Alsup, John E., *The Post-Resurrection Appearance Stories of the Gospel Tradition* (Calwer Theologische Monographien 5; Stuttgart: Calwer, 1975).

Armstrong, Arthur H., "Gnosis and Greek Philosophy," in D. M. Scholer, ed., *Gnosticism in the Early Church* (Studies in Early Christianity 5; New York: Garland, 1993) 33–70.

Attridge, Harold W., and Elaine H. Pagels, "The Tripartite Tractate: Introduction," in Harold W. Attridge, ed., *Nag Hammadi Codex 1 (The Jung Codex):*

Introductions, Texts, Translations, Indices (NHS 22; Leiden: Brill, 1985) 159–90.

Aune, David E., "The Apocalypse of John and the Problem of Genre," *Semeia* 36 (1986) 65–96.

Avila, Charles, *Ownership: Early Christian Teaching* (Maryknoll, NY: Orbis Books, 1983).

Barnes, Timothy D., "Legislation Against the Christians," *JRS* 58 (1968) 32–50.

Barton, John, "Source Criticism," *ABD* 6.162–65.

Barrett, C. K., "Paul Shipwrecked," in B. P. Thompson, ed., *Scripture: Meaning and Method; Essays Presented to Anthony Tyrrell Hanson for his Seventieth Birthday* (Hull: Hull University Press, 1987) 43–58.

Barry, Catherine, *La Sagesse de Jésus Christ* (Bibliothèque Copte de Nag Hammadi Section Textes 20; Quebec: Les Presses de l'Université Laval, 1993).

Baus, Karl, *From the Apostolic Community to Constantine* = Hubert Jedin, ed., *Handbook of Church History*, vol. 1 (New York: Herder, 1965).

Beauvoir, Simone de, *The Second Sex*, (New York: Vintage-Random House, 1974).

Benko, Stephen, "Pagan Criticism of Christianity During the First Two Centuries A.D.," *ANRW* 2.23.2 (1980) 1055–1114.

Benson, Edward White, *Cyprian: His Life, His Times, His Work* (London: Macmillan, 1897).

Bianchi, Ugo, "Documento finale," in idem, ed., *Le Origini dello Gnosticismo* (Studies in the History of Religions 12; Leiden: Brill, 1967) xxvi–xxix.

————. *Selected Essays on Gnosticism, Dualism and Mysteriosophy* (Studies in the History of Religions 38; Lieden: Brill, 1978).

Bienert, Wolfgang A., "The Picture of the Apostle in Early Christian Tradition," in W. Schneemelcher, ed., *New Testament Apocrypha* (2 vols; Philadelphia: Westminster/ John Knox, 1992) 2.5–27.

Bowersock, Glen W., *Martyrdom and Rome* (Cambridge: Cambridge University Press, 1995).

Brauer, George C., *The Age of the Soldier Emperors* (Park Ridge, NJ: Noyes, 1975) 19–57.

Broek, Roelof van den, "The Authentikos Logos: A New Document of Christian Platonism," *VC* 33 (1979) 260–86.

Brown, Peter, *The Body and Society: Men, Women, and Sexual Renunciation in Early Christianity* (Lectures on the History of Religions 13; New York: Columbia University Press, 1988).

Brown, Raymond E., *The Gospel According to John (xiii–xxi)* (AB 29a; Garden City, NY: Doubleday, 1970).

Brown, Scott Kent, "James: A Religio-Historical Study of the Relation Between Jewish, Gnostic, and Catholic Christianity in the Early Period Through an Investigation of the Traditions About James the Lord's Brother" (Ph.D. dissertation; Brown University, 1972).

———. "Jewish and Gnostic Elements in the Second Apocalypse of James," *NovT* 17 (1975) 225–37.

Brun, Lyder, *Die Auferstehung Christi in der urchristlichen Überlieferung* (Giessen: Töpelmann, 1925).

Budge, E.A. Wallis, *The Egyptian Heaven and Hell* (1925; repr. La Salle, IL: Open Court, 1994).

Bultmann, Rudolf, *History of the Synoptic Tradition* (rev. ed.; London: Blackwell, 1963).

———. *The Gospel of John: A Commentary* (Philadelphia: Westminster, 1971).

Büchsel, Friedrich, "ἀλληγορέω," *TDNT* 1.260–63.

Cameron, Ron, *Sayings Traditions in the Apocryphon of James* (HTS 34; Philadelphia: Fortress, 1984).

Canfield, Leon H., *The Early Persecutions of the Christians* (Studies in History, Economics and Public Law 2; New York: Columbia University Press, 1913).

Clarke, G. W., "Double-Trials in the Persecution of Decius," *Historia* 22 (1973) 651–63.

———. "Some Observations on the Persecution of Decius," *Antichthon* 3 (1969) 63–76.

Collins, John J., "Apocalypse: The Morphology of a Genre," *Semeia* 14 (1979) 1–20.

Collins, Raymond F., *Letters That Paul Did Not Write* (Good News Studies 28; Wilmington, DE: Michael Glazier, 1988).

Copenhaver, Brian P., trans., *Hermetica* (Cambridge: Cambridge University Press, 1992).

Craig, William L., "From Easter to Valentinus and the Apostles' Creed Once More: A Critical Examination of James Robinson's Proposed Resurrection Appearance Trajectories," *JSNT* 52 (1993) 19–39.

Cunningham, Agnes, *The Early Church and the State* (Sources of Early Christian Thought; Philadelphia: Fortress, 1982).

Daly, Cahal B., *Tertullian the Puritan and His Influence: An Essay in Historical Theology* (Dublin: Four Courts, 1993).

Dibelius, Martin, *James: A Commentary on the Epistle of James* (Philadelphia: Fortress, 1976).

Dodd, Charles, H., "The Appearances of the Risen Christ: an Essay in Form-Criticism of the Gospels," in D. E. Nineham, ed., *Studies in the Gospels:*

Essays in Memory of R. H. Lightfoot (Oxford: Blackwell, 1957) 9–35.

Dörrie, Heinrich, and Dörries, Hermann, "Erotapokriseis," in *RAC* 6 (1966) 342–70.

Doty, William G., *Letters in Primitive Christianity* (New Testament Series; Philadelphia: Fortress, 1973).

Driver, S. R., *An Introduction to the Literature of the Old Testament* (9th ed. rev.; Edinburgh: T. & T. Clark, 1929).

Duhm, Bernhard von., *Die Theologie der Propheten als Gundlage für die innere Entwicklungsgeschichte der israelitischen Religion* (Bonn: Marcus, 1875).

⸺. *Israels Propheten* (Tübingen: Mohr, 1922).

Dumeige, Gervaise, "Le Christ médecin dans la litterature chrétienne des premiers siécles," *Revista di archeologia cristiana* 48 (1972) 115–41.

Dupont, Jacques, *The Sources of the Acts* (New York: Herder and Herder, 1964) 75–112.

Ferguson, Everett, *Backgrounds of Early Christianity* (2d ed.; Grand Rapids, MI: Eerdmans, 1993).

Ficker, Gerhard, "Petrusakten," in Edgar Hennecke, ed., *Neutestamentliche Apokryphen in Verbindung mit Fachgelehrten in deutscher Übersetzung und mit Einleitungen* (Tübingen: Mohr, 1904) 383–423.

⸺. "Petrusakten," in E. Hennecke, ed., *Handbuch zu den Neutestamentlichen Apokryphen in Verbindung mit Fachgelehrten* (Tübingen: Mohr, 1904) 395–491.

⸺. "Actus Vercellenses," in E. Hennecke, ed., *Neutestamentliche Apokryphen in Verbindung mit Fachgelehrten in deutscher Uebersetzung und mit Einleitungen* (2nd ed.; Tübingen: Mohr, 1924) 226–49.

Filoramo, Giovanni, *A History of Gnosticism* (Oxford: Blackwell, 1990).

Francis, James A., *Subversive Virtue: Asceticism and Authority in the Second-Century Pagan World* (University Park, PA: Pennsylvania State University Press, 1995).

Frend, W. H. C., *Martyrdom and Persecution in the Early Church* (Garden City, NY: Doubleday, 1967).

—————. "Prelude to the Great Persecution: The Propaganda War," *JEH* 38 (1987) 1–18.

Fuller, Reginald H., *The Formation of the Resurrection Narratives* (Philadelphia: Fortress, 1980).

Furman, James E., "Leading to Light: A Christian Reading of a Nag Hammadi Text," *Coptic Church Review* 6 (1985) 22–26.

Genette, Gérard, *Narrative Discourse: An Essay in Method* (Ithaca, NY: Cornell University Press, 1980).

Georgii, H., "Zur Bestimmung der Zeit des Servius," *Philologus* 71 (1912) 518–26.

Gilhus, Inguild S., *The Nature of the Archons: A Study in the Soteriology of a Gnostic Treatise from Nag Hammadi* (Studies in Oriental Religions 12; Weisbaden: Harrassorvitz, 1985).

Grant, Michael, *Gladiators* (Pageant of History; London: Baylis and Son, 1967).

—————. *The Army of the Caesars* (New York: Charles Scribner's Sons, 1974).

Grant Robert M., *Gnosticism and Early Christianity* (2d ed.; New York: Columbia University Press, 1966).

—————. *Heresy and Criticism* (Louisville: Westminster/ Knox, 1993).

Green, Henry A., *The Economic and Social Origins of Gnosticism* (SBLDS 77; Atlanta: Scholars Press, 1985).

Groningen, G. van, *First Century Gnosticism: Its Origin and Motifs* (Leiden: Brill, 1967).

Guillamont, Antoine,"De Nouveaux Actes Apocryphes: Les Actes de Pierre et des Douze Apôtres," *RHR* 4 (1979) 141–52.

————, Henri-Charles Puech, Gilles Quispel, Walter C. Till and Yassah 'Abd al Masīh, trans., *The Gospel According to Thomas* (Leiden: Brill, 1959).

Haas, Christopher J., "Imperial Religious Policy and Valerian's Persecution of the Church," *CH* 52 (1983) 133–44.

Haas, Yves, "L'exigence du renoncement au monde dans les Actes de Pierre et des Douze Apôtres, les Apophtegmes des Pères du Désert, et la Pistis Sophia," in Bernard Barc, ed., *Colloque international sur les textes de Nag Hammadi* (Québec, 22–25 août 1978) (Bibliothèque Copte de Nag Hammadi Section Études 1; Quebec: Les Presses de l'Université Laval, 1981) 295–303.

Hall, Robert G., "Isaiah's Ascent to See the Beloved: An Ancient Jewish Source for the Ascension of Isaiah?" *JBL* 113 (1994) 463–84.

Harnack, Adolf von, *Die Apostelgeschichte* (Beiträge zur Einleitung in das Neue Testament 3; Leipzig: Hinrichs, 1908).

————. *The Mission and Expansion of Christianity in the First Three Centuries* (New York: Harper, 1961).

Hedrick, Charles W., "The Apocalypse of Adam: A Literary and Source Analysis," *SBLSP* 2 (1972) 581–90.

————. *The Apocalypse of Adam* (SBLDS 46; Atlanta: Scholars Press, 1980).

————. "Kingdom Sayings and Parables of Jesus in the Apocryphon of James: Tradition and Redaction," *NTS* 29 (1983) 1–24.

Hills, Julian V., *Tradition and Composition in the Epistula Apostulorum* (HDR 24; Minneapolis: Fortress, 1990).

Himmelfarb, Martha, *Tours of Hell: An Apocalyptic Form in Jewish and Christian Literature* (Philadelphia: University of Pennsylvania Press, 1983).

———. *Ascent to Heaven in Jewish and Christian Apocalypses* (Oxford: Oxford University Press, 1993).

Holtzmann, Heinrich-Julius, *Die synoptischen Evangelien: Ihr Ursprung und ihr geschichtlicher Charakter* (Leipzig: Engelmann, 1863).

Horman, John, "The Source of the Version of the Parable of the Sower in the Gospel of Thomas," *NovT* 21 (1979) 326–401.

Hübner, Jörg, "Christus medicus: Ein Symbol des Erlösungsgeschehens und ein Modell ärztlichen Handelns," *KD* 31 (1985) 324–35.

Jackson, Howard M., *The Lion Becomes Man: The Gnostic Leontomorphic Creator and the Platonic Tradition* (SBLDS 81; Atlanta: Scholars Press, 1985).

Janssen, L. F., "'Superstitio' and the Persecution of the Christians," *VC* 33 (1979) 131–59.

Jasper, R. C. D. and G. J. Cuming, *Prayers of the Eucharist: Early and Reformed* (3d ed.; New York: Pueblo, 1987).

Joly, Robert, *Le dossier d'Ignace d'Antioche* (Université libre de Bruxelles, Faculté de Philosophie et Lettres 69; Brussels: Éditions de l'Université de Bruxelles, 1979).

Kaestli, Jean-Daniel, "Les principales orientations de la recherche sur les actes apocryphes des apôtres," in François Bovon, ed., *Les Actes Apocryphes des Apôtres* (Geneva: Labor et Fides, 1981) 57–67.

Kee, Howard C., *Medicine, Miracle and Magic in New Testament Times* (SNTSMS 55; London: Cambridge University Press, 1986).

Keegan, Terence J., *Interpreting the Bible: A Popular Introduction to Biblical Hermeneutics* (New York: Paulist, 1985).

Keller, Carl A., "De La Foi à La Connaissance: Le Sens des 'Actes de Pierre et des Douze Apôtres' (NHC VI,1)," *RTP* 110 (1978) 131–37.

Kendall, Daniel, and Gerald O'Collins, "The Uniqueness of the Easter Appearances," *CBQ* 54 (1992) 287–307.

Keresztes, Paul, "Two Edicts of the Emperor Valerian," *VC* 29 (1975) 81–95.

―――. "The Decian Libelli and Contemporary Literature," *Latomus* 34 (1975) 761–81.

Klijn, A. F. J., "The So-Called Hymn of the Pearl," *VC* 14 (1960) 154–64.

Knipfing, John R., "The Libelli of the Decian Persecution," *HTR* 16 (1923) 345–90.

Krause, Martin and Pahor Labib, *Gnostische und hermetische Schriften aus Codex II und Codex VII* (Abhandlungen des deutschen archäologischen Instituts Kairo, koptische Reihe 2; Glückstadt: Augustin, 1971).

―――. "Die Petrusakten in Codex VI von Nag Hammadi," in idem, ed., *Essays in Honor of Alexander Bohlig* (NHS 3; Leiden: Brill, 1972) 36–58.

―――. "Der Dialog des Soter in Codex III von Nag Hammadi," in idem., ed., *Gnosis and Gnosticism* (NHS 8; Leiden: Brill, 1977) 13–34.

Kruse, Heinz, "The Return of the Prodigal: Fortunes of a Parable on its Way to the Far East," *Orientalia* 47 (1978) 163–214.

Kurz, William S., *Farewell Addresses in the New Testament* (Zacchaeus Studies: New Testament; Collegeville, MN: Michael Glazier/ Liturgical Press, 1990).

Lawson, John, *A Theological and Historical Introduction to the Apostolic Fathers* (New York: Macmillan, 1961).

Layton, Bentley, *The Gnostic Treatise on Resurrection from Nag Hammadi* (HDR 12; Atlanta: Scholars Press, 1979).

George W. MacRae, George W., "A Nag Hammadi Tractate on the Soul," in C.J. Bleeker, ed., *Ex orbe religionum: Studia Geo Widengren oblata* (Supplements to Numen 21; 2 vols.; Leiden: Brill, 1972) 1.471–79.

Malherbe, Abraham J., *The Cynic Epistles* (SBLSBS 12; Missoula, MT: Scholars Press, 1977).

Ménard, Jacques É., *La Lettre de Pierre à Philippe* (Bibliothèque Copte de Nag Hammadi Section Textes 1; Quebec: Les Presses de l'Université Laval, 1977).

————. *L'Authentikos Logos* (Bibliothèque Copte de Nag Hammadi Section Textes 1; Quebec: Les Presses de l'Université Laval, 1977).

————. *Le Traité sur la Résurrection (NHC 1,4)* (Bibliothèque Copte de Nag Hammadi Section Textes 12; Quebec: Les Presses de l'Université Laval, 1983).

————. *La Gnose de Philon d'Alexandrie* (Paris: Cariscript, 1987).

Meyer, Marvin W., *The Gospel of Thomas: The Hidden Sayings of Jesus* (San Francisco: Harper, 1992).

Miles, Margaret R., "Martyrdom, Gnosticism, and the Early Church," in idem., *Fullness of Life: Historical Foundations for a New Asceticism* (Philadelphia: Westminster, 1981) 19–36.

Moldenke, Harold N., and Alma I., *Plants of the Bible* (Plant Science Books 28; Waltham, MA: Chronica Botanica, 1952).

Myszor, Wincenty, "Dzieje Piotra: Przeklad z koptyjskiego," *Studia theologica Varsaw* 15 (1977) 169–75.

Nussbaum, Martha C., *The Therapy of Desire: Theory and Practice in Hellenistic Ethics* (Martin Classical Lectures 2; Princeton, NJ: Princeton University Press, 1994).

Oborn, George T., "Why Did Decius and Valerian Proscribe Christianity?" *CH* 2 (1933) 67–77.

Osiek, Carolyn, *Rich and Poor in the Shepherd of Hermas: An Exegetical-Social Investigation* (CBQMS 15; Washington, DC: Catholic Biblical Association, 1983).

Pagels, Elaine, *The Gnostic Gospels* (New York: Random House, 1979).

———. "Gnostic and Orthodox Views of Christ's Passion: Paradigms for the Christian's Response to Persecution?" in B. Layton, ed., *The Rediscovery of Gnosticism*, vol. 1: *The School of Valentinus* (Studies in the History of Religions 41; Leiden: Brill, 1980) 262–83.

Painchaud, Louis, *Le Deuxième Traité du Grand Seth* (Bibliothèque Copte de Nag Hammadi Section Textes 6; Quebec: Les Presses de l'Université Laval, 1982).

Parrott, Douglas M., "The Acts of Peter and the Twelve Apostles," in idem, ed., *Nag Hammadi Codices V,2–5 and VI with Papyrus Berlinensis 8502,1 and 4* (NHS 11; Leiden: Brill, 1979) 197–229.

———. "Gnostic and Orthodox Disciples in the Second and Third Centuries," in C. W. Hedrick and R. Hodgson, eds., *Nag Hammadi, Gnosticism and Early Christianity* (Peabody, MA: Hendrickson, 1986) 193–219.

———. "Gnosticism and Egyptian Religion," *NovT* 29 (1987) 71–93.

———. "The Acts of Peter and the Twelve Apostles (VI,1)," in J. M. Robinson, ed., *The Nag Hammadi Library in English* (2d ed.; San Francisco: Harper, 1988) 287–89.

———. "The Acts of Peter and the Twelve Apostles," in Aziz S. Atiya, ed., *The Coptic Encyclopedia* (10 vols.; New York: Macmillan, 1991) 1.61–63.

———. *Nag Hammadi Codices III,3–4 and V,1 with Papyrus Berolinensis 8502,3 and Oxyrhynchus Papyrus 1081* (NHS 27; Leiden: Brill, 1991).

———. "The Acts of Peter and the Twelve Apostles," *ABD* 5.264–65.

Patterson, Stephen J., "The Gospel of Thomas: Introduction," in John S. Kloppenborg et al., eds., *Q-Thomas Reader* (Sonoma: Polebridge, 1990) 77–127.

———. "Sources, Redaction and Tendenz in the Acts of Peter and the Twelve Apostles (NH VI,1)," *VC* 45 (1991) 1–17.

Pearson, Birger A., *Gnosticism, Judaism, and Egyptian Christianity, Studies in Antiquity and Christianity* (Minneapolis: Fortress, 1990).

———. "Jewish Elements in Gnosticism and the Development of Gnostic Self-Definition," in idem, *Gnosticism*, 124–35.

———. "Gnosticism as Platonism," in idem, *Gnosticism*, 148–64.

———. "Philo, Gnosis, and the New Testament," in idem, *Gnosticism*, 165–82.

———. "Gnosticism in Early Egyptian Christianity," in idem, *Gnosticism*, 194–213.

Peel, Ellen, "Subject, Object, and the Alternation of First and Third Person Narration in Novels by Alther, Atwood, and Drabble: Toward a Theory of Feminist Aesthetics," *Critique* 98 (1989) 107–122.

Perkins, Pheme, "Peter in Gnostic Revelation," *SBLSP* 2 (1974) 1–13.

———. *The Gnostic Dialogue* (Theological Inquiries; New York: Paulist, 1980).

———. "Pistis Sophia," *ABD* 5.375–76.

———. *Gnosticism and the New Testament* (Minneapolis: Fortress, 1993).

Peterson, Daniel, *The Roman Legions Recreated in Colour Photographs* (Europa Militaria 2; London: Windrow & Greene, 1992).

Phan, Peter C., *Social Thought* (Message of the Fathers of the Church 20; Wilmington: Glazier, 1984).

Philips, E. D., *Greek Medicine* (Aspects of Greek and Roman Life; London: Thames and Hudson, 1973).

Poirier, Paul-Hubert, *L'Hymne de la Perle des Actes de Thomas* (Homo Religiosus 8; Liege: Louvain-la-Neuve, 1981).

Porter, Stanley E., "The 'We' Passages," in Bruce W. Winter, ed., *The Book of Acts in its First Century Setting*, vol. 2: *Graeco-Roman Setting* (Grand Rapids, MI: Eerdmans, 1994) 545–74.

Quispel, Gilles, "The Study of Encratism: A Historical Survey," in Ugo Bianchi, ed., *La Tradizione Dell'Enkrateia: Motivazioni Ontologiche e Protologiche* (Rome: Dell'Ateneo, 1985) 35–81.

Rahner, Karl, *Penance in the Early Church* (Theological Investigations 15; New York: Crossroad, 1982).

Ramsey, Boniface, *Beginning to Read the Fathers* (New York: Paulist, 1985).

————. "Christian Attitudes to Poverty and Wealth," in Ian Hazlett, ed., *Early Christianity: Origins and Evolution to A.D. 600* (Nashville: Abingdon, 1991) 256–65.

Robbins, Vernon, "By Land and By Sea: The We-Passages and Ancient Sea Voyages," in C. H. Talbert, ed., *Perspectives on Luke-Acts* (Special Studies Series 5; Edinburgh: T. & T. Clark, 1978) 215–42.

Robinson, Gesine, "The Trimorphic Protennoia and the Prologue of the Fourth Gospel," in J. E. Goehring, C. W. Hedrick, eds., *Gnosticism and the Early Christian World: In Honor of James M. Robinson* (Sonoma, CA: Polebridge, 1990) 37–50.

Robinson, James M., "Jesus from Easter to Valentinus (or to the Apostles' Creed)," *JBL* 101 (1982) 5–37.

Rollinson, Philip, *Classical Theories of Allegory and Christian Culture* (Pittsburgh: Duquesne University Press, 1981).

Rose, H. J., *Religion in Greece and Rome* (New York: Harper, 1959).

Runia, David T., *Philo in Early Christian Literature: A Survey* (Minneapolis: Fortress, 1991).

Sainte Croix, G. E. M. de, "Aspects of the Great Persecution," *HTR* 47 (1954) 75–113.

———. "Why Were the Early Christians Persecuted?" *Past and Present* 26 (1963) 6–38.

———. "Why Were the Early Christians Persecuted? — A Rejoinder," *Past and Present* 27 (1964) 28–33.

Salvoni, F., "Un Nuovo Apocrifo: Gli Atti di S. Pietro e dei 12 Apostoli," *Ricerche bibiche e religiose* 15 (1980) 35–42.

Sage, Michael M., *Cyprian* (Patristic Monograph Series 1; Cambridge: Philadelphia Patristic Foundation, 1975).

Salisbury, F. S., and H. Mattingly, "The Reign of Trajan Decius," *JRS* 14 (1924) 1–23.

Schenke, Hans-Martin, "Die Taten des Petrus und der zwölf Apostel," *TLZ* 98 (1973) 13–19.

———. "The Acts of Peter and the Twelve Apostles," in W. Schneemelcher, ed., *New Testament Apocrypha* (2 vols.; Louisville: Westminster/ Knox, 1992) 2.412–25.

Schmidt, Carl, *Die alten Petrusakten im zusammenhang der apocryphen Apostellitteratur nebst einem neuentdeckten Fragment* (TU 24; Leipzig: Hinrichs, 1903).

———. "Studien zu den alten Petrusakten," *ZKG* 43 (1924) 321–48.

Schneemelcher, Wilhelm, "Introduction: Second and Third Century Acts of Apostles," in idem, ed., *New Testament Apocrypha* (2 vols; Louisville: Westminster/ Knox, 1992) 2.78–83.

Schoedel, William R., "The First Apocalypse of James, V,3:24.10–44.10," in D. M. Parrott, ed., *Nag Hammadi Codices V,2–5 and VI with Papyrus Berlinensis 8502,1 and 4* (NHS 11; Leiden: Brill, 1979) 65–104.

———. *Ignatius of Antioch: A Commentary on the Letters of Ignatius of Antioch* (Hermeneia; Philadelphia: Fortress, 1985).

Scholer, David M., ed., *Gnosticism in the Early Church* (Studies in Early Christianity 5; New York: Garland, 1993).

Scholes, Robert, and Kellogg, Robert, *The Nature of Narrative* (New York: Oxford University Press, 1966).

Scott, Walter, ed. and trans., *Hermetica* (repr.; Boston: Shambhala, 1993).

Seesemann, Heinrich, "πεῖρα κτλ." *TDNT* 6.23–36.

Segal, Alan F., "Heavenly Ascent in Hellenistic Judaism, Early Christianity and their Environment," *ANRW* 2.23.2 (1980) 1333–1394.

Sell, Jesse, "A Note on a Striking Johannine Motif Found at CG VI:6,19," *NovT* 20 (1978) 232–40.

———. "Simon Peter's "Confession" and The Acts of Peter and the Twelve Apostles," *NovT* 21 (1979) 344–56.

———. "Jesus the "Fellow-Stranger" — A Study of CG VI:2,35–3,11," *NovT* 23 (1981) 173–92.

Sherwin-White, A. N., "Early Persecutions and the Roman Law Again," *JTS* 3 (1952) 199–213.

———. "Why Were the Early Christians Persecuted? –– An Amendment," *Past and Present* 27 (1964) 23–27.

Smith, Terence V., *Petrine Controversies in Early Christianity* (WUNT 15; Tübingen: Mohr-Siebeck, 1985).

Smith, Wesley D., *The Hippocratic Tradition* (Ithaca, NY: Cornell University Press, 1979).

Söder, Rosa, *Die apokryphen Apostelgeschichten und die romanhafte Literatur der Antike* (Stuttgart: Kohlhammer, 1932).

Staden, Heinrich von, trans., *Herophilus: The Art of Medicine in Early Alexandria* (Cambridge: Cambridge University Press, 1989).

Stead, G. C., "In Search of Valentinus," in B. Layton ed., *The Rediscovery of Gnosticism*, vol. 1: *The School of Valentinus* (Studies in the History of Religions 41; Leiden: Brill, 1980) 75–102.

Streeter, B. H., *The Four Gospels: A Study of Origins* (London: Macmillan, 1924).

Tabor, James D., "Ascent to Heaven," *ABD* 3.91–94.

Tardieu, Michel, *Écrits gnostiques: Codex de Berlin* (Sources gnostiques et manichéennes 1; Paris: Cerf, 1984).

————, and Jean-Daniel Dubois, *Introduction à la littérature gnostique* (Initiations au christianisme ancien; Paris: Cerf, 1986).

Temkin, Owsei, *Hippocrates in a World of Pagans and Christians* (Baltimore: Johns Hopkins University Press, 1991).

Thomas, Christine M., "The Acts of Peter, the Ancient Novel, and Early Christian History" (Ph.D. dissertation; Harvard University, 1995).

Thomassen, Einar, ed., L. Painchaud and E. Thomassen, trans., *Le Traité Tripartite (NH 1,5)* (Bibliothèque Copte de Nag Hammadi Section Textes 19; Quebec: Les Presses de l'Université Laval, 1989).

Tiller, Patrick A., *A Commentary on the Animal Apocalypse of 1 Enoch* (Early

Judaism and its Literature 4; Atlanta: Scholars Press, 1993).

Trevett, Christine, *A Study of Ignatius of Antioch in Syria and Asia* (Studies in the Bible and Early Christianity 29; Lewiston, NY: Mellen, 1992).

Tuckett, C. M., *Nag Hammadi and the Gospel Tradition: Synoptic Tradition in the Nag Hammadi Library* (Studies of the New Testament and its World; Edinburgh: T. & T. Clark, 1986).

Turner, John D., *The Book of Thomas the Contender* (SBLDS 23; Missoula, MT: Scholars Press, 1975).

Vallee, Gerard, *A Study in Anti-Gnostic Polemics: Irenaeus, Hippolytus and Epiphanius* (Studies in Christianity and Judaism 1; Waterloo, Ontario: Wilfid Laurier University Press, 1981).

Veilleux, Armand, *La Première Apocalypse de Jacques (NH V,3). La Seconde Apocalypse de Jacques (NH 5,4)* (Bibliothèque Copte de Nag Hammadi Section Études 17; Quebec: Les Presses de l'Université Laval, 1986).

Vielhauer, Philipp, "Introduction: The Testimonies of the Early Church Regarding Jewish-Christian Gospels," in W. Schneemelcher, ed., E. Hennecke, rev., and R. McL. Wilson, trans. ed., *New Testament Apocrypha* (2 vols; Philadelphia: Westminster, 1963) 1.126–30.

Vööbus, Arthur, trans., *The Synodicon in the West Syrian Tradition* (CSCO 368; Louvain: Secrétariat du CSCO, 1975).

Vorster, Willem S., "The religio-historical context of the resurrection of Jesus and resurrection faith in the New Testament," *Neotestamentica* 23 (1989) 159–75.

Walsh, William J., and John P. Langan, "Patristic Social Consciousness — The Church and the Poor," in John C. Haughey, ed., *The Faith that Does Justice: Examining the Christian Sources for Social Change* (Woodstock Studies 2; New York: Paulist, 1977) 113–51.

Wellhausen, Julius, *Geschichte Israels* (Berlin: Reimer, 1878).

Whitman, Jon, *Allegory: The Dynamics of an Ancient and Medieval Technique* (Cambridge: Harvard University Press, 1987).

Williams, Jacqueline A., *Biblical Interpretation in the Gospel of Truth from Nag Hammadi* (SBLDS 79; Atlanta: Scholars Press, 1988).

Wilson, Robert McL., *The Gnostic Problem: A Study of the Relation between Hellenistic Judaism and the Gnostic Heresy* (London: Mowbray, 1958).

———. "Philo and Gnosticism," in D. T. Runia, ed., *The Studia Philonica Annual: Studies in Hellenistic Judaism*, vol. 5 (Atlanta: Scholars Press, 1993) 84–92.

Wimbush, Vincent L., "Sophrosyne: Greco-Roman Origins of a Type of Ascetic Behavior," in J. E. Goehring, C. W. Hedrick, eds., *Gnosticism and the Early Christian World: In Honor of James M. Robinson* (Sonoma, CA: Polebridge, 1990) 89–102.

———. ed., *Ascetic Behavior in Greco-Roman Antiquity: A Sourcebook* (Studies in Antiquity & Christianity; Minneapolis: Fortress, 1990).

Wink, Walter, *Naming the Powers: The Language of Power in the New Testament* (Philadelphia: Fortress, 1984).

———. *Unmasking the Powers: The Invisible Forces That Determine Human Existence* (Philadelphia: Fortress, 1986).

———. *Engaging the Powers: Discernment and Resistance in a World of Domination* (Minneapolis: Fortress, 1992).

———. *Cracking the Gnostic Code: The Powers in Gnosticism* (SBLMS 46; Atlanta: Scholars Press, 1993).

Wisse, Frederik, "The Use of Early Christian Literature as Evidence for Inner Diversity and Conflict," in idem, D. M. Scholer, ed., *Gnosticism in the Early Church*, 365–79.

Wissowa, Georg, *De Macrobii Saturnaliorum fontibus capita tria* (Vratisslaviae: Koebnerum, 1880).

Workman, Herbert B., *Persecution in the Early Church* (Oxford: Oxford University Press, 1980).

Yamauchi, Edwin M., *Pre-Christian Gnosticism: A Survey of the Proposed Evidence* (Grand Rapids, MI: Eerdmans, 1973).

————. " Pre-Christian Gnosticism, the New Testament and Nag Hammadi in Recent Debate," in F. Wisse, D. M. Scholer, eds., *Gnosticism in the Early Church*, 26–32.